2RN AND THE ORIGINS OF IRISH RADIO

By the same author

Oscar Wilde (1983/97)

The Dublin Gate Theatre 1928–1978 (1984)

The Dandy and the Herald: manners, mind and morals from Brummell to Durrell (1988)

Brian Friel and Ireland's Drama (1990)

Lawrence Durrell: the Mindscape (1994)

The Thief of Reason: Oscar Wilde and Modern Ireland (1995)

The Diviner: the art of Brian Friel (1999)

edited or co-edited by Richard Pine

All for Hecuba: the Dublin Gate Theatre 1928–1978 (1978)

Dark Fathers into Light: Brendan Kennelly (1994)

Music in Ireland 1848–1998 (1998)

To Talent Alone: the Royal Irish Academy of Music 1848–1998 (1998)

2RN

and the origins of Irish radio

Richard Pine

FOUR COURTS PRESS

Set in 10 on 13 point Janson Text by
Mac Style, Scarborough, N. Yorkshire for
FOUR COURTS PRESS LTD
Fumbally Lane, Dublin 8, Ireland
e-mail: info@four-courts-press.ie
and in North America
FOUR COURTS PRESS
c/o ISBS, 5824 N.E. Hassalo Street, Portland, OR 97213.

A catalogue record for this title
is available from the British Library.

ISBN 1-85182-603-3 hbk
ISBN 1-85182-604-1 pbk

Printed in Great Britain
by MPG Books, Bodmin, Cornwall.

For Bruce

Contents

Foreword

In greeting the appearance of this first volume in the series 'Broadcasting and Irish Society' I am conscious of how multi-faceted is the history of RTÉ, and how intimately RTÉ, since its inception in 1926, has engaged with Irish society, reflecting, and contributing to, its development.

It is perhaps a commonplace to refer to RTÉ's influence on the social, cultural and political fabric of the lives of Irish people. Yet when we consider how very fundamentally radio and television have been part of our day-to-day communication, we can see how that engagement is defined and transformed by the complex nature of communication itself: it is never stable for too long, never eligible for complacency, always challenged and always challenging.

Radio came to Ireland at a critical time. Today, the question of what defines a 'national' broadcaster, working in the public service, and the even more pressing twin question of 'value for money', indicate another critical juncture. It is evident from this initial excursion into our history that the origins of the electronic media in Ireland were part of a much larger debate on the role of communication in Irish society, which continues to the present day. Origins are strange phenomena: the excitement of the *first* broadcast, the *first* radio achievement in sports or music or current affairs, is always tempered by the struggle and uncertainty of the newborn. Every succeeding achievement, of whatever scale of magnitude, encounters that same complexity.

In tracing the origins and early years of Radio Éireann, Richard Pine, the series editor of 'Broadcasting and Irish Society', has pointed us towards many aspects of our political and social culture which continue to concern us. I believe that the co-existence of excitement and uncertainty, now with the perspective of seventy-five years of broadcasting wisdom, will be reflected in future volumes of the series, as it is in the life of RTÉ itself as we celebrate this milestone in the public service of Ireland.

Bob Collins
Director-General, RTÉ

Preface

During my first term as a student in Dublin, on New Year's Eve 1967, I was sitting in a bar on South William Street when the volume of the radio – in those years a widely favoured form of background susurrus – was raised. It was 6.40 p.m. and the voice of Éamon de Valera, with which until then I had not been familiar, began to seduce the room. It was a Presidential broadcast of only five minutes' duration, commemorating the centenary of the Fenian rising, but as he spoke of Ireland it became clear that this was a form of communication which was a regular, expected and implicit part of Irish culture and society and of the broadcasting system which served it.

'Broadcasting' had been a feature of Irish communications long before radio existed. At Daniel O'Connell's 'monster meetings' it was obviously impossible for the human voice to carry, unaided, to the huge crowds assembled. So, in the absence of electronic apparatus, men would stand just within hearing distance and would shout the speech to the next man, and thus the Liberator's words were communicated by these 'broadcasters' from crowd to crowd and eventually from village to village. Word of mouth has, in all its aspects and ramifications, always been a central feature of information in Ireland.

Radio, when it arrived, fulfilled the function of previous organs of mass communication such as the popular press; *The Nation*, the medium of the Young Ireland movement, had enjoyed a readership or, more to the point, a listenership, far in excess of the numbers actually sold, since it was read aloud at village gatherings throughout Ireland. Radio came to serve a similar function. '*I heard it on the radio*' was to become a commonplace acknowledgement of the centrality of Radio Éireann in the country's information system and indeed of its cultural and social life. As Norris Davidson remarked in 1966, on the occasion of the fortieth anniversary of RTÉ, public service broadcasting truly exists 'when the public relies on the broadcasting service without realising that it is relying on it'.*

Radio has a continuing magic which is not available to television. The mental pictures evoked by the place-names on the dials of our parents' and grandparents' sets (as Seamus Heaney said of 'Stockholm' in his Nobel lecture) became indefinite friends in a world of possibilities for generations of

---

*In a radio broadcast on 16 December 1966, RTÉ Sound Archives tape no 32/68C.

youngsters: 'Berlin', 'Prague', Leningrad', 'Aberdeen' were not so much places inhabited by real people as ideas, suggestions of cultures and mysteries. For me, 'Hilversum' represented a palace of the exotic – it was long after childhood that I realised that my fascination was probably due to the anagrammatic possibility of the 'silver hum' which I always associate with the older sets. Eventually 'Athlone' took its place on this dial among the radio stations of the world, sending out Irish voices to remote destinations, its inaugural broadcast carrying the words of Éamon de Valera.

This book is not a history of radio in Ireland: it is simply an account of the way in which the radio service was established in the Irish Free State. Up to now that process has been totally neglected in histories of the period, despite the fact that it is an episode in the earliest years of the independent state which reveals serious flaws in the way that state was conducting itself. Chapter Five ('2RN – the opening years') does not purport to log all its achievements, simply to give a flavour of the way 2RN was received and the chief avenues down which it developed. In many ways the process by which Irish radio came into existence is of more interest than its actual early life – perhaps that is true of all life.

If I had intended a comprehensive history I would, for example, have addressed the topic described in Rex Cathcart's history of the BBC in Northern Ireland which had preceded 2RN in 1924 (*The Most Contrary Region*, 1984) but I believe there is a valid distinction to be made between the origins of 'Irish' radio and the origins of radio in Ireland: BBC activity in Northern Ireland has been predominantly one of regional policy rather than indigenous growth.

There is indeed a much larger story to be told, including the sociological dimension of the way that the presence of radio effected a change in people's homes. It is be hoped that future volumes of *Broadcasting and Irish Society* will help to achieve that.

Although the Irish and the British experiences may seem disparate – both quantitatively and qualitatively – I have included references to the early history of the BBC, largely drawn from the first volume of Asa Briggs' monumental study *The Birth of Broadcasting* (1961), because, up to 1922, Ireland and Britain had shared a legal and administrative structure, and therefore in the mid-1920s the evolution of radio in each country, however different their societies may have been, followed cognate paths.

Also, the experience in Finland replicates the Irish story in several respects and I have occasionally referred to this parenthetically. Finland bears a remarkable similarity to Ireland: a largely agrarian population; a history of suppression by more powerful neighbours; independence followed quickly by civil war; two languages and cultures (Finnish and Swedish) within the same society, served by separate print and broadcast media, one of them quite distinct from, and unconnected with, the languages and cultures which surround it; and a country to this day territorially divided by politics. Comparative study between the Irish and Finnish radio experiences would, I believe, be fruitful and instructive.

The progress of radio over the past century has only served to underline the fact that its early uses remain its continuing strengths. 'Nation shall speak unto nation' may be part of the larger story, embracing – or perhaps contained by – 'culture shall speak unto culture'. Within that story, however, are many minor narratives: the fact that in 1926 a Kerry listener might hear for the first time the accents of an Ulsterman; that speakers of Munster Irish could discover their difference from speakers of Donegal Irish. The recent advent of 'community radio' has completed a cycle of signification first conceived in the world's first (and illegal) news bulletin of 1916. The early story of 2RN can be so easily read as a parable of modern Irish radio, while the concept of radio as a tool of rural development, articulated as it was in the planning of the service, has been – and is still being – borne out in societies such as Kenya, Egypt, India and Sri Lanka.

When I consider how we have arrived today at a media crossroads at which the talk is of two factors – control and the speed of technological change – I am amazed but also reassured that, in order to keep public service broadcasting in sight, we are continually re-inventing the wheel. Eighty years ago, Irish people were beginning to ask themselves the same inevitable questions posed by Michael D. Higgins in his Green Paper on broadcasting in the 1990s. But the fact that those *are* the questions, and that they *are* still being asked, is, I believe, the safeguard that public service broadcasting requires. This part of the history has been written in that belief.

Inishnee,
New Year's Day, 2001

Acknowledgments

I was very gratified when, on my retirement from RTÉ in 1999, the Director-General, Bob Collins, invited me to undertake the general editorship of the series *Broadcasting and Irish Society* and to write the initial volume, celebrating the seventy-fifth anniversary of Irish radio with an account of the inception of '2RN'. Along the way he has been very supportive of the series and of my involvement in it. It has been a pleasure to work with the Director-General's Special Assistant, Adrian Moynes, who has enabled me to progress with a sense of the continuing ethos of public service broadcasting. I am also extremely grateful to Peter Feeney, RTÉ's Freedom of Information Officer, for smoothing my path within the administrative echelons of the organisation with an enthusiasm and an appreciation of my task which stem from his own involvement in current affairs broadcasting.

Other former colleagues in RTÉ provided professional assistance, most notably RTÉ's Archivist, Brian Lynch, who alerted me to the destruction at some unknown date of files in the Department of Posts and Telegraphs relating to the early years of broadcasting. In the RTÉ Reference and Illustrations Library, Con Bushe and Jane Hall provided research facilities and Malachy Moran and Leni McCullagh were particularly helpful in sourcing rare material. Former colleagues Máire Ní Mhurchú and Diarmuid Breathnach were kind enough to provide me with a modern transcription (as well as translation) of Séamus Clandillon's letters to Douglas Hyde. The staff of the Sound Archives, Ian Lee, Robert Canning and Joan Murphy were as fastidiously helpful as always.

Helen Andrews of the Royal Irish Academy's research project *Dictionary of Irish Biography* was informative as ever and Emilie Pine was, once again, a diligent and effective research assistant.

During the 1980s, when I researched much of the background to this book (and delivered a fragment of it to a meeting of the American Conference of Irish Studies at University College, Dublin, in 1987), I was skilfully guided by the staff of the State Paper Office, then housed in Dublin Castle and now incorporated in the National Archives; I am pleased to acknowledge that assistance so many years later. Séamus Haughey of the library of Dáil Éireann provided essential information on former members of the Dáil.

Finally, my friend Dr Michael Laffan, of the Department of Modern History in University College, Dublin, was kind enough to read the text with a critical eye and was able to save me from some lamentable errors, and I am deeply grateful to him for his attention and constructive suggestions for improvements and clarifications.

Radio and Irish society, 1898–1934: a chronology*

1898	**Guiglielmo Marconi conducts radio experiments between Rathlin Island and Ballycastle.**	
1901	**Marconi establishes wireless telegraphy stations at Crookhaven Co. Cork and Rosslare, Co. Wexford.**	
	First experiments in trans-Atlantic wireless between Poldhu, Cornwall and St John's, Newfoundland.	
1903	**Marconi station established at Malin, Co. Donegal.**	
1905–7	**Marconi station established at Clifden, Co. Galway.**	
1907	**Amalgamated Radio Telegraph Company establishes trans-Atlantic station at Tralee, Co. Kerry.**	
1912	**Marconi stations established at Letterfrack, Co. Galway and Ballybunion, Co. Kerry.**	
1913	**Dublin Wireless Club founded.**	
1914	**Marconi station established at Valentia Island, Co. Kerry.**	
	May	Final reading of Home Rule Bill in UK Parliament (enacted and suspended in September for duration of the first world war).
	July	Erskine Childers' *Asgard* accomplishes gun-running to Irish Volunteers at Howth Harbour.
	August	World War 1 begins.
1916	April	Easter Rising; proclamation of the Irish Republic; announcement 'broadcast' from O'Connell Street.
	May	Execution of leaders of the Rising.
1917	October	Éamon de Valera elected President of Sinn Féin.
1918	November	World War 1 ends.
	December	General Election: Sinn Féin wins 73 of 105 seats in Ireland.
1919	January	Meeting of 'First Dáil Éireann'.
	March	**First east-west wireless telephony signals transmitted from Ballybunion to Louisberg, Nova Scotia.**

*Sources: J.E. Doherty and D.J. Hickey, *A Chronology of Irish History since 1500*; R.F. Foster, *Modern Ireland 1600–1972*; Paddy Clarke, *Dublin Calling: 2RN and the Birth of Irish Radio*; Maurice Gorham, *Forty Years of Irish Broadcasting*.

	April	de Valera elected President of Dáil Éireann; Seán T. O'Kelly elected Ceann Comhairle.
	June:	Alcock and Brown land at Marconi Station, Clifden, after the first transatlantic light.
	September	Dáil Éireann declared illegal.
1920	February	Curfew in Dublin.
	March	'Black and Tans' arrive in Ireland.
	June	Dáil reconvenes.
	November	'Bloody Sunday'.
1921	May	General Election: Sinn Féin wins 124 of 128 seats, abstains from assembly which meets in June.
	August	Sinn Féin constitutes 'Second Dáil Éireann'.
	October-December	Anglo-Irish negotiations leading to the Treaty.
	December	de Valera denounces the Treaty.
1922	January	Dáil Éireann approves Treaty by 64 votes to 57.
		de Valera resigns as President of Dáil Éireann; Arthur Griffith elected President of Dáil Éireann; Provisional Government under Chairmanship of Michael Collins; Collins formally takes control of Dublin Castle; Collins chairs Committee to draft constitution of Irish Free State (Darrell Figgis vice-chairman).
	February	Civic Guard (Garda Siochána) founded. **First broadcast by Marconi Company from Writtle (UK).**
	March–April	Discussions between Provisional Government and southern Unionists.
	May	Collins-de Valera electoral pact (repudiated by Collins in June).
	June	Constitution of Irish Free State agreed with British Government.
		General Election: Pro-Treaty 58, Anti-Treaty 36; Labour 17, Farmers 7, Independent 6, Dublin University 4.
		Civil War begins.
	July	**Marconi station at Clifden captured.**
	August	Arthur Griffith dies; Michael Collins shot.

		W.T. Cosgrave becomes chairman of the Provisional Government (and in September President of Dáil Éireann).
	September	Army Emergency Powers.
	October	Irish Free State Constitution enacted. 'Alternative [Anti-Treaty] Dáil' elects de Valera 'President of the Irish Republic'.
	November	First executions of the civil war, including Erskine Childers. **BBC starts broadcasting.**
	December	Saorstat Éireann [Irish Free State] officially comes into existence. **Radio Society of Ireland founded.**
1923	January	W.T. Cosgrave's home burnt.
	February	T.F. O'Higgins shot.
	April	**First notices inviting applications for broadcasting licences.**
	May	End of Civil War.
	July	11,316 military prisoners in Irish Free State. **Radio Association of Ireland founded.** Censorship of Films Act.
	August	Public Safety (Emergency Powers) Act. **Broadcasting relay from Dun Laoghaire to Royal Dublin Society.** General Election.
	September	Irish Free State admitted to the League of Nations. Fourth Dáil assembles; W.T. Cosgrave elected President. **White Paper on Wireless Broadcasting.**
	November	W.B. Yeats awarded Nobel Prize for Literature.
	December	First Free State National Loan. **Dáil Committee on Broadcasting established.** *Irish Radio Journal* **first published.**
1924	January	14th. **Wireless Committee meets.** 15th. **Wireless Committee issues 1st Interim Report.** 31st. **Wireless Committee issues 2nd Interim Report.** Public Safety Act renewed. Reduction of old-age pension by 1 shilling.

	March	13th. **Wireless Committee issues 3rd Interim Report.**
		26th. **Wireless Committee issues Final Report.**
		27th. **Dáil orders Reports to be published with full supporting documents.**
		Army Mutiny.
		Messrs Hempenstall import Burndept radio van.
	April	Boundary Commission established.
	May	Dublin Corporation dissolved (until 1930).
	August	Dáil Éireann occupies previous RDS premises at Leinster House.
		Marconi transmissions in Dublin.
	September	**BBC Belfast station starts transmission.**
	December	*Freeman's Journal* ceases publication.
1925	June	**Department of Finance agrees to proposals for Dublin broadcasting station.**
	September	**Amalgamation of Dublin Wireless Club and Radio Society of Ireland to form Wireless Society of Ireland.**
	October	Suicide of Darrell Figgis.
		Irish Radio Review **first published.**
	November	**First Wireless Exhibition.**
		IRA sets up 'Army Council'.
		Séamus Clandillon appointed Director of 2RN.
		2RN starts test broadcasts.
	December	**2RN outside broadcast tests.**
1926	1 January	**Opening broadcast of 2RN.**
	May	Foundation of Fianna Fáil.
	August	**First sports broadcast by 2RN.**
	November	Public Safety (Emergency Provisions) Act.
		Wireless Telegraphy Bill introduced.
		Second Wireless Exhibition.
	December	**Wireless Telegraphy Act.**
1927	February	**John Logie Baird demonstrates his 'Televisor' in Dublin.**
	April	**Cork broadcasting station (6CK) opens.**

	June	General Election: Cosgrave re-elected President; Fianna Fáil refuses to take oath of allegiance.
	July	Kevin O'Higgins shot.
	July–August	Emergency legislation enacted.
	August	de Valera takes oath.
		Electricity Supply Board founded.
	September	General Election: Cosgrave re-elected President.
1928	March	**Irish Radio News first published.**
		Seán Lemass describes Fianna Fáil as a 'slightly constitutional party'.
	July	Ireland wins first Olympic gold medal.
	August	Foundation of Taibhdhearc na Gaillimhe.
	October	Foundation of Dublin Gate Theatre.
	December	New Free State currency.
1929	July	Censorship of Publications Act.
		First screening of Ireland's first sound film.
	November	*Ireland* – documentary film made by the Government.
1930	September	Ireland elected to Council of League of Nations.
1931	September	Éamon de Valera founds *Irish Press*.
	October	IRA declared illegal (until March 1932).
1932	February	Formation of Army Comrades Association (Blueshirts).
		General Election.
	March	de Valera forms first Fianna Fáil administration.
	June	Eucharistic Congress held in Dublin.
		Test broadcasts from high-power transmitter at Athlone.
	July	'Economic war' between Ireland and Britain starts.
	September	de Valera becomes Chairman of the League of Nations Assembly.
1933	January	General Election: Fianna Fáil achieves an overall majority.
	February	**de Valera inaugurates Athlone station.**
	May	Oireachtas removes oath of allegiance from the Constitution.

	September	Cumann na nGaedheal, National Centre Party, Blueshirts unite to form Fine Gael.
1934	May	Premiere of film *Man of Aran*.
	November	**Séamus Clandillon removed as Director of 2RN.**

CHAPTER 1

Introduction

He suggested that he could be of invaluable service ... It had come to his knowledge that some members of the Government were not above making money commercially, and he thought he might just as well follow their example ... He further stated that he had considerable influence with the members of the Cabinet ... I told him I would allow him the sum of £[---] per month whilst he was working in our interests ... He several times mentioned the difficulties he was experiencing in getting finance to fight his election, and ... I allowed him to draw a cheque for £[-] ... to help him in this matter ... I again allowed him to draw a second cheque for £[-], making a total of £[---] received from me on the strength of statements made regarding his great influence with the Government and his unique knowledge of the resources of Ireland, and his ability to secure work and contracts for us, all of which I have since found to be untrue.

In the political climate of the 1990s and 2000s, with a plethora of tribunals and judicial enquiries into bribery and corruption of senior public figures, such a witness, revealing payments to a leading politician, would have been one of many. The allegations have the same timbre as those made in 1999 and 2000 in relation to the election expenses of Government ministers and the issuing of radio licences.

Yet they were made in 1922, and relate directly to the complex social and political web of vested and incipient interests in the aftermath of the Irish Civil War, and in particular to the establishment of the inaugural national radio service, '2RN'. The history of the introduction of radio to the Irish Free State in 1923–6, and of its early development, is the narrative of a young medium in a new and dangerous political environment. Out of this period came a 'station', initially named from its call-sign,[1] which grew into Radio

---

1 A 'call-sign' was the signal by which a radio station identified itself. The London station, for example, was designated '2LO'. For the derivation of '2RN' and mistaken interpretations of its significance, see below, p. 40.

Éireann, Ireland's public service broadcaster, and which became a major factor in the development of Irish culture and society and a central presence in the Irish household. The mere fact that the term 'station' was employed to identify and describe the broadcasting function places a particular concept of location, control and traffic in communication at the centre of the semantics of radio and later television.

But the identity and function of 2RN were not at all clear at the outset. The central document in this history is entitled *First, Second and Third Interim Reports and the Final Report of the Special Committee to consider the Wireless Broadcasting Report together with Proceedings of the Committees* [sic], *Minutes of Evidence and Appendices* (1924) which in itself suggests the tentative nature of many of the emergent state's negotiations with its structure and proceedings: the 'Wireless Broadcasting Report' was in fact the White Paper prepared by and for the Postmaster-General (PMG), as he was called at that time.[2]

As W.T. Cosgrave was to inform the Dáil during the debate on this *Report*, 'This was the first Committee which was formed to deal with a subject like this'.[3] This episode in modern Irish history is a classic example of a country, its elected representatives severally and collectively, and its government feeling their way in unknown territory. That a concept as fundamental and yet as elusive as human communication could find itself at the centre of such a 'subject', and that the apparent red herrings of extraneous matter could prove not to be red herrings at all, but integral elements in a narrative of such complexity and relevance to Irish life, is a matter for profound reflection.

In his biography of Bryan Cooper, the Sligo landowner and Independent TD for South Co. Dublin 1923–30, who was responsible for urging the publication of the full version of that narrative, Lennox Robinson refers to this Report, together with that of the Committee of Public Accounts and that of the Army Inquiry as 'furnish[ing] the secret history of Ireland from 1921 to 1926'[4] and certainly, as a mirror held up to the internal workings of the Irish mind and the Irish conscience, the *Report* (as I shall refer to it) is a remarkable document. Central though it is, surrounding it are many other documents, some of them government memoranda, others works of fiction, still more the straightforward aspirations and observations of businessmen, scientists, radio

2 The office of Postmaster-General became that of Minister for Posts and Telegraphs following the Ministers and Secretaries Act, 1924; subsequent administrations have changed the designation of the portfolio to 'Minister for Communications' and 'Minister for Arts, Heritage, Gaeltacht and the Islands'.
3 Dáil Éireann Parliamentary Debates 15 February 1924, vol. 6, cols. 1107–8 – subsequently cited as 'DD 6' etc. During the early years of the Free State, the PMG/Minister for Posts and Telegraphs was an 'Extern Minister' – that is, not a member of the Executive Council (Cabinet); the office became a Cabinet post in 1927 when the 'extern' status was abolished.   4 L. Robinson, *Bryan Cooper* (London: Constable, 1931) p. 163.

enthusiasts, investors, retailers and ordinary citizens reflected in the popular press of the day.

Surrounding the *Report* and the entire process of establishing 2RN are also the social, cultural and economic realities of Ireland, newly independent but still with post-Treaty ties to the apron of its former occupier and with palpable evidence throughout the country of that occupation in law, infrastructure and mindset. As Mary MacSwiney, newly elected to the Dáil in 1921 in succession to her late brother Terence, put it in the debate on the Treaty: 'Can you not realise the slave mind it took a hundred years to create, it will require a few years of freedom to bring us back'.[5] The phase commonly known today as 'post-colonial' was just beginning, and the introduction of radio – a little understood phenomenon – as a means of Irishmen and Irishwomen speaking to one another over the airwaves of freedom illustrates the uncertainties and anxieties of that 'secret history'.

The man against whom these allegations were made was himself a creature of complexity: Darrell Figgis, poll-topping Independent TD for Co. Dublin 1922–5,[6] novelist, poet and critic, who aided Erskine Childers in the Howth gun-running in 1914, was Secretary of Sinn Féin 1917–19, acting chairman (under Michael Collins) of the Committee which drafted the Constitution of the Irish Free State, and – most relevant to the charges made against him – secretary of the Committee of Inquiry into the Resources and Industries of Ireland. The resources of Ireland had been one of the chief factors in the mobilisation of an intellectual middle-class momentum in mid-nineteenth-century Ireland,[7] and were to be so again in the early years of the new state. In his pamphlet *The Gaelic State* (1917) Figgis had anticipated this initiative:

> The unused mineral resources of the country … are, as is well-known, very considerable, and one of the first tasks of an Irish State would be to see that they were used.[8]

Figgis had also been a judge of the 'Dáil Courts' set up in 1919 to adjudicate in land claims. This, too, he had anticipated in *The Gaelic State*, as he had certain aspects of the Constitution, which he saw as a replication of the historic Irish polity which had pre-existed the English invasion.[9] Figgis' unwilling – and in

5 *Official Report of Debate on the Treaty* (Dublin: Dáil Éireann, 1922) p. 230. 6 Figgis received 15,087 votes in the election of 1922; however, at the 1923 election he slipped to a poll of 2,923 and took the eighth seat. 7 Sir Robert Kane, 'The Industrial Resources of Ireland' (Dublin: Loyal National Repeal Association, 1845 – 2nd edn); cf. also R. D. Lyons, *The Intellectual Resources of Ireland* (1873). 8 D. Figgis, *The Gaelic State in the Past & Future* (Dublin: Maunsel, 1917) p. 81. 9 Cf. ibid. pp. 22–3 on the role of the brehons as civil arbitrators, and pp. 66–9 on the appropriate composition and accountability of the government, which predicted the concept of Extern ministers.

some respects unwitting – involvement in Irish politics, which he at one point called 'ignoble', was, in fact, based on an extraordinarily profound awareness of Irishness, and his explication of the historical reasons for the need for a radical revision of Ireland under Irish governance can hardly be bettered.

The man who made the allegations was a London-based businessman of Irish extraction, Andrew Belton, who wished to use Figgis as a front man for his investments in the lucrative business of 'reconstruction' which Ireland offered in the aftermath of its long and destructive struggle towards independence. Belton claimed to have been a major in the British army, of which he had been a boxing champion, 'Commander-in-Chief of the Army of the Emperor of Morocco'[10] and instrumental in raising a loan for the government of British Guiana. Figgis' suicide in 1925 was, I believe, due not merely to other unhappy circumstances of his life but directly to the revelations about his part in Belton's affairs.

Their acrimonious and short-lived relationship permeates the 600 pages of the *Report*, occupying the hearts and minds of all the participants and colouring the already embarrassed and embarrassing issue of policy with the innuendo of 'influence'. That Figgis may have suggested to Belton that he could become 'Minister for Reconstruction' and that Belton could have seen him as a potential leader of the Irish government (and had contemplated harnessing the forces of Lord Beaverbrook and Winston Churchill as well as the southern Irish unionists to infiltrate Irish politics and politicians at the highest level – Arthur Griffith, W.T. Cosgrave and Michael Collins) lends characteristics to this narrative which one encounters more often in the fiction of the period such as Figgis' own *The House of Success* (1921) and Eimar O'Duffy's *roman à clef The Wasted Island* (1919) in which Figgis appears in the character of Cyril Umpleby.

That the *Report* should read sometimes like pages from a novel – and that at one point the participants should refer explicitly to the concatenation of fact and fiction[11] – is due only in part to the Figgis-Belton intrigue. The sense of unreality which imbues much of the *Report* is due also to the lack of pointers as far as the nature of radio was concerned – its potency as a medium, its uses and applications, its cost. At one and the same time we see the members of the Committee groping in the dark and yet providing brilliant glimpses of that potential.

---

10 In the words of Senator Colonel Maurice Moore: *First, Second and Third Interim Reports and the Final Report of the Special Committee to consider the Wireless Broadcasting Report together with Proceedings of the Committees* [sic], *Minutes of Evidence and Appendices* (Dublin: Stationery Office, 1924) document 556 – referred to hereafter as *Report*: the evidence given to the Committee was numbered by paragraph, while the appendices containing the documentation were numbered by document. 11 Cf. William Magennis: 'taking the fiction writer's imagination … if anyone deliberately intended to pervert things, and had the novelist's power, he could do it': *Report* para. 2714.

Ireland was not alone in trying to understand radio.[12] Only a very few, like the Belarus-born American David Sarnoff (1891–1971), were intelligent and clear-sighted enough at the beginning to see how to 'make radio a household utility'.[13] In 1892, for example, four years before Sarnoff's employer, Guglielmo Marconi, had arrived in London to introduce his radio discoveries, an English scientist, Sir William Crookes, 'had described as "bewildering" the prospect that global communication could be carried on without wires'.[14] The chief architect of the BBC, J.C.W. (later Lord) Reith forecast that 'rightly developed and controlled, it will become a world influence with immense potentialities for good – equally for harm, if its function is wrongly or loosely conceived'.[15] The question – obvious to us now but not universally perceived in the 1910s and 1920s – was what distinguished 'right' from 'wrong' in the process of conception.

Elsewhere, Reith said:

> Broadcasting ... presents for reflection characteristics which are unique in their constitution and significance. It is not subject to the limitations which handicap so many of the great endeavours which are instituted to promote unity of thought or action in matters of high moment, national or international, or undertaken on behalf of individual or corporate intelligence. It operates on a plane of its own, and is therefore the more commanding in its interest for those who are associated with its development.[16]

In 1966, critic and actor Gabriel Fallon, who was an early participant in radio drama, observed:

> 'Change is inevitable' said Disraeli. In a progressive country change is constant. This is certainly true of broadcasting. The metamorphosis of 2RN into Radio Telefís Éireann has a ... speedy and rather frightening complexity. It was as if the canal boat we once knew had suddenly turned into some huge atomic battleship. The aesthetic growth has been no less marked ... Whenever I chance to visit the studios ... I feel I'm a stranger in a strange land, and I sometimes wonder if that room,

12 I employ the term 'wireless' where the contemporary circumstances require it; elsewhere I refer to 'radio', in agreement with a writer in 1923 who objected to 'wireless' – 'why describe a thing as a negation?': quoted in A. Briggs, 'The Image and the Voice' *Twentieth Century* vol. 166 no. 993, November 1959. 13 Quoted in A. Briggs, *The History of Broadcasting in the United Kingdom 1: The Birth of Broadcasting 1896–1927* (Oxford: Oxford University Press, 1995) p. 24. 14 Quoted in Asa Briggs, 'Past, Present and Future in Headlines' in A. Briggs and D. Snowman (eds.), *Fins de Siècle: how centuries end 1400–2000* (London: Yale University Press, 1996) p. 179. 15 Quoted in A. Briggs, *The Birth of Broadcasting* pp. 305–6. 16 J.C.W. Reith, *Broadcast over Britain* (London: Hodder and Stoughton, 1924) p. 222.

with its solitary microphone, in [Little] Denmark Street, is not just part of some vague, adventurous dream.[17]

One of the chief actors in this narrative, Thomas Johnson, leader not only of the Labour Party but also of the Opposition in the Dáil (due to the boycott by anti-Treaty deputies supporting Éamon de Valera), saw something of the future: 'if what we read about men being able to carry receiving sets in their watch pockets, attach them to their umbrellas, and receive messages, is likely to be true, then the chances of licensing every set are very small indeed'.[18] Bryan Cooper himself, alluding in the Dáil to H.G. Wells' vision of the scientific future, said 'I look upon broadcasting as only the beginning of a potential asset which may be of extraordinary value to the State ... which should not be in private hands, but which the State should control and scrutinise'.[19]

As we shall see in Chapter 2, the military and subversive uses of radio had already been demonstrated in wartime Ireland, thus requiring that the State should take a protective stance, but, as Chapter 3 indicates in alarming detail, it was by no means a presumption that in peacetime the operation of radio should be the responsibility of the State. It is worth recalling that at the time of the White Paper and subsequent deliberations (1923–4) the BBC – for most of its history upheld as the embodiment of public service principles – was a consortium of commercial radio interests entitled the British Broadcasting *Company*, which only on 1 January 1927 became the British Broadcasting *Corporation*.

That the issue of public policy for broadcasting should have been so haphazardly discussed is an indication of the fact that the polity of the Irish Free State was in formation, that Irish citizens were only beginning to think in positively Irish ways and to organise Irish society in the areas beyond the experience of the underdog. Had not the Figgis-Belton intrigue been uncovered, that discussion might not have taken place at all.

Lennox Robinson also wrote in his life of Bryan Cooper that

> till the end of this century there will be two schools of thought in Ireland: one school which thinks that Ireland can express herself best by hugging herself tighter and ever tighter and accepting nothing from outside, and the other school which thinks that Ireland will sacrifice nothing by becoming international, accepting everything from outside and shaping it to her own image.[20]

---

17 In a programme broadcast on 2 December 1966: RTÉ Sound Archives tape 32/68A. **18** DD 6, 15 February 1924, col. 1090. Johnson was speaking in reply to the PMG's anxiety about allowing unlicensed radios. The licence requirement for radio was abolished in 1972. **19** Ibid. 3 April 1924, col. 2883. **20** L. Robinson, op. cit., p. 157.

This, too, exercised the Committee and the Dáil, but while, in the light of the unequivocal tone of Douglas Hyde's inaugural address on the opening night of 2RN (see Appendix 2) we might expect it to have been a central and pervasive plank in its proceedings, it seems to have been less obvious a preoccupation but perhaps more subliminal. In fact, it appears that certain cultural as well as pragmatic assumptions were made regarding the possible debate of Irish-Ireland versus cosmopolitanism in relation to the set-up of radio – and certainly we find far less debate than attended the inception of Telefís Éireann in the late 1950s and early 60s or the creation of the second television channel in 1978.[21]

Nevertheless, a cultural condition which we might best describe as *anxiety* did stimulate conditions which went beyond the cultural, as the participants recognised, if only subliminally, that the issue of identity was, if not at stake, certainly at risk. Conor Cruise O'Brien, whose observations as Minister for Posts and Telegraphs on the origins of Irish radio will be considered in Chapter 2, has underlined the fact that communication, and the issue of freedom of speech, affects our sense of fundamental rights and fundamental values:

> Any legislation on broadcasting … necessarily raises very fundamental issues: essentially those of freedom in a democratic state and the limits of such freedom … unavoidably touching on central issues of political philosophy… We are not really afraid of broadcasting … we are afraid of what we may do to ourselves and to one another *with* broadcasting.[22]

There is in this almost an echo of the British Postmaster-General in 1926, who told the House of Commons 'If once you let broadcasting into politics, you will never be able to keep politics out of broadcasting'.[23] It alerts us to the wider question of the power of the media, and especially the assembling of multinational media empires by such modern moguls as Rupert Murdoch and Silvio Berlusconi, and to the various attempts to address these developments in international forums such as that of UNESCO on communications and the 'new world order', chaired by Seán MacBride in the 1970s.[24] But although the scale of the problem has escalated to this extent, the essential point remains one of principle: the control and transmission of information and opinions *via* electronic, unseen media. The fact that the medium of radio was relatively unknown and not understood in the early 1920s increases rather than diminishes that sense of anxiety.

21 These topics will be addressed in future volumes of the 'Broadcasting and Irish Society' series by, respectively, John Bowman and Muiris Mac Conghail.   **22** C. Cruise O'Brien, *Herod: reflections on political violence* (London: Hutchinson, 1978) pp. 110–11, 142.   **23** *Hansard* vol. 199, 12 November 1926. **24** *Communication and Society Today and Tomorrow: Many Voices, One World: report by the International Commission for the Study of Communication Problems* (Paris: UNESCO, 1980).

Throughout the proceedings of the Wireless Committee we encounter the issues of control and content: where was the appropriate *locus* of authority, and what was the desired nature of programme content? In examining the debate surrounding the founding of 2RN, it is useful to conflate two definitions: one, Harold Lasswell's classic view of media analysis: 'who says what by what means to whom and with what effect?';[25] the other, Sidney Verba's observation that 'political culture regulates who talks to whom and who influences whom'.[26] In the Irish context both definitions suggest that political culture and state-controlled communications were developing coterminously. But we must also bear in mind the fact that broadcasting policy *appears* to have been indeterminate rather than determinate, and not necessarily consonant with the declaratory spirit of the Constitution. This is especially difficult when we consider that 2RN was not so much concerned with who *said* what as with who *sang* what, since its early programming was predominantly musical. We will not find in the early schedules of 2RN any extensive indication of the 'reconstruction' or nation-building in which W.T. Cosgrave's Cumann na nGaedheal government was so passionately engaged in the 1920s, but, as I shall argue in Chapter 5, we can detect a subliminal sense of what that reconstruction involved, and a working out of what role a radio service might play in the development of Irish culture.

One further aspect of anxiety was the question of the Irish language, which in the case of radio was occluded rather than illuminated. One of the central figures in the creation of 2RN, P. S. O'Hegarty, Secretary of the Department of Posts and Telegraphs, had written in 1924:

> Whether Ireland will survive at all, will depend, not on further political changes, but on the character and the institutions which she produces. And that is the gravest problem which confronts her. In its forefront is the question of the revival of Irish, and it is the vital question ... If we do not revive and develop Irish, we must inevitably be assimilated by one of these two communities [Britain or America], or by the combined power which they must eventually form, and in that case our name and tradition and history will vanish out of human ken, and our national individuality will be lost.[27]

With his political master, J.J. Walsh, O'Hegarty strove unsuccessfully to persuade Dáil Éireann to ensure that the Irish language became one medium

25 H. Lasswell, 'The Structure and Function of Communication in Society', in L. Bryson (ed.), *The Communication of Ideas* (New York: Harper and Row, 1948). 26 S. Verba, 'Conclusion: Comparative Political Culture' in L. Pye and S. Verba (eds.), *Political Culture and Political Development* (Princeton NJ: Princeton University Press, 1965) p. 519. 27 P.S. O'Hegarty, *The Victory of Sinn Féin: how it won it and how it used it* (Dublin: Talbot Press, 1924, repr. UCD Press 1998) p. 127.

of reconstruction, that it was a vital element in the Irish character which was being reasserted. That they so signally failed, and that the Irish language would wait fifty years for the radio service which Walsh asserted was essential,[28] is an indication of the ambivalence of politicians towards this symbol of cultural identity. There was plentiful evidence, in the wake of the first world war, of the fate of 'a small nation' – which Darrell Figgis was to describe at the time (1916) as 'a great war that is no less than a toppling civilization'.[29] While Ireland's political freedom was assured, it faced the internal dangers of an unstable democracy, while externally its cultural and economic vulnerability would become increasingly evident. It was the task of O'Hegarty and Walsh to establish a communications channel between the government and the Irish people which would be trusted and respected and which would contribute to that reconstruction. That they so nearly put the service as a whole in the hands of an English merchant adventurer is one of the most extraordinary episodes in the history of that reconstruction.

In two respects, the Figgis-Belton affair foreshadowed the type of inquiry with which this Introduction opened, and which has been such a feature of public and private life in recent years and decades, beginning with the privacies of the 'Kerry Babies' inquiry in the 1980s and reaching into the 1990s and 2000s with the tribunals relating to payments to politicians (chaired by Justices Flood and Moriarty). At one point in the Wireless Committee's enquiry into the Figgis-Belton affair, a sworn judicial inquiry was called for, eliciting the clairvoyant observation by William Magennis that, if that were the path taken, 'we shall have nothing else to do for the rest of our existence'.[30] At another, when Bryan Cooper's motion to publish the full documentation was being debated, deputies foresaw the Freedom of Information Act 1997: if everything were published, it would lead 'to a doubt in the minds of officials … as to how far they were likely to have anything they said more or less confidentially … made public at any particular moment'.[31] As W.T. Cosgrave so wrongly put it, 'Departmental files … cannot be made the subject of publication. That is fairly obvious'.[32] The story of this episode of the Irish media is full of its future.

---

28 Raidió na Gaeltachta started broadcasting in 1972.   29 D. Figgis, *Æ (George W Russell): a Study of a Man and a Nation* (Dublin: Maunsel, 1916) p. 156.   30 DD 6, 22 February 1924, col. 1396.   31 Ibid. 14 February 1924, col. 1070.   32 Ibid. col. 1071.

CHAPTER 2

The scientific, political
and social background

GUGLIELMO MARCONI AND THE
INTRODUCTION OF RADIO INTO IRELAND

In his influential textbook of the 1960s, *Understanding Media* (1964), Marshall McLuhan, famous today for the expression 'the medium is the message',[1] drew attention to the fact that the world's first broadcast occurred in Dublin on 25 April 1916.[2] Up to that time, radio signals were *narrowcast*; that is, they were transmitted from one point to another, the receiver(s) being known to, and intended by, the sender, and *vice versa*. With the advent of broadcasting, the certainty of point-to-point transmission was replaced, or superseded, by the indeterminate nature, number and location of the receivers.

The occasion in April 1916 – the 'Easter Rising' – cannot have had more significant connotations, nor can it have offered a more pointed example of the confusion between, and the gradual separation of, wireless telegraphy – the sending of a message over a deliberate distance – and wireless telephony – the sending of sound into the airwaves.

The leaders of the Rising had planned that they would take over the premises of the Irish School of Wireless Telegraphy, situated above Reis's fancy goods shop at 10/11 Lower Sackville (today O'Connell) Street, at the junction with Lower Abbey Street. The commander of the post, Captain Tom Weafer, was killed by a sniper's bullet during the first attempt to erect an aerial on the roof of the building. Nevertheless, on Tuesday 25th April, his unit succeeded in transmitting in Morse code on the shipping wavelength, in the hope of informing the outside world, in statements written by James Connolly, that the Irish Republic had been proclaimed the previous day and that republican forces occupied the centre of Dublin city. Transmissions continued until midday on Wednesday 26th, when British artillery fire made

---

1 The title of his 1967 publication (co-authored with Q. Fiore).   2 M. McLuhan, *Understanding Media* (London: Routledge, repr. 2001) p. 332

further activity impossible. Even then, they succeeded in carrying the transmitter across O'Connell Street to the GPO where the rising was fated to expire.

It is almost certain that the transmissions were undetected by any receivers (although news of the Rising was sent *via* the Marconi station at Valentia and appeared in American newspapers). But, as Maurice Gorham points out, 'whether or not the broadcasts reached their objective, it showed great imagination for the men who planned the Rising to think of using wireless for such a purpose as early as 1916. They were of course ahead of their time'.[3] Although there had been a genuine intention to establish a republican radio (or wireless telegraphy) station – an intention which was not realised – the exercise proved the point of McLuhan's overall perspective of the media – that the medium *was* the message: the symbolic nature of the gesture, as symbolic and as futile as the leaders knew the Rising itself to be, *was* in itself the message, sent out to an unwitting world. The predominance of sign over fact, as Maurice Goldring has noted, sets the scene for the triumph of symbols over that which they symbolise: 'the beauty of a gesture [carries the day] over tactical accuracy'.[4]

In the 1970s Conor Cruise O'Brien, as Minister for Posts and Telegraphs, became well-known for his commentary on this incident:

> It was of course illegal, both under the domestic laws of the state in which it occurred, and under the international radio regulations then governing wireless telegraphy. It was also war propaganda, the transmission of words to win support for violent action. And like most war propaganda it was designedly inaccurate and misleading ... The painful conclusion is, I think, inescapable. Broadcasting was conceived in sin. It is a child of wrath. There is no knowing what it may not get up to.[5]

O'Brien's anxiety came from several areas of his responsibility: two years previously he had felt obliged to introduce the Broadcasting Authority (Amendment) Bill 1975 (which passed into law in 1976) in the context of controlling the appearance on the airwaves of subversive organisations;[6] in 1977 a heated debate was in progress as to the nature of the planned second television channel; and throughout the 1970s attempts had been made to control, and legislate for, the illegal 'pirate' radio broadcasting which had

3 M. Gorham, *Forty Years of Irish Broadcasting* (Dublin: Talbot Press, 1967) p. 3. **4** M. Goldring, *Faith of Our Fathers: the Formation of Irish Nationalist Ideology 1890–1920* (Dublin: Repsol, 1982) p. 43. **5** 'Nation shall speak peace unto nation among other things': address to the Dublin Symposium on Direct Satellite Broadcasting organized by the European Space Agency and the European Broadcasting Union, 23 May 1977, in C. Cruise O'Brien, *Herod* p. 142. **6** Section 31 of the Broadcasting Authority Act 1960 had first been invoked in 1971.

proliferated in Ireland.[7] In the period 1973–7 O'Brien, as Minister, was involved in all aspects of these issues. As he stressed in addressing a Satellite Broadcasting symposium, 'I am a minister in a sovereign state, having responsibility to see that domestic laws and international agreements regarding broadcasting are respected'.[8] Over sixty years after the 1916 transmission, it was still possible for someone with these responsibilities to be apprehensive about the nature of a potentially dangerous medium:

> I think our history, both in the more remote past and recently, has placed us today in a situation where the defence of the democratic state, together with the liberal values and civil rights for all citizens which that kind of state alone sustains, requires a high degree of intelligent vigilance and that such vigilance should be turned on our use of words and images and particularly on the broadcasting of these.[9]

O'Brien's views had been partially expressed in 1924 by the Postmaster-General: – 'Considering the dangerous instrument provided through the medium of wireless I do not see how a nation could leave [it] at the mercy of any but reliable citizens … Nobody can say at the moment how wireless is going to develop'[10] – and echoed by at least one technical expert: 'there is no knowing what may develop … there may be all sorts of unknown developments, so much so that there is a possibility … that it may be necessary for the State to take it over'.[11] Moreover, in his *Victory of Sinn Féin*, published in 1924, the PMG's departmental secretary, P.S. O'Hegarty, had repeatedly emphasised the provisional and speculative nature of Irish society: 'the "Island of Saints and Scholars" is burst, like Humpty Dumpty, and we do not quite know yet what we are going to get in its place'.[12]

There is an important radio analogy to the Irish situation. As Reith wrote in 1924:

> The operations of broadcasting are dependent for their propagation on the mysterious and fascinating medium we call ether. When we speak of the ether, we speak more or less as fools, for the more is discovered, the more apparently contradictory facts are revealed. It would seem to have properties which formerly were regarded as mutually exclusive. While it fascinates, it mystifies; and the more it fascinates and the more it is explored the more it mystifies. With all manner of its characteristics and

7 The first use of the word 'pirate' to describe illegal radio activity occurred in Britain in 1922, A. Briggs, *The Birth of Broadcasting* p. 100. **8** C. C. O'Brien, op. cit., p. 142. **9** 'Broadcasting and Terrorism', pp. 118–19. **10** *Report* paras. 69, 96. **11** Ibid. para. 1108, evidence of E. C. Handcock MIEE. **12** P.S. O'Hegarty, op. cit. p. 91.

properties definitely and mathematically proved, it is still only a conception of the mind. When we attempt to deal with ether we are immediately involved in the twilight shadows of the borderland ... as knowledge increases, so does ignorance.[13]

'Propaganda' – the term used by Conor Cruise O'Brien to describe the 1916 broadcast – was much in evidence during the meetings of the Wireless Committee, as it wrestled with the nature of broadcasting and, indeed, the uses of language. In *The Victory of Sinn Féin* O'Hegarty had also referred to the onset of the civil war as 'an extraordinary example of the power of words',[14] and now he found himself in the thick of a debate which focussed on that power.

There are therefore profound connotations in Walsh's statement to the Committee on 16 January 1924 'when I use the word propaganda I intend it to cover everything supplied through the medium of a broadcasting station'[15] – a point which he repeated a few minutes later: 'Everything that comes from a broadcasting statement is propaganda'.[16] While one might pedantically observe that *propaganda* strictly speaking means 'to be propagated' or 'disseminated', and that therefore everything intended for transmission by radio was *propaganda*, there is a much more startling aspect to Walsh's point: his experience of the war of independence and of the civil war was – as was that of all in the committee room at that moment – a cultural as well as a military or political experience. Ireland had been the site of a 'propaganda war' in which Arthur Griffith had established a Department of Propaganda (later Publicity), one of whose functions was to label the anti-Treaty faction as 'the Irregulars', another to transmit news to Britain by telegraph.[17] It was another drama in which the control of the medium was at least as important as what was transmitted, if not more so.[18]

As Walsh went on to say very forcefully on the question of whether a broadcasting station should be Irish-controlled for Irish audiences, or simply a means of re-transmitting material from England:

---

13 J.C.W. Reith, *Broadcast over Britain*, pp. 222–3.   14 P.S. O'Hegarty op. cit. p. 85.   15 *Report* para. 390.   16 Ibid. para. 403. It must be assumed that 'statement' is a stenographer's error for 'station'. 17 In 1925 Richard Hayward, writing in the *Irish Radio Journal* (the article was a partial reprint of his speech to the Publicity Club) referred to the upcoming Dublin Broadcasting Station as 'the most important weapon in the Government's armoury of publicity and the sweetest and most efficient instrument in its advertising band' – *Irish Radio Journal* vol. 2, no. 23, 16 November 1925. The juxtaposition of the musical and the military metaphors is instructive.   18 Paddy Scannell and David Cardiff, in their *Social History of British Broadcasting* vol. 1, *1922–1939 Serving the Nation* (Oxford: Blackwell, 1991) describe Reith's attempts to have 'controversial' matter allowed on the BBC: 'Under the present terms the BBC was falling behind enlightened practice in other countries. In Italy and Russia ... the national broadcasting systems were used for political and cultural propaganda, in Holland radio was used for religious propaganda, in the United States there was complete freedom, and in Germany – which Reith regarded as the most relevant example – controversial subjects were positively encouraged' – pp. 41–2.

> There are and have been people in this country who have been
> prepared to sacrifice their lives for ideals. Language is one of these
> ideals, and these people who are prepared to sacrifice their lives for
> ideals would not certainly look kindly on the victimization of the Irish
> language.[19]

Radio came to Ireland at a critical juncture. The *Report* indicates, much more
clearly and explicitly than any other document, including the subsequent Dáil
debates, that its significance could not be dissociated from the experience and
aftermath of the past five years, especially in the light of continuing political
instability. Walsh spoke for the consensus within Dáil Éireann when he
continued:

> As an Irishman who looks to some kind of bright future for this coun-
> try of ours, some kind of a Gaelic future, I feel that every element
> which is likely to bring about that brightness and that Gaelic spirit
> ought to be seized upon by men who think as I do. I see in this broad-
> casting one of the most potent elements in modern development for
> the shaping of the minds and the outlook of the people ... We [the
> Department] are unanimous and fixed in our view that the Irish people
> will insist on this great medium – the future of which no man can
> perceive at the moment – being in their own hands for their own shap-
> ing and their own making ... I would not entertain the idea for one
> instant that I should be the means of depriving the Irish people of an
> instrument which will go far to their making or, should it fail, to their
> undoing.[20]

Whether the station was to be used for entertainment, education, public
announcements or political speeches, it must be controlled both as to its right
to broadcast and as to its content – by 'men who think as I do'. What level of
control was to be put in place was negotiable, but the concept was sustained
throughout by Walsh and his department officials for reasons which dwelt in
the collective and recent memory.

Thirty years later Maurice Gorham, who was himself to be Director of
Radio Éireann 1953–60, was to write:

> In my view even the most truthful broadcasting becomes propaganda
> as soon as it sets out to influence listeners' thinking, attitudes, and
> actions, as well as merely to inform or entertain. It does not matter

---

19 *Report* para. 391.   **20** Ibid. paras. 392, 395.

whether you call it 'morale' broadcasting or 'counter-propaganda'; it is still propaganda, even though it may be propaganda on the right side.[21]

Once again, the perspective of what may be 'right' or 'wrong' could be especially divisive in the Irish context. The fact that during the civil war the Marconi Station at Clifden could be fought over not once but twice was a sign as much as it was a fact.

Looking behind the unique phenomenon of the 1916 broadcast, we find a series of radio episodes which in a sense predict it. It is a commonplace that any scientific development of natural resources or phenomena can be employed as easily for harmful or negative ends as for creative and positive. The 'Evil be thou my Good' of Milton's Satan which makes 'darkness visible' is a useful analogy. To employ the invisible medium of the airwaves to carry an audible message is only one step on the way to being able to carry the *visible* signals of television.[22] The fact that Guglielmo Marconi is often credited (not least by himself) with the *invention* of radio neatly obscures the deeper fact, that to *invent* literally means to *discover*, which was the real achievement of Marconi, who had been experimenting in Ireland since 1898.

In *The Power behind the Microphone* (1941) P.P. Eckersley, one of the pioneers of BBC radio, confirmed this when he wrote:

> No one invented wireless ... Its sudden birth as a practical means of communication was the result of many new conceptions which were not noticed by the man in the street because they seemed the normal result of the labours of research ... Indeed, Marconi was one who had the ability to collect bits from the scrap-heap of unrelated discovery and use them to build up a working system. He did not so much invent as adapt the work of others to a specific purpose.[23]

Like Reith, Marconi himself foresaw both the advantages and dangers of radio:

> Communication between peoples widely separated in space and thought is undoubtedly the greatest weapon against the evils of misun-

21 M. Gorham, *Broadcasting and Television since 1900* (London: Dakers, 1952) p. 10. Guglielmo Marconi's later career as an ambassador of Italy – in the USA and at the Paris Peace Conference – and his role in the inauguration of Vatican Radio in 1931 involved him as the direct mouthpiece of propaganda. On one occasion he was asked by Mussolini to put Italy's case on the Abyssinian war in a BBC broadcast, which Reith refused to allow – J.C.W. Reith, *Into the Wind* (London: Hodder and Stoughton 1949) p. 236. **22** In the 1920s a priest in the border area of South Armagh is said to have succeeded in transmitting television pictures over a short distance by means of equipment which he had designed, manufactured and patented himself: I am obliged to Paddy Clarke for this information. **23** P.P. Eckersley, *The Power behind the Microphone* (London: Cape, 1941) pp. 25–6.

derstanding and jealousy, and if my fundamental invention goes some way towards averting the evils of war I shall not feel that I have lived in vain.[24]

Because his 'invention' was so fundamental, he also recognised its enormity:

The more a man bends the phenomena of nature to his will the more he discovers and the more he will discover: because of this he will increasingly realize the infinity of the infinite.[25]

As Asa Briggs noted when he began to publish his history of the BBC, it is difficult in the modern world to imagine society without mass communications or even cars and aeroplanes. In Ireland, however, due to particular circumstances, it is not as difficult as Briggs suggests to achieve 'an effort of the imagination to stretch back to 1922'.[26]

It was not entirely fortuitous that Marconi had come to Ireland, since he himself was half Irish, his mother, Annie, being a member of the Enniscorthy branch of the Jameson whiskey distilling family. In 1905 Marconi himself married an Irishwoman, the Hon. Beatrice O'Brien, daughter of the 14th Baron Inchiquin of Dromoland Castle, Co. Clare. The marriage was dissolved in 1924.

Marconi's place in history as the Gutenberg of wireless is early and decisive, but by no means unique. In fact by 1899 a textbook had already appeared entitled *A History of Wireless Telegraphy*, plotting the growth of knowledge in the various areas and applications of electrical science, and *Punch* magazine had published predictions of broadcast entertainment as early as 1850. It was Marconi's genius which harnessed what Eckersley called 'unrelated discovery' – which could be seen to have begun with the revolution in physics in seventeenth-century France – and made of it a new use for the constituent elements. Marconi acknowledged this:

By availing myself of previous knowledge and working out theories already formulated, I did nothing but follow in the footsteps of Howe, Watt, Edison, Stephenson and other illustrious inventors. I doubt very

24 *The Popular Wireless Weekly*, January 1924. **25** Quoted by George Waters, in 'Guglielmo Marconi 1874–1937: the Man and the Medium', text of RTÉ broadcast lecture 25 April 1974. Darrell Figgis said much the same of George Russell: 'The history of Science proves well enough that every great discovery comes in some rare and lucid intuition, when the knowledge hidden in the depths of man's being, and borne unwittingly by him through his days in some tacit function of that being, suddenly – evoked may be, though not necessarily, by the sight of a little part of the universe working in picture in a test-tube – flashes before his thinking brain. For discoveries, indeed are less discoveries than recoveries' – D. Figgis, *Æ* pp. 52–3. **26** A. Briggs, 'Broadcasting and Society' *The Listener* 22 November 1962.

much whether there has ever been a case of a useful invention in which all the theory, all the practical applications and all the apparatus were the work of one man.[27]

Up to the middle of the nineteenth century, signalling had been operated through the unreliable means of semaphore. With the invention of the electric telegraph, communication was revolutionised: cable carried Morse messages instantaneously, a development which reached its apogee with the laying of the trans-Atlantic cable in 1866, the European end being sited at Valentia, Co. Kerry. Even here, the dangers of such a form of communication would have been apparent: John Mitchel at that time had asked: 'Will a lie told at one end come out truth at the other?'[28]

But, as Maurice Gorham so eloquently put it, with Morse 'wireless could communicate but it could not speak or sing'.[29] When, as a young man, Marconi encountered the work of Heinrich Hertz on electro-magnetic radiation he realised that the two branches of science could be united to enable signals to be sent without the use of cable, and in 1894 he succeeded in transmitting such signals across short distances, and, after he had detected the significance of the aerial and the earth, across increasingly longer distances. By the following year he could transmit over one kilometre and by 1896 – the year which also saw the first demonstration of cinema and the first motor show – he had filed the first patent application in London. In 1897 the 23-year-old founded the Marconi Company. The fact that Marconi could 'see the future' with his associative habit of mind meant that he would eventually own a wide range of patents with wireless relevance and, as we shall see, would thus exercise a lucrative control over its exploitation. The fact that in the 1920s his company would advertise the 'Marconiphone' as 'the triumph of the Master Mind' is a telling indication of his sense of self-importance.

Marconi's professional arrival in Ireland was *via* London, where he had obtained an introduction to the Engineer-in-Chief of the Post Office, W.H. Preece. As a result Marconi was commissioned to demonstrate his methods to the Post Office and the War Office, and with their resources was able to increase the power of his transmissions across distances of $4\frac{1}{2}$ miles on Salisbury Plain and 9 miles across Bristol Channel.

Wireless had been recognised as a tool in military operations. Meanwhile, its usefulness to shipping (either in ship-to-shore or ship-to-ship) was developing,[30]

27 G. Marconi, unpublished memoirs, quoted in A. Briggs, *The Birth of Broadcasting* p. 29. Others working parallel to Marconi included a Dane, Valdemar Poulsen, an Englishman, William Duddell, the Canadian R. A. Fessenden and the Russian A.S. Popoff: cf. ibid. pp. 19, 24–5.   **28** Figgis had quoted this in his encomium of George Russell ('Æ'): D. Figgis, *Æ* p. 43.   **29** M. Gorham, *Broadcasting and Television* p. 20.   **30** The arrest in 1910 of the murderer H. H. Crippen as a result of ship-to-shore transmission of information is a commonplace of the history of both communications and criminal

with the Marconi Company fitting out ships, lighthouses and shore stations with the transmitting and receiving equipment. Its social application was soon to manifest itself in Ireland also. In July 1898 the Dublin *Daily Express* and *Evening Mail* employed the Marconi Company to transmit results of the races in the Royal St George Yacht Club's regatta from a vessel in Kingstown [Dún Laoghaire] harbour to the harbourmaster's house on the shore, which were relayed thence by telephone to the newspaper offices in Dublin. This was the first journalistic use of wireless in the world.[31] In the same month, Lloyds of London commissioned Marconi to install a wireless link between Rathlin Island and Ballycastle, Co. Antrim, for the purpose of facilitating the shipping reports from the dangerous waters in that region, resulting in the world's first commercial use of wireless.[32]

It was in the extension of transmission power by means of thermionic radio valves[33] that the worldwide significance of radio became obvious: Marconi's persistence in increasing the distances over which radio signals could be carried culminated in 1901 in the first semi-successful transatlantic transmissions which have been described as 'defy[ing] the theoretical laws of physics'.[34] Marconi established his European station at Clifden and the North American station at Cape Breton, Nova Scotia. The Clifden station was a hub of transatlantic wireless traffic until the Civil War disturbances caused its closedown. 'Marconigrams' carried messages at a cost of 5*d.* per word for ordinary messages and 2½*d.* per word for press reports [equivalent to 40p or 20p at 2000 prices; €0.5 or €0.25] – half the cost of the equivalent service available on the cable from Valentia. Three operators transmitted at 30 words per minute, compared with the 22 words-per-minute capacity of Valentia. Overall, the station employed 150 permanent staff (including 10 engineers and 25 operators at full capacity), with approximately 140 casual seasonal turf-cutters who fuelled the generators – a substantial benefit to the region, reckoned to have put Clifden about 20 years ahead of the rest of Connemara in economic terms.[35]

One of the first messages transmitted, on 17 October 1907, came from David Lloyd George, then President of the Board of Trade in Britain:

> Every improvement in the Communications between various parts of the British Empire helps to consolidate and strengthen it. All

detection, while in 1912 the ship-to-ship alert of the sinking of the *Titanic* resulted in a number of passengers being saved by the nearby *Carpathia*. **31** P. Clarke, *Dublin Calling: 2RN and the birth of Irish Radio* (Dublin: RTÉ, 1986) p. 4. **32** Ibid. 'Marconi's Cottage', a small hut on Rathlin which it is alleged (perhaps erroneously) that Marconi built, became the subject of a poem which provided the title of a volume by Medbh McGuckian (1991). **33** The invention of which has been attributed to both Sir Ambrose Fleming and Lee de Forest. **34** G. Waters, op. cit. **35** P. Clarke, 'The Marconi Wireless Station at Derrygimla-Clifden and Letterfrack' – RTÉ information brochure 1987.

well–wishers of the Empire will welcome, therefore, every project for facilitating contact between Britain and the great Dominion across the Atlantic.[36]

(Ironically, Lloyd George cannot have known that within a few years radio installations would form a vital part of the negotiations on an Anglo-Irish treaty, or that his later involvement with the Marconi company would imperil his career.) In contrast, one of the next transmissions was from a member of Galway County Council to President Roosevelt, congratulating him on his presidency and appealing for his support in obtaining self-government for Ireland.[37]

On 25 July 1922 the anti-Treaty forces attacked the station, destroying the receiving house and inflicting severe damage on the condenser, and on 15 August it was retaken by the Free State Army, the news being announced to Marconi headquarters in London *via* a Marconigram:

> ON TUESDAY MORNING 15TH INST NATIONAL TROOPS UNDER COMMAND OF COL COMMANDANT A BRENNAN LANDED IN TWO PLACES ON THE WEST COAST OF GALWAY AND PROCEEDED TO SURROUND CLIFDEN THE LAST STRONGHOLD OF THE IRREGULAR FORCES IN THE WEST AT 6AM THE ATTACK OPENED ON THE IRREGULAR POSTS WHICH WERE STRONGLY FORTIFIED AFTER AN ENGAGEMENT OF 45 MINUTES THE NATIONAL TROOPS RUSHED THE BARRACKS WITH BAYONETS AND BOMBS UNDER THE COVER OF MACHINE GUN FIRE ONLY TO FIND THAT THE MAJORITY OF THE GARRISON HAD FLED IN DISORDER TO THE MOUNTAINS ON THE APPROACH OF THE NATIONAL TROOPS ARMS AND A LARGE QUANTITY OF AMMUNITION BOMBS AND EXPLOSIVES WERE ABANDONED TWO OF THE OUTPOSTS WERE CAPTURED AND MADE PRISONERS THREE MINES WERE LOCATED AND DISCONNECTED ALL BARRACKS AS WELL AS THE WIRELESS STATION ARE NOW HELD BY NATIONAL TROOPS.[38]

On 25 October 1922 the Postmaster-General announced to the Dáil that the station had been destroyed by Republicans, and that the question of its reopening would be investigated. In the meantime, Clifden was recaptured by the Republicans on 29 November; the Government troops now stationed at the Marconi site were forced to retire to Galway, and it was not until 9 December that the town and the Marconi station were re-occupied by the Government forces. The question of compensation for the wartime damage,

---

36 Ibid.   **37** Ibid.   **38** Marconigram dated 7.14 p.m. 17 August 1922 illustrated in ibid. p. 7.

which had rendered repairs to the Marconi station at Clifden uneconomic, would recur in the deliberations of the Wireless Committee.[39]

POLITICAL DEVELOPMENT IN IRELAND, 1916–1923

The capture and recapture of the Marconi station at Clifden in 1922 were by no means the only incidents indicating the power of radio in an unstable society, but they were to reverberate in the deliberations of the Dáil's Wireless Committee two years later. Together with events concerning Marconi's work in Britain and his involvement with the incipient BBC, it was to colour much of the Postmaster-General's original proposal for the foundation of an Irish Broadcasting Company (IBC). When J.J. Walsh gave evidence to the Committee regarding his intention to exclude the Marconi Company from the proposed IBC, he said:

> We are not able to penetrate the political or financial wall of the Marconi mind, except we feel we are in the grip the whole time of a very dangerous institution, and nothing will shake us free of that feeling.[40]

Although ostensibly the PMG's objections were concerned with what he believed to be Marconi's determination to secure the Irish radio franchise, there is a further, and more serious, suggestion that he had allowed the idea of the Marconi Company and of the medium of radio itself to become indissoluble and indistinguishable. Thus he could regard the company and the service it provided as 'a very dangerous institution' – the expression is redolent of Conor Cruise O'Brien's later view of broadcasting as 'conceived in sin ... a child of wrath'.

The Irish Free State in 1923–4 was itself both 'a very dangerous institution' and greatly endangered. It was Kevin O'Higgins who commented on the first meeting of the Provisional Government that it consisted of 'simply eight young men in the City Hall standing amidst the ruins of one administration, with the foundations of another not yet laid, and with wild men screaming through the keyhole. No police force was functioning through the country, no system of justice was operating, the wheels of administration hung idle, battered out of recognition by rival jurisdictions'.[41]

---

39 Paddy Clarke (*Dublin Calling* p. 6) points out additionally that the Clifden operation was becoming redundant since the increase in transmitting power enabled stations in Wales to service the trans-Atlantic traffic, and as a consequence the Letterfrack and Ballybunion stations were also closed. **40** *Report* para. 19. **41** Quoted in Terence de Vere White, *Kevin O'Higgins* (Tralee: Kerryman, 1966) p. 84.

The decade from the achievement of independence in 1922 to the accession of Fianna Fáil to government in 1932 was one of instability and anxiety, during which the twin and rival forces of the pro- and anti-Treaty factions moved in parallel. These factions could be said on the surface to deny the principle of electro-magnetism, so important to radio, that like forces repel and unlike forces attract; yet this polarisation and divisiveness were in fact due more to their likeness than their dissimilarity: the issue of violence which had separated them initially gave way to the apparently ideological issue of taking an oath to the British monarch. This in its turn evaporated when in 1927 Éamon de Valera, calling the oath 'an empty formula', proved the point made three years earlier when P.S. O'Hegarty had called it 'nothing but eyewash ... devised to save faces ... one of the most harmless oaths ever devised'.[42] As with so many occasions of civil war, such as the USA and Spain, it was the passionate urge towards a commonly conceived destiny which both bound together the protagonists and then divided them. Their continuing divisions would be evident in the pages of the *Report* as war gave way to a barely negotiated peace and the first attempts at civil government, during which the internal stability of the fledgling Cumann na nGaedheal party was at times severely threatened, with personalities on either side of the ideological divide present in the committee room of the wireless investigation.[43]

In addition to the danger of civil disturbance, Ireland in the 1920s was vulnerable to severe economic conditions, and to the concept of demographic change as the urban-rural balance began to shift significantly. As Darrell Figgis said in 1923, 'Constitutions made at a time, such as the present, when social and political ideas are rapidly shifting and changing must needs indicate the likelihood of change in certain directions; and make allowance for such changes'.[44]

The need for educational reform, for social improvements such as rural electrification, for the transformation of cultural institutions, all had a bearing on the way a national broadcasting service was conceived and born. But the issue of security was uppermost.

When the Wireless Committee came to consider the question of who should control the broadcasting station, the military issue was at its shoulder at every turn. So also was the potential of radio. When Thomas Johnson, Labour leader and effectively leader of the opposition, asked the PMG what degree of freedom the station might have, the words used carried unspoken and undiscussed echoes of the recent war and the overall implications of the project of Irish freedom in which they were all deeply concerned:

42 P.S. O'Hegarty, op. cit., pp. 114–15. **43** Cf. John M. Regan, *The Irish Counter-Revolution 1921–1936* (Dublin: Gill and Macmillan, 1999) pp. 227–9, 248, 233–4. **44** D. Figgis, *The Irish Constitution explained by Darrell Figgis* (Dublin: Mellifont Press, 1923) p. 58.

Deputy Johnson — Is there any objection to a person having a crystal set[45] without a licence?

Postmaster-General — Well, there would not be any great objection, but naturally we want to know what he is getting the set for. He is not getting it for nothing....

— The argument, very strongly, I think, is used that the possibility of wireless on the minds of a nation is so great and may be far greater than the influence of the Press. Does not that rather tend to the conclusion that you must give as great freedom as it is possible to give for the communications that may be made, and not to control these communications in any way?

— Well, in what particular way do you suggest that we intend to control that to the detriment of your idea of free intercourse?

— First, control of the kind of material that is to be sent out from the single broadcasting station which is going to influence the minds of people is in the hands of a company.[46] The second and ultimate control is in the hands of the Postmaster-General, who may be broad-minded or narrow-minded, who may have certain opinions as to what ought to go out and what ought not to go out, but the censorship on that tremendous influence is in these hands, the private company, of which the public has no control except through the Postmaster-General, and his influence is an indirect one, through an official.

— The responsibility for the material sent out in the first instance lies with the company; in the second instance and only when called upon to play a part, with the Postmaster-General, and in the third and final instance with the Dáil, which controls the Postmaster-General. It is the public which controls the Dáil.[47]

At this point the Secretary of the Department, P.S. O'Hegarty, intervened:

Mr O'Hegarty — As a matter of fact is it not a fact, and is it not evidenced by the experience in other countries, that a private company running an undertaking of this sort will give far more freedom and far more variety than a Government Department will, and is it not a fact that in England they have done so[?].

Deputy Johnson — You are jumping to a conclusion. You are concluding that my question is directed to a certain argument. I see from the statement of the Postmaster-General and what I am learning as I go along

---

45 For an explanation of the various radio sets available at the time, see below p. 41.   **46** At this stage of the proceedings (16 January 1924) the PMG's White Paper, proposing the formation of an Irish Broadcasting Company, was the only model under discussion.   **47** *Report* paras. 464, 467–8.

on this question is that the influence is, or may be, a very, very great one, and therefore it requires a very great deal of care and attention which, no doubt, the Postal Department has given to it. But it has to be considered from the point of view of the influence upon the minds of the people and those who control that influence, and I suggest that we, at least, ought to consider whether there is any possible practical way of securing as great an amount of freedom in the sending out of information as it is possible to secure. I am very doubtful whether a company of this kind is going to guarantee that amount of freedom. It may be the only practical method. I have not arrived at a conclusion, but I realise in this matter that we are entering upon an entirely new field, which may ultimately alter our whole conception of human relations and ethical considerations.[48]

As Lennox Robinson's observation (quoted in my Introduction) indicates, there were two opposing views as to the future of Ireland, which were not necessarily identical or coterminous with the politically divided parties. In his important study *Building Democracy in Ireland: political order and cultural integration in a newly independent nation* (1986) Jeffrey Prager equates these parallel political viewpoints with two opposing 'traditions' within Irish society and politics at the time of independence – 'Irish-Enlightenment' and 'Gaelic-Romantic' – and explores the experience of the first decade of the Free State as an attempted accommodation between the two.[49] Although Prager's thesis over-emphasises the polarisation between these two concepts and thus obscures some of the complexities and contributions of those who occupied the middle ground,[50] his work in general is sufficiently valuable for us to explore it as a model for what happened in the case of radio.

Prager defines the Irish-Enlightenment tradition, 'articulated first by the Protestant Ascendancy, which helped shape many of the institutions of Irish society', as offering 'a conception of Ireland as a modern urbane nation, like other European nations, committed to nonsectarianism and parliamentarianism'.[51] Its 'distinctive values and aspirations' were based on a 'preeminent' belief in Irish independence:

Ireland should be subordinate to no external force or control. It ought to be self-determining, capable of directing the affairs of the population,

---

48 Ibid. paras. 468–9. **49** J. Prager, *Building Democracy in Ireland: Political Order and Cultural Integration in a Newly Independent Nation* (Cambridge: Cambridge University Press, 1986). **50** As criticism of Prager, cf. J. Regan, op. cit. p. 380: 'As provocative as his theory and interpretation are they tend, like all such models, towards enforcing rather than recording an order which explains politics and political actors. What is most significant about the post-revolutionary settlement is not the exclusivity of vying political cultures but their commonality.' **51** Ibid. p. 38

with the Irish people together determining the course of their history ...
Ireland was capable of making its own contribution to world or Western
culture by being cognizant of its own history and tradition ... Irish-
Enlightenment norms [with parliamentarianism and 'legitimate structures of authority' at their centre] constituted a firm commitment to
democratic individualism ... Ireland was viewed as a moral community
in which all men and women, as members, possessed inalienable rights
but also responsibilities to other members, irrespective of status.[52]

By contrast, the Gaelic-Romantic tradition 'emerged in the nineteenth
century as a significant system of national meaning':

> The nation ought to strive to re-create its past and resist those changes
> that seemed to challenge the basic meaning of Ireland as embodied in
> its traditions. Modern Ireland was to be celebrated as a preindustrial
> nation; its identity was to be found in its rural character. The sanctity
> of the family was to be preserved, the Church was to remain a central
> social institution second only to the family, and the farm was to serve as
> the backbone for a healthy, thriving society ... In place of a commit-
> ment to a moral order of free individuals, a belief was expressed in the
> power of the Irish people to create a self-sufficient, agricultural, and
> autonomous nation unlike any other modern nation, and one where
> Gaelic principles would become preeminent despite centuries of
> suppression ... Gaelic-Romantic republicanism embodied a belief in
> the immanence of the Republican ideal ... contingent upon the aboli-
> tion of the evils of cosmopolitanism from the Irish landscape ...
> Hierarchy and authority [were] illegitimate in the organization of social
> relations ... Force and violence were necessary to purge the Irish of
> British influence ... Physical force came to be understood ... as an Irish
> rejection of parliamentary negotiation and constitutionalism.[53]

Thus Prager sees the Irish-Enlightenment as envisaging and articulating
'modern secular aspirations for the Irish nation', while the Gaelic-Romantic
'yearn[ed] for a social order protective of the values and patterns of interac-
tion'.[54] Prager's thesis, which he explores through three case studies – the
drafting of the Free State Constitution, the failure of the Boundary
Commission in 1925, and the political consequences of the assassination of

---

52 Ibid. pp. 40–1. 53 Ibid. pp. 42–6; we should however recall that the Sinn Féin pamphlet of 1917,
'The Ethics of Sinn Féin', emphasised 'the individual rather than ... his adhesion to a social group or
class' (cf. Maurice Goldring, *Faith of Our Fathers* p. 21) – the essential point being that a metamorphosis of political and social thinking was undertaken under the generic name of 'Sinn Féin' during this
period. 54 Ibid. p. 16.

Kevin O'Higgins (Minister for Justice) in 1927 – is that

> through these two distinct cultural traditions, Irishmen came to under-
> stand the problem of Irish modernity in decisively different ways. Each
> formulation was national in scope, each identified strongly with the
> Irish nation, and each offered a view of the appropriate features of the
> national community. Both condemned the British rule of Ireland. But
> as competing cultural responses to a modern nation, their coexistence
> after independence proved no longer possible.[55]

It can by no means be said that Cumann na nGaedheal, the forerunner of
Fine Gael, was exclusively the cosmopolitan, 'Irish-Enlightenment' party, or
that Sinn Féin was merely the political representative of Irish-Ireland or
'Gaelic-Romantic'. For example, the outlooks of Arthur Griffith and W.T.
Cosgrave (Cumann na nGaedheal) were decidedly parochial, producing, in
the cultural sphere, the two censorship acts which inhibited artistic awareness
and development, yet theirs was the bedrock on which the programme for
reconstruction was based, whereas, in Éamon de Valera and Seán Lemass,
Fianna Fáil, which eventually held power for 35 of the 41 years from 1932,
had statesmen of international stature and wide interests, yet whose inward
looking approach to government was to cause economic and cultural hardship.

Griffith, credited by Prager with embodying Irish-Enlightenment norms,
was fiercely anti-cosmopolitan, declaring 'Cosmopolitanism never produced
a great artist nor a good man yet and never will'.[56] And W.B. Yeats, who was
the subject of Griffith's spleen on that occasion, was precariously ambivalent
on the question of nationalism and identity.[57] Thus one cannot presume that
the pragmatic strategies adopted in any particular case were necessarily indicative of deeply held beliefs – Griffith's model for Irish independence of a 'dual
monarchy' (similar to that in Hungary) was a lesser solution than the Republic
which, he recognised, could not be achieved.

In *The Gaelic State* Figgis himself had said quite unambiguously that the
centuries-old suppression of the Irish polity had caused a centuries-old resent-
ment of, and antagonism towards, the foreign force effecting that suppression,
culminating in the risings of the nineteenth century, and that if it did not have
as its aim the restoration of that polity, any attempted protest against English
rule, or accommodation with it, would be completely misguided and alien to
the true expression of the Irish people.[58] Yet he was capable, between writing
this and taking his seat in the 1922 Dáil, of making his own accommodation

---

55 Ibid. p. 50.   56 *United Irishman* 21 October 1903.   57 Cf. Declan Kiberd, 'Inventing Irelands',
The Crane Bag vol. 8 no. 1, 1984.   58 D. Figgis, *The Gaelic State* pp. 5–7.

with the new realities and with the evolved pragmatism of Sinn Féin, thus effecting a *transitus* from Gaelic-Romantic to Enlightenment mindsets, or at least a *rapprochement* between them.

Although Prager's reading of the Gaelic-Romantic mind is generally impressive, he misses the significance of shifts in attitude such as Figgis', which constitute one of the chief ironies of the period in both political and intellectual terms: in Prager's thesis, there could have been no place in Gaelic-Romantic Ireland for Figgis – broadly regarded as 'Anglo-Irish' in background. Yet Figgis, in his writing on George Russell, and in *The Gaelic State*, displays not only a very firm grasp of the Gaelic-Romantic ideal, but also the intellectual capacity to move from it towards the Irish-Enlightenment model:

> Nationality meaning now a tissue of live interests instead of a medley of ancient catchwords, clearer political thinking resulted ... The State for which we work in the future in answer to the problems of the present is the State that dwelt in our past. It is a conception of civiliza-tion that is our peculiar heritage ... Ireland has fought long against England with no other hope than to make another England of Ireland. That is only to break a political union to make a union of ideals; and that again is to abrogate nationality while espousing its cause. It is a hard thing to say, but true notwithstanding, that many of our later heroes [Tone, Emmet, O'Connell, Butt, Grattan] have stood for noth-ing more than this ... They opposed England with Ireland, which was fine; but they did not oppose English civilization with Irish civilization, and that is a great difference.[59]

Observing that 'Grattan's Parliament'[60] excluded Irish-Ireland, Figgis demon-strated that both polities could be accommodated if there were sufficient lati-tude of thought:

> The intuitions of a nation are not lost, though they be deliberately repressed; and what those intuitions first achieved as a conceivably fair civilization they will achieve again, though with the differences atten-dant on the different conditions affecting the accidentals of life. For those intuitions are nationality; and without them nationality is but a windy word. If wise statesmanship were to act from such intuitions, looking within at the continuing mind of its own nation instead of

---

59 D. Figgis, *Æ* pp. 87, 117–18, 121–2. **60** 'Grattan's Parliament' is the sobriquet commonly applied to the Irish Parliament 1783–97 during which period it operated effectively independent of the parlia-ment in London.

looking without at the mind of other nations, and give a political place to such economic and social units – political, that is to say, in the sense of being a unit in the Polity or State of the Nation – the conditions would repeat themselves even as in the past, and the State of the past would simply and automatically repeat itself in the future.[61]

In *The Gaelic State* he wrote:

> The old Irish State was a good organisation, because it is almost impossible to think of it apart from the life which it contained and conveyed, so nearly identical were the two things. The stateships were the people and the people were the stateships ... The modern state of Ireland is not, in that sense, an organisation at all; it is simply a configuration imposed upon its life, not fitting that life at all.[62]

It is clear from Figgis' explication of the Free State Constitution, which, like the Treaty, was a negotiated and a disputed document, that he had moved towards the pragmatic acceptance of the 'Irish-Enlightenment' perspective without abandoning this espousal of the 'Gaelic-Romantic' position.

The process of 'reconstruction' to which the Cumann na nGaedheal government was committed, and with which it proceeded amid the constant experience of violence, hiatus and disruption, occurred in the absence of Fianna Fáil from the Dáil and therefore it can be argued that it did so in the absence of any consensus. Ironically, under British rule the 'first Dáil' of 1919 had been an illegal assembly – 'a situation wherein we in Ireland had two governments' as O'Hegarty put it[63] – and under the Free State there were two competing or alternative 'treaties' (that signed by the Irish representatives with the British government, and de Valera's 'Document no. 2')[64] and two Constitutions – one enacted by Dáil Éireann, the other its draft or shadow.[65] As Conor Cruise O'Brien has argued,[66] there was an ambivalence concerning the legitimacy of the Irish Free State predicated on the deeply divisive question of whether or not the political achievements of the Treaty were a sufficient basis for regarding the new State as an integral entity, delivering the fullness of freedom and independence as conceived by Irish republicanism.

---

61 Ibid. pp. 125–6. Figgis' observations are impregnated with Russell's own writing: cf. *The National Being* (Dublin: Maunsel, 1916) *passim* and *Co-operation and Nationality* (Dublin: Maunsel, 1912) p. 33: 'A social order of some kind we must have in rural districts, which will bring men into mutually beneficial relations with each other, which will create or draw out the highest economic, political and human qualities in the people, and remind them daily that they are units of a society from which they receive benefits, and to which their loyalty and affection will naturally flow'. **62** D. Figgis, *The Gaelic State* pp. 55–6. **63** P.S. O'Hegarty op. cit. p. 25. **64** For contemporary elucidation of this point, cf. ibid. pp. 58–63. **65** Cf. Prager, op. cit. pp. 67–94. **66** C. Cruise O'Brien, *Herod* pp. 128–40.

Seán Lemass's statement in 1928, that 'Fianna Fáil is a slightly constitutional party',[67] and de Valera's of the following year, 'I still hold that your right[68] to be regarded as the legitimate Government of this country is faulty, that this House itself is faulty',[69] remind us of this ambivalence.

The tensions between the pro- and anti-Treaty factions emanated from the fundamental split between those who believed that, after the planned 'blood sacrifice'[70] of 1916 further violence was unnecessary and undesirable, and those who to this day believe that the bullet is the natural ally of the ballot in achieving a full 32-county republic. No-one exhibited the former more effectively than P.S. O'Hegarty, whose *Victory of Sinn Féin* is predicated on the need to eliminate violence, and, in association with Figgis' novel *The House of Success* and his *Recollections*, and Eimar O'Duffy's *The Wasted Island*, offers a model of the metamorphosis of violence into urbanity. Perhaps the inherent contradictions within that metamorphosis are best exemplified by the fact that between 17 November 1922 and 2 May 1923, seventy-seven Republican prisoners were executed by the Free State government – the ultimate act of violence being necessary in order to gain a state of non-violence.

In his *apologia* for the Constitution (dedicated to the memory of Arthur Griffith) Darrell Figgis, who was to stand at the centre of the radio débâcle, displayed the utmost ambivalence to the document in which he had been so deeply involved. Originally published as a series of eight articles in the *Irish Independent*, Figgis' book is notable for the attacks on the very structure of the Constitution, as regards the way in which the popular will is translated into law and carried out by the administration and the judiciary. Acutely conscious of the dichotomies within the Constitution, he wryly quoted l'Abbé Caspard: 'A people is not susceptible to more than one form of government at the same period' and went on to deliver this anecdote: 'During the early days of the second French Republic a customer entered a bookseller's and asked: "Have you a copy of the French Constitution?" "We do not", the bookseller politely replied, "deal in periodical literature".'[71] The life expectancy of the Free State Constitution must have seemed equally temporary in these years.

Thus two views of the Irish present, and therefore of its future, were formulated; the anti-Treaty parties, for the first five years of the Cumann na nGaedheal government, lived in the shadowlands of dissent. As Prager puts it, 'with no real parliamentary opposition, many critical questions concerning the

---

67 DD 22, 21 March 1928, col. 1615.   68 He was addressing the Dáil which he had entered in 1927.
69 DD 28, 14 March 1929, col. 1398.   70 Cf. P.S. O'Hegarty op. cit. p. 120: 'it was agreed ... that it was our duty to make a forlorn hope insurrection if the time came when some such desperate measures were necessary in order to recall the nation to self-respect and decency'. In his *Recollections* Figgis also wrote of 'Padraic [*sic*] Pearse, looking for the spiritual renewal of a nation in a sacrifice of blood' – p. 134.   71 D. Figgis, *The Irish Constitution* pp. 5, 15.

course of the new nation went undiscussed'.[72] Postmaster-General Walsh would be quick to point out to the Wireless Committee that a significant section of the elected Dáil was conspicuous by its absence. Radio was one of the vital issues which very nearly remained in the shadows where the pragmatic struggled with the ideological.

In the early 1920s this sense of a 'split', of mutual suspicion and secret manoeuvres, was prevalent, with supposedly dependable persons and reliable positions betrayed, and betraying themselves, in the highly volatile political and cultural environment. It goes back to the Parnell scandal in 1890, and it moved into the business of the Wireless Committee. During its sittings, when Figgis was being interrogated on his motives and connections with various business interests, he retaliated with the suggestion that others involved in the application for radio licences might also have vested interests, but that they had concealed those interests, whereupon Deputy William Magennis exclaimed 'Committee Room 15!'[73] – the isolated remark having the power to summon from the collective memory the *locus* of the betrayal of Parnell and all the emotional impedimenta which it carried.

As with the fall and death of Parnell, the 'uncrowned king', so in August 1922 the deaths of both Collins and Griffith were a major loss to the pro-Treaty parties, destabilising their confidence and sense of direction. Richard Mulcahy said at Collins' graveside 'We are all mariners on the deep, bound for a port still seen only through storm and spray, sailing on a sea full of dangers and hardships and bitter toil'.[74] It is no coincidence that Reith would use the same metaphor to describe the uncertainty of radio – 'uncharted seas'.[75]

The Army Mutiny of 1924, the fiasco of the Boundary Commission of 1925, and the assassination of Kevin O'Higgins (deputy leader of the Government, Minister for Justice and External Relations) in 1927 were, as Prager has shown, testing grounds for the solidity and flexibility of the new democratic structures. Even as the Government was preparing, in 1923, for the establishment of a broadcasting station, the Postmaster-General had to write to the Minister for Defence asking for the removal of 'the military ban on broadcasting and wireless'[76] while in 1925 the GPO, which was to be Irish radio's symbolic home for forty years, was still being rebuilt after its destruction in the 1916 Rising.

---

72 J. Prager op. cit. p. 137.   73 *Report* para. 2779; only a few minutes earlier Magennis had quoted the explicit reference: 'a certain member of the Irish Party, defending Mr Parnell, said "If the private lives of other members could be inquired into as yours was, Mr Parnell, they would be found to be just as big a blackguard as you are yourself" ' (ibid. para. 2618).   74 Quoted in J.J. Lee, *Ireland 1912–1985: Politics and Society* (Cambridge: Cambridge University Press, 1989) p. 174.   75 J.C.W. Reith, *Broadcast over Britain* p. 23.   76 *Report* doc. 56.

Among the actors in the proceedings of the Wireless Committee were several who had been instrumental in creating the environment in which this reconstruction could take place. J.J. Walsh, for example, had been one of the most prominent figures in the inauguration of Dáil Éireann in 1919, and was one of those who pushed forward the idea of a committee system within the Dáil to ensure the active participation of deputies as opposed to passive acquiescence in the 'dictatorship' of the Cabinet – the first such Committee being that responsible for drafting a Constitution, 'suitable to the democratic needs of this country' as Walsh's motion had it,[77] a Committee of which Darrell Figgis became the effective chairman.

Thomas Johnson had been the chief architect of the Democratic Programme which had provided the basis for the operation of the Free State and for the drafting of the Constitution – a Programme which demonstrated the capacity for compromise between Johnson's rigorous socialism and what was acceptable to the dominant Sinn Féin party.[78] Like Walsh, Johnson had also pushed the point about the lack of opportunity for TDs to participate, calling the Cabinet domination of the Dáil 'party rule' rather than 'democratic rule'.[79] When during the 'Army crisis' it appeared that the Government (the Executive Council) was being manoeuvred into a subordinate position *vis-à-vis* the Army Council, it was Johnson who, only one month after the Final Report of the Wireless Committee, made public what was widely known and feared as a State-within-a-State:

> The Executive Council in deciding to ask for the resignation of military officers from particular posts, not in asking them to resign their commissions, was in itself a kind of admission that these officers were in a position of independence – or semi-independence – of the Executive Council.[80]

Figgis, too, had supported change in social and economic organisations, on a co-operative basis (he passionately admired the work of George Russell in agricultural co-operation),[81] in which he was joined by a future Minister for Posts and Telegraphs, P.J. Little, at that time editor of the Sinn Féin weekly *New Ireland*.[82] In his posthumously published *Recollections* Figgis wrote: 'Since the days of the Parnell split, when family was divided against family and son

---

77 Arthur Mitchell, *Revolutionary Government in Ireland: Dáil Éireann 1919–22* (Dublin: Gill and Macmillan, 1995) pp. 12, 46. **78** Cf. A. Mitchell op. cit. pp. 15, 17. **79** Cf J. Prager, op. cit. p. 109; cf. also P.S. O'Hegarty, op. cit. p. 54: 'the second Dáil was like the first – a collection of mediocrities in the grip of a machine'. **80** DD 6, 20 March 1924, col. 2246. **81** Figgis also contributed to *The Irish Statesman* edited by Russell. **82** P.J. Little's father had been Prime Minister of Newfoundland and he himself was a Dáil representative to South Africa and South America during the 'propaganda war': cf. A. Mitchell op. cit. p. 343.

against father, there has been a horror in Ireland of political divisions, a horror that has led to false unities and crushed out the practice (the rare, the vital, the manly practice) of friendship in opposition and a brave giving and taking of criticism'.[83] And if we seek further evidence of Figgis' capacity to embrace the positive sides of the 'two traditions' or mindsets, his epitaph on the anti-Treaty activist Cathal Brugha indicates that, while they may have held differing views on how to achieve them, they were largely *ad idem* in their aspirations: 'his life in the dream of the Republic – a Republic of name, without definition or constitution – was his reality. The public declaration of the name was all that to him was required to complete the reality that existed indivisibly in his mind'.[84]

Prager exhibits Emile Durkheim (1858-1917) as a sociological guide to 'the moral underpinning of society' and 'the interpenetration of the cultural and political institutional realms' and states Durkheim's major thesis to be that 'the primary tasks of the modern state are to reflect upon, articulate, implement, and transform the collective consciousness of its constituency' on which stability depends.[85] If, as Prager suggests, we adopt a Durkheimian perspective on the democratic state, especially in the relation of the political élite to society, and in the way that political legitimacy is articulated in the state 'as the organ of social thought', then we could expect to find that the programme for radio development would demonstrate to us the Irish Free State's project for national recovery. As Figgis himself wrote in an essay on 'Irish Nationality' in 1913,

> the whole struggle of Ireland down the centuries is a meaningless riddle unless this fierce desire for the preservation of its institutions be understood and fairly recognised ... The situation is essentially a simple one. She has her polity, her civilisation, her institutions, in which things she has couched her nationality, and in which things she is attesting every day that her nationality is still a breathing and vital thing awaiting its renewed expression.[86]

It is inconceivable that the medium of radio could have been overlooked as a vehicle for such strategies and emotions, but with the exception of J.J. Walsh's defence of the Gaelic heritage as a justification for founding 2RN, executed with patriotic fervour but constantly desiccated by his preoccupation with apprehending licence evaders, it was never explicitly discussed as such, until 2RN was operative and listeners were able to react to its programming.

83 D. Figgis, *Recollections* p. 205.   84 Ibid. p. 220.   85 J. Prager, op. cit. pp. 6–7.   86 D. Figgis, 'Irish Nationality', *The English Review* vol. 14, June 1913.

There are, indeed, baffling inconsistencies and contradictions in both the planning and implementation of the service, due to the inherent doubts and misconceptions of the planners about the nature and function of radio. Lest it be thought that this was a uniquely Irish situation, brought about by the war of independence and the civil war, let us recall that in the establishment of the BBC the same doubts and misconceptions were encountered. Some in Britain – not least the Prime Minister, Ramsay MacDonald – discounted and even dismissed radio as an unimportant medium.[87]

It appears to have been a general fact that, despite the large number of radio retailers in Dublin in particular, many people were unaware of radio, or at least unconscious of its presence in their lives. One example from Prager's analysis of post- and pro-Treaty reconstruction is appropriate: in the Dáil debate on the Treaty Piaras Béaslaí said

> The plain blunt man in the street ... sees in this Treaty the solid fact – our country cleared of the English armed forces, and the land in complete control of our own people to do what we like with. We can make our own Constitution, control our own finances, have our own schools and colleges, our own courts and our own flag, our own coinage and stamps, our own police.[88]

Béaslaí's obvious aspiration was to replace the emblems and structures of British rule with those of Irish freedom, but one might also expect to find more positive ambitions towards new expressions of Irishness which might extend the native culture in new directions, beyond merely wiping out the symbols of suppression. In such a context, not least because he spoke in the year in which Britain was setting up its own radio service, Béaslaí – whose Irish-language plays were to be broadcast in the early years of 2RN[89] – might have mentioned the possibility of independent Ireland finding its own voice through the medium of radio. Instead, ironically or not, that aspiration result-ed in the diminution of such media – the Censorship of Films Act 1923 being one of the first (and the Censorship of Publications Act 1929 being one of the most hotly contested) manifestations of the Free State's need to control the 'words and images' available to its citizens.

When 2RN came on the air, Cosgrave himself spoke on St Patrick's Day 1926 of solidarity and inter-dependence, emphasising that 'we must look upon all our citizens as Brother-Irishmen' and that 'the good of each is the good of all';[90] he was thus asserting the common goals which characterise not only the

---

87 Cf. A. Briggs, *The Birth of Broadcasting* p. 247. **88** *Official Report of Debate on the Treaty* p. 177. **89** Recollection of Maighréad Ní Ghráda, RTÉ Sound Archives tape 32/68A. **90** SPO S/5/111/1 – National Archives.

Cumann na nGaedheal Government but also that of Fianna Fáil, which took control in 1932.

> The building up of the State is a long task. It cannot be accomplished in a few years; it is the work of many generations. It is but a little time since we undertook responsibility for our household – there have been many changes even in that short period. New institutions, consonant with our new responsibilities, have been set up; old institutions have been remodelled to bring them into harmony with our new conditions; big schemes of construction and development have been initiated.[91]

'Responsibility for our household' meant a thorough recrudescence of a domestic 'economy',[92] which had never in the past 120 years been other than provincial and derivative.[93] But Cosgrave, in closing his broadcast with the words 'the people are awakening to their responsibilities' implied that the national project of recovery and reformation had been mobilised on an institutional and schematic basis.

Cosgrave's address on 2RN was not unique. He was constantly arguing the need for rebuilding on the foundations of inherent Irishness. A few months later he asserted:

> the aim and purposes of the Cumannn na nGaedheal Organisation are an ordered society, hard work, constant endeavour, a definite settled policy of reconstruction and rehabilitation.[94]

It had been a consistent approach of principle above party. In 1919, Griffith had said at the Sinn Féin Ard Fheis:

> Sinn Féin is not a party. It is a national composition. If it is a party at all, it is a composite party. No part of that composition may claim its own individual programme until the national ideal of freedom has first been attained. Then we may press forward our separate ideals. Until then we must sink ourselves that the nation may gain from our unity.[95]

If, as Prager comments, this 'reads like a Protestant assault on an Irish Catholic sensibility', especially in seeking to quench the passion that had

---

91 Ibid.   **92** I am using the word 'economy' as an analogy to Cosgrave's 'household' to emphasise that the word derives from the Greek oikonomos meaning 'manager of the household' or 'steward'. **93** The words might have been borrowed directly from Russell's (Æ's) *The National Being*: 'it would be a bitter reproach on the household of our nation if there were any unconsidered, who were left in poverty, and without hope and outside our brotherhood', p. 55.   **94** W. Cosgrave, 'Policy of the Cumann na nGaedheal Party' quoted in J. Prager, op. cit. p. 202.   **95** quoted by D. Figgis, *Recollections* p. 259.

brought Irish nationalism to a head',[96] then it illustrates how much Cumann na nGaedheal sought an accommodation between Irish-Enlightenment and Gaelic-Romantic cultures – which, as Prager demonstrates, culminated in Cosgrave's capitulation and transfer of power to de Valera in 1932. Nowhere is this better expressed than in O'Hegarty's *The Victory of Sinn Féin*: 'a comprehensive national movement which combined the revolutionary emotion of the aftermath of the insurrection with the clear intellectuality of Sinn Féin – a Revolutionary Movement which had a revolutionary aim and an evolutionary method'.[97] It is ironic that that same reconstruction was the attraction both to speculators like Andrew Belton, who so nearly gained control of the prospective Irish Broadcasting Company, and to those of the Gaelic-Romantic school such as Séamus Clandillon, who became 2RN's first Director.

Like the Constitution, which embodied the restrictions on the revolutionary spirit which are necessary to contain its volatile energy, the radio service would become a stabilising agent, reflecting the 'public morality' against which the Constitutional guarantee of freedom of expression had to be measured. It can therefore be assumed that, like the explicit Censorship Acts, 2RN would exercise an implicit gamekeeping role on who gained access to the microphone and what they said.

Radio Éireann could not have fulfilled this role without finding its audience in the Gaelic-Romantic tradition of Irish culture, yet it fulfilled Cosgrave's model by doing so within an Enlightenment perspective. As such, it became one of the chief agents in the legitimation of the modern Irish state, but until de Valera took office did so implicitly rather than explicitly. It did not enunciate any policy (except in Hyde's opening speech and Cosgrave's St Patrick's Day broadcast) nor did it become the instrument of any conscious programme of cultural development or *dirigisme*.

That it functioned in an air of uncertainty at every level and in every aspect of the Free State is illuminated by the statement of Patrick Hogan, Minister for Agriculture,[98] who said in 1927:

> We were all younger four or five years ago. We have learned since …
> There were a lot of things put into the Constitution which lead to
> confusion and the instability that confusion always brings about.[99]

The arguments about the programme content of 2RN can thus be seen as arguments (largely subliminal) about what the State should become and what its broadcasting service should reflect.

---

96 J. Prager op. cit. pp. 202–3.   97 P.S. O'Hegarty, op. cit. p. 6.   98 Not to be confused with Patrick Hogan, Labour TD for Clare, who was to be a member of the Wireless Committee.   99 DD 20, 27 July 1927, col. 1003.

THE LAW AND THE MARKET-PLACE

The basic legislation governing radio activity in the period in question was the Wireless Telegraphy Act 1904. Part of the confusion regarding telegraphy and telephony stemmed from the fact that the same Act had been deemed to relate to both activities. The distinction between the two was only imperfectly understood at the time. However, that confusion was succinctly summed up by the Solicitor to the Post Office, George Reid, when he stated that 'the Acts previous to the Act of 1904 were not dealing with wireless, except by way of anticipation'.[100] These included the Telegraph Act of 1869 which recognised the phenomenon of telegraphy but naturally was ignorant of the possibility of the transmission of sound. However, in 1881 that Act had been invoked in respect of the telephone, in a case in which it was decided that 'a telephone is a telegraph within the meaning of the Telegraph Acts, and a conversation held through a telephone is a communication transmitted by telegraph for the purpose of the Telegraph Acts ... Any apparatus for transmitting messages by electric signals is a "telegraph" whether a wire is used or not'.[101] As Reid observed, the judges 'say it is perfectly obvious. They quoted a lot of learned and scientific men who made inventions, and they said it was obvious they had in their minds the possibility of transmitting messages without a wire at some future date'.[102]

It also transpired that 'transmission' included within its legal meaning both sending and receiving, which elicited this exchange:

> *Deputy McGarry* — How could transmission be receiving?
> [*Witness*] — It is the law.
> — Well, the law is a 'hass'.
> — It is very often ... It may be wrong, but that is the law.[103]

The power to control telegraphy, which therefore included telephony, was vested in the Postmaster-General who thus had 'an absolute right to refuse to allow any man to have wireless apparatus on his premises'.[104] It was, however, quite legitimate to offer a wireless for sale, and even to own one, provided it was not used for the purpose for which it was intended, and this perplexing situation was to exasperate the members of the Committee when they came to consider the matter of licences. The Solicitor to the Post Office, although certain that no new legislation was required to empower the PMG to control radio activity, advised that it *was* necessary in respect of the licensing situation

---

100 *Report* para. 2214.   **101** Evidence of G. Reid, *Report* para. 2235 and Memorandum from Reid to PMG 17 December 1923, ibid. doc. 543.   **102** Ibid. para. 2251.   **103** Ibid. paras. 2248–2251. **104** Ibid. para. 2238.

in the light of this anomaly: 'if there is unlimited liberty to the public to sell and to buy such apparatus, obviously the temptation to use it without having obtained a Licence will be very great, and in fact such freedom to buy and sell must undoubtedly lead to a great amount of wireless operating without any Licence'.[105]

The PMG was initially adamant that without special licences, some of which had been issued to *bona fide* experimenters, ownership was illegal, and the civil war had made it necessary to explicitly revoke any such licence. (Approximately twenty-five had been issued prior to the outbreak of civil war.) A departmental memorandum dated 'August '23' and entitled 'Wireless Telephony' baldly states the circumstances in which war had disrupted radio development:

> After the transfer of the Post Office Services from the British Government on the 1st April, 1922, permits for the installation and working of wireless receiving apparatus were issued by the Irish Postmaster-General to experimenters and other persons who complied with the conditions laid down as regards the apparatus and aerial to be used and on payment of a fee of 10s. a year [10 shillings = half a pound (i.e. 50p) and would be equivalent to £10 at 2000 values; €12.5]. On the outbreak of the disturbances in the country in July, 1922, these permits were withdrawn at the request of the Military authorities and all persons in possession of wireless apparatus were required to surrender it to the Post Office for safe custody. The sale, importation or manufacture of wireless apparatus was also prohibited. The general prohibition against the use of wireless apparatus has not yet been removed. For some time past, however, special permits have been given on specified conditions with the approval of the Military Authorities for wireless receiving demonstrations at Fetes and other entertainments organised for charitable and public objects.[106]

Walsh had a perfectly watertight legal argument for insisting that using an unlicensed set was illegal, even though in practice it made him look somewhat ridiculous. No doubt arguing from the experience of the 'disturbances', he pointed out that the State should have 'an opportunity of controlling and tracing the whereabouts of every instrument in the country'.[107] It was this conviction which permeated the text of the Wireless Telegraphy Act 1926, rather than the determination to provide Ireland with the most appropriate, and adequately supported, public service broadcasting system.

105 Memorandum from Reid to O'Hegarty, 21 December 1923, ibid. doc. 295. 106 Ibid. doc. 117.
107 Ibid. para. 345.

In an ironically prescient expression, Walsh in fact predicted the situation which would develop in 1939 with the outbreak of the second world war, when he spoke of the need for State control:

> It might conceivably happen that within the next few years a situation would arise ... a time of national emergency ... I do not say that it will arise ... I cannot forsee any danger, but these instruments are naturally looked upon as potent forms of communication in times of national strain. I can take my mind back to the situation, twelve months ago, when it would, possibly, have been regarded as a criminal offence of the worst type to be in possession of one of these instruments.[108]

In fact, radio activity, in the sense of receiving BBC signals, was already widespread, and to a small but significant extent in experimentation. One witness, Prof. J.J. Dowling of UCD, told the Committee:

> For a long time before what is called in this country the 'Black and Tan era' I was carrying out research work with wireless apparatus, and neither the British military nor the Black and Tans nor our own forces or the other forces that operated in Ireland recently ever interfered with me, and no doubt I was, technically, at any rate, acting illegally the whole time.[109]

On 19 January 1924, during the meetings of the Committee, the Dublin newspapers carried a 'leak' to the effect that the Post Office planned to take action against owners of unlicensed sets. It was in fact the third occasion on which such action had been contemplated. Walsh stood on his legal dignity when he told the Committee on 21 January:

> The military controlled broadcasting up to three or four months ago, when it was officially handed over to us [the Post Office]. We had a suspicion at that time that some people were taking in sets, and unless we took some such action broadcasting would get out of our hands. We issued notices in the Press to the effect that anybody who dealt in broadcasting violated one of the laws of the State. Notwithstanding that, they continued to do so.[110]

---

108 Ibid. paras. 2063, 2065. The wartime, or 'emergency' experiences of Ireland, with the German Minister, Eduard Hempel, transmitting information from a radio in the back of his car in the Dublin mountains, and two men of Irish extraction – William Joyce and Francis Stuart – broadcasting from Germany and a third, Brendan Bracken, responsible for Churchill's propaganda, underline Walsh's prescience. **109** *Report* para. 3083. **110** Ibid. para. 886.

The issue of unlicensed radios would continue to vex the PMG and would dominate the Wireless Telegraphy Bill which he introduced into the Dáil two years later.

The international dimension of broadcasting also preoccupied the Committee. In the light of our knowledge today of international conventions and awareness of such organisations as the European Broadcasting Union, it seems extraordinary that in 1922-4 the concept of international regulation of broadcasting wavelengths was so hard to grasp, but here, too, the Wireless Committee found itself at sea.

The relevant convention was in fact under consideration at the time of the Wireless inquiry, and was frequently mentioned. It caused a chauvinistic outburst on the part of deputies McGarry and Magennis:

> *Mr Mulligan* [Post Office Engineer] — The wave length will be 377 metres.
> *Deputy McGarry* — How will you fit that in?
> *Mr Mulligan* — We will fit it in all right. We have already an arrangement with the British Post Office, and the matter is being referred to the Imperial Communications Committee …
> — Why is it agreed to, and a Committee sitting here?
> — It is not a matter of this Committee agreeing to it. This Committee cannot fix anything in connection with it.
> *Deputy Magennis* — … Now we are told that there are certain things that we need not trouble to ask about, because they are decided already. If we are told that, it is unconstitutional to say the least of it.
> *J. J. Walsh* — I do not think anyone suggested that for a moment, but as a necessary preliminary it is essential to ascertain through those Conventions in wireless as to the wave length to be permitted in any particular country…
> *Mr O'Hegarty* — It is a matter of international agreement.[111]

As Conor Cruise O'Brien was to point out fifty years later, 'the electro-magnetic spectrum, unlike newsprint and ink, is public property' and must be controlled 'by the state on behalf of the community, basically through an inherent monopoly in the allocation of frequencies'.[112] Therefore internationally an inter-State body was required to supervise allocation to individual States.

Ireland was also confined in certain specific aspects of international communications by the terms of its Treaty with Britain, which stipulated that

---

111 Ibid. paras. 116-17.   112 C. Cruise O'Brien, op. cit. p. 116.

the establishment of radio stations 'for communication with places outside Ireland' must be agreed by the British Government and that the latter retained the right to establish such stations. Furthermore, it provided for the closure of the wartime signalling stations and for the Free State to take them over for commercial purposes, subject to Admiralty inspection. This Walsh hoped to do, believing that there was still a considerable revenue to be derived from wireless telegraphy to Atlantic shipping from the stations at Malin and Valentia, and, on taking up office, had immediately assured himself that it was in order by seeking the opinion of the Attorney-General, who advised: 'the British Government is to have a voice in the matter as regards Imperial Defence but in no other respect ... they could not prohibit the purely commercial use of any installation as (say) for a special news service'.[113]

On this point also, it appeared, the Radio Convention was instrumental. In January 1924 Walsh told the Wireless Committee that the League of Nations had given notice of a conference to be held in London that summer to 'draw up regulations regarding radio, telegraphy, and telephony, including broadcasting, for which there are at present no international regulations whatever'.[114] By November 1924 things were little or no further forward: when the planned conference failed to materialise, the Norwegian representative at the League, the Arctic explorer Fridtjof Nansen, complained that the rapid development of unregulated radio activity was 'threatening a species of anarchy in the ether'.[115] Walsh informed the Executive Council:

> Until the question of control is definitely settled, it is not possible to determine what attitude we should adopt towards the British Imperial Wireless Chain;[116] neither is it possible to take advantage of the opportunities for development which these Stations provide. The advantages of possession are obviously great, as with improved equipment we should be able to attract most of the Atlantic Shipping messages through these two Stations, with a corresponding increase in revenue ... The messages sent to and received from ships of other Countries and the accounting and correspondence in relation to them with Foreign Administrations would enhance the status of our own

---

113 Attorney-General, 'Opinion on construction of Annex to Treaty in particular relation to ownership of certain Wireless Stations' 13 March 1922, SPO S 3669a (National Archives). The AG went on to say 'In my opinion the Irish Government would be entitled to object to any such station being established [by the British Government] for any purpose other than that of Imperial Defence'.   114 *Report* para. 2114.   115 Quoted in A. Briggs, *The Birth of Broadcasting* p. 283.   116 The 'Chain' (or 'Scheme' as it was otherwise called) was a projected linkage of countries within the British Empire which was mooted first in 1906, was resurrected in 1912–13 and set aside during world war 1, and again revived during the 1920s – cf. A. Briggs, ibid. pp. 294–6; W.J. Baker, *A History of the Marconi Company* (London: Methuen, 1970) pp. 116, 143–7, Ch. 25 *passim*. It was this project which precipitated the 'Marconi scandal' in Britain: see below, pp. 74–5.

Government. From the National point of view alone therefore the possession of these Stations is an important consideration.[117]

Since all Irish radio allocations remained within the remit of the British Post Office, the designation of '2RN' was decided in London. As Maurice Gorham notes, 'some of these call-signs were arbitrary, like Manchester 2ZY, but some suggested the place where the station was, like London 2LO'.[118] (Others were 2BE [Belfast], 6BM [Bournemouth] and 6LV [Liverpool].) There is, however, no basis for his further assertion[119] that '2RN' was intended to evoke the song 'Come back *to Erin*'.

In fact an international regulating agency – L'Union Internationale de Radiodiffusion, which P. P. Eckersley referred to as 'a broadcasting League of Nations'[120] – was formed in March 1925 but it was a further year before wavelengths were agreed by international convention, to which Ireland was a party.[121] Thus again a year later the matter had not yet been fully addressed. A memorandum of November 1925 indicates that at that stage there was still a delay and an uncertainty about the way forward:

> Until the Convention is called we cannot establish a Wireless Station for communication with places outside Ireland and we have a very important proposal recently from the Associated Press of America whereby they would undertake, if and when a Wireless Station were established here, to guarantee the State against any loss. The combine would arrange that all their European work would pass through the Irish Station.[122]

The momentum for an Irish radio service was, however, building up with a palpable public interest in, and growing demand for, radio broadcasting as a medium of entertainment. This contrasted – and conflicted – sharply with the current political situation.

There was some reluctance on the part of the PMG in the early stages of the Committee to accept the prevalence of radio ownership, but the growth in the radio trade in the period 1920–4 had been substantial, and at least in some quarters its significance and potential was recognised: in 1925 George Russell ('Æ'), whose preoccupation was the development of Irish rural life through agricultural co-operation, was to write in the *Irish Radio Review* that

---

117 PMG to Secretary, Executive Council, 5 Samhain 1924 – SPO S 3669a (National Archives). 118 Gorham, op. cit. p.23. 119 Ibid. 120 P.P. Eckersley, op. cit. p. 81. 121 The other participants were Austria, Belgium, Czechoslovakia, Denmark, Finland, France, Germany, Great Britain, Holland, Hungary, Italy, Norway, Spain, Sweden and Switzerland. 122 Minister for Posts and Telegraphs to Executive Council, 27 November 1925, SPO S 3669a (National Archives).

radio could induce 'myriad changes in the mentality of the country folk ... within a generation' through a proliferation of sets capable of receiving London, Paris, Berlin and the USA.[123]

By 1925–6 there were in fact approximately 10,000 wireless sets in Ireland, of which 3,000 were licensed at a fee of £1 (equivalent to £20 today; €25) under the scheme which was introduced in the interim between the publication of the Wireless Report and the start-up of 2RN, by which stage the licence fee had been reduced – after much resistance by the Department of Finance – to 10 shillings (50p). The number of sets rose by the end of 1926 to an estimated 25,000, and the new legislation introduced a more efficient and effective licensing system. On 20 April 1927 Bryan Cooper asked in the Dáil what had been the revenue from the importation tax on wireless sets in the previous financial year and was told that it amounted to £19,008.[124] A few minutes later he enquired as to the licence fees paid in the previous three months and was told £8,315.10.0[125] – in other words 16,631 licences. (One expert, in evidence to the Wireless Committee, had said that one third of households in Ireland [200,000] would probably buy and licence a radio in the first year of the indigenous service, rising to two-thirds [400,000] in the second year – an estimate which was thus proved to be wildly wrong.)[126]

A crystal set, operating without a battery, which could be heard by multiple listeners using headphones, could be purchased for 7/6d. (37½p or £7.50 at 2000 values; €9.4), with more powerful sets at £1-£2 plus £1 for headphones, while valve sets, using an amplifier and a loudspeaker, which required an expensive 'wet battery', cost from £4.16.0 (£4.80) for a 2-valve model to as much as £60 (£1200 in 2000; €1500) for a sophisticated set. Crystal sets would receive effectively at distances of up to 10 or 20 miles from the transmitter, while the more powerful one-valve sets would receive over distances of 50 miles, and much larger distances could be covered for listeners with two- or three-valve radios. The Committee and the Dáil would be greatly concerned as to the location of the broadcasting transmitter, since poorer listeners with crystal sets would be discriminated against if they lived more than twenty miles from the station.

Moreover, the same expert, Dr J. O'Doyle, told the Committee in 1924 that 'the sets on view in most of the windows in Dublin at present ... are sets manufactured two years ago when broadcasting was starting in England. As time went on the British public got to know there was something deficient in these sets and they would not buy them.'[127]

123 Quoted in P. Clarke, *Dublin Calling* p. 32. This echoed his expectation of 1912, voiced in *Co-operation and Nationality* (p.41) that 'we will yet see the electric light and the telephone in rural districts'. **124** DD 19, 20 April 1927, col. 1208. **125** Ibid. col. 1213. **126** Dr J. O'Doyle, *Report* paras. 2911–16. In the UK, 35,000 licences were issued in 1922, rising to 2 million by the end of 1926 – A. Briggs, 'The Image and the Voice', *The Twentieth Century* vol. 166 no. 993, November 1959. **127** Ibid. para. 2920.

O'Doyle also referred to the defects of amateur broadcasters. 'Sets constructed at the present moment in Dublin are constructed by amateurs, and these people no doubt will ruin broadcasting. It is impossible to tune them out. There is somebody sending in Blackrock on a power of 20 watts; that power is sufficient to get to the east of England or France … He goes so far as a speech every night and turns on a gramophone'.[128] This view of amateur activity was in sharp contrast to the views of the amateurs themselves, who had written to the PMG in September 1923 to remonstrate over their exclusion from the 'conference' which was being held with the prospective IBC: 'The Dublin Wireless Club is the only body in Ireland which represents the interests of amateurs and experimenters, and my Executive are strongly of the opinion that in the matter of Broadcasting which will to a great extent depend upon the support of amateurs and experimenters, the Dublin Wireless Club which has fostered the growth of Amateur Wireless in Ireland is reasonably entitled to be represented.'[129] This was not a view which the PMG shared at that stage, since he was so strongly convinced that the IBC would prove to be the only viable option, and it appears not to have been considered subsequently, unlike the situation in Finland, where the amateurs in fact organised the earliest official broadcasting, handing over the service to the BBC-model Finnish Broadcasting Company when it was ready to take it on.[130]

The Radio Society of Ireland was formed in 1922, followed the next year by the Radio Association of Ireland (with the *Irish Radio Journal* as its official organ); the Dublin Wireless Club amalgamated with the Radio Society in 1925 to form the Wireless Society of Ireland, with the *Irish Radio and Musical Review* as its mouthpiece. By 1924, according to Seán McGarry, one of these societies had 600 members paying a subscription of one guinea (£1.05).[131] Where the two former were trade organisations, the *Evening Herald* referred to the Wireless Society of Ireland as 'composed of people interested in the many branches of wireless science and including in its roll of membership physicists, engineers and experimenters of all grades of skill'.[132]

In addition to the *Review* and the *Journal*, the *Irish Radio News* appeared from 1928 to provide a forum for discussion of radio topics and a further eighteen British radio periodicals were also available in the Irish newsagents. In Britain also, wireless societies provided much of the impetus for the early development of radio. In Ireland, they were to contribute significantly to the debate taking place between the defeat of the White Paper proposals and the putting in place of 2RN, and continued to comment on the quality of programming.

128 Ibid. para. 2923.   **129** A.C. Bridle, Hon. Sec. Dublin Wireless Club to PMG, 15 September 1923, ibid. doc. 152.   **130** Rauno Endén (ed.), *Yleisradio 1926–1996: a History of Broadcasting in Finland* pp. 16–18   **131** *Report* para. 43.   **132** *Evening Herald* 11 November 1925.

There were four schools where the skills of wireless could be learned – an Atlantic College at Cahirciveen, Co. Kerry, established by Morris Fitzgerald in 1911, and a sister school in Dublin's Henry Street in 1917 which later moved to Leeson Park; the Irish School of Wireless Telegraphy where broadcasting had begun in O'Connell Street in 1916, the year of its foundation by P.K. Turner; and a School of Wireless Telegraphy set up by Harold Hodgins in Kevin Street Technical Schools, equipped by the Marconi Company.[133]

What would today be called 'high street' shopping for radio was prevalent in Dublin by 1924, when in July the Irish and Continental Trading Company opened a 'Radio Salon' at 6 Lower Ormond Quay. Other traders included Robinson's and Meldon's (both in South Anne Street), the Irish Radio Trader at 34 Dame Street (the address of the *Irish Radio Journal*), Thomas Dockrell in South Great George's Street, Lambert Brien and Co. and Yeates and Sons (both in Grafton Street), Irish Radio Stockists (3 Crow Street) and the Marconi Company (at 3 College Green). Although there was no indigenous radio service, listeners could receive several of the BBC stations, especially after the service in Belfast (2BE) came on air in September 1924, its first announcement being made by Tyrone Guthrie (then an inexperienced twenty-three-year-old who was in charge of all programming except music,[134] and who was to pioneer the medium of radio drama and to become one of the greatest stage directors of his time): 'Hello, hello, this is 2BE, the Belfast Station of the British Broadcasting Company calling'.

Radio became mobile when Messrs Dixon and Hempenstall, with premises in Dublin's Suffolk Street, imported a motor van built in the shape of a Burndept 'Ethophone V' wireless to which they attached four loudspeakers and drove around the city relaying programmes from the BBC. W.D. Hogan, who had a 'Radio House' at 56 Henry Street, also fitted out a vehicle with a radio receiver which he brought to various social functions such as tennis and golf parties. In April 1926 he installed the equipment on the Dublin-Cork train and provided radio entertainment from the newly established 2RN.

By 1925 the trade was considered sufficiently developed to hold the first Dublin Wireless Exhibition at the Round Room of the Mansion House, promoted by the Wireless Society of Ireland, at which 24 of the 37 Irish-based companies exhibited, alongside two from the UK. (It was from here that the first test broadcasts of 2RN were made). The following year the venture was repeated, under the auspices of the Society of Irish Wireless Traders. Listeners were able to hear many relays from the BBC, including the London Wireless Orchestra conducted by Sir Edward Elgar, a speech by the British Prime Minister, Stanley Baldwin, and another by Sir Oliver Lodge, one of the

133 Information in this paragraph is derived from P. Clarke, *Dublin Calling* p. 30. Hodgins became Secretary of the Wireless Society of Ireland. **134** Cf. T. Guthrie, *A Life in the Theatre* (London: Hamish Hamilton, 1960) pp. 31–3.

English radio pioneers. The Marconi stand offered a two-valve set for £7.10.0. with a 'Mellovox' loudspeaker at £2.8.0. extra.

Coinciding with the first Exhibition the *Evening Herald* published a four-page supplement which included a contribution by the Minister, detailing the advantages of the new service in respect of information, expressed the hope that homesteads would enjoy 'varied and well balanced programmes of interesting and instructive matter' and that 'this amelioration of winter in the country would be a profound benefit to the nation as a whole', and announcing the early establishment of a sister station to be situated in Cork.[135] 'Powerful as the written word may be', Walsh said, 'how much more powerful is the living voice which adds to the matter of the discourse the impetus of that subtle quality of personality of the speaker? ... I am [for] using the broadcasting service to the utmost limits of its great power to promote the happiness and prosperity of the country.' The *Irish Times* reported him as saying that 'perhaps the most important use to which broadcasting can be put is as an instrument of educational planning'[136] – a view which may surprise us, considering the case which he was to argue in defence of the White Paper.

A curious social and linguistic point concerns the use of the terms 'broadcasted' and 'listening-in' or 'listener-in'. Asa Briggs has observed that 'imprecision of language is itself an indication of a certain lack of precision of mind',[137] and in Britain it took some time before these terms were deleted from the provisional vocabulary. There, an Advisory Committee on Spoken English, which included Robert Bridges (the Poet Laureate), G.B. Shaw and Rudyard Kipling, suggested that 'to broadcast' should be conjugated like the verb 'to cast',[138] while Reith himself found the term 'listener-in' to be objectionable: 'This is a relic of the days when he actually did listen in to messages not primarily intended for him; now he is the one addressed, and he accordingly listens. Only the unlicensed listen in'.[139] Thus the concept of eavesdropping by legitimate listeners was replaced by a direct link between broadcasters and their public. Considering how closely the Irish Post Office was monitoring the British situation, it is surprising to note that the previous terms continued in use throughout the proceedings of the Wireless Committee in 1924, unless of course one allows for the fact that the PMG's insistence on the ever-present illegality of utilising a radio set meant that their users continued to be 'listeners-in' in the new Reithian sense.

The term had received a social twist of some consequence when, on 1 October 1923, the Abbey Theatre staged Seán O'Casey's one-act play *Cathleen Listens-In*, a satire of contemporary politics employing the radio idiom as a metaphor for eavesdropping. It was revived in March 1925, and was followed

135 *Evening Herald* 11 November 1925. 136 *Irish Times* 11 November 1925. 137 A. Briggs, *The Birth of Broadcasting* p. 92. 138 Ibid. p. 221. 139 J.C.W. Reith, *Broadcast over Britain* p. 162.

in May that year by a similarly inspired revue at the Olympia Theatre, *Dublin Listening* by John McDonagh.

In 1923 the *Irish Times* had carried a piece from an English paper, 'The Woes of Wireless' which began:

> Timidly she advances, wearing on her face the look of one who almost expects the treatment before her. It has happened so often! She goes towards her husband who has been ensconced in the one comfortable armchair in the room for the past three hours. Not a word has passed his lips, nor has she dared to speak. But now speech has become imperative, and so, with a smile calculated to call forth civility even from a tube official, she tentatively whispers –
> 'John dear, I –'
> 'Sh'sh!' The command is hissed at her with all the venom of a snake.
> 'But John, you –' she tries again.
> 'Be quiet!' he snaps, glowering with positive hatred in his eyes.
> It is useless for her to try and explain that an urgent message has arrived, requesting John's presence at the bedside of a rich and very sick uncle. Experience – bitter mentor – has taught her to refrain from interrupting her husband when he wills otherwise. You see, he's 'listening-in'.[140]

Two years later the *Evening Herald* carried a report that 'radio wrinkles are the latest dread of American women who see their faces marred by folds and creases brought on by the strain of listening to wireless programmes'.[141] All this ran contrary to the promise held out by a Dundalk retailer, Edgar Arnott, who advertised radio as a medium for 'Nights of Pleasure!'

On 17 May 1922 the Marconi Company, through its representative in Ireland, J.J. Kelly,[142] had applied formally for a licence to broadcast, but received no positive response; on 10 August Kelly enquired of the PMG again and was told: 'owing to the present disturbed conditions in Ireland the issue of licences for the installation or use of apparatus for Wireless Telephony is suspended'.[143]

A week later, the *Daily Express* made a similar application, which was supported by the soon-to-be Governor-General of the Free State, T.M. Healy.[144] It is possible that Lord Beaverbrook, its proprietor, saw radio as a threat to the newspaper industry, or, alternatively, that he saw its implications as a new medium of propaganda. (A year later, the *Daily Express* would clash

---

140 *Irish Times* 4 April 1923. 141 *Evening Herald* 6 February 1925. 142 He was an Alderman of Dublin Corporation at the time. 143 *Report* doc. 18. It also appears (doc. 61) that the Siemens Company of Berlin had expressed an interest, as had Messrs Uebersee Handel, also of Berlin, through their Irish agent W.A. Doyle Kelly – ibid. docs. 136–38. 144 Ibid. docs. 8–10.

with the British Post Office over the conduct of radio and, as in Ireland, would be refused a broadcasting licence.)

One application which appears to have caused considerable amusement all round was received from Francis J. Lowe, describing himself as Secretary of the Friends of the Irish Free State, New York, who proposed 'to erect an aerial [1500 feet high, on the Hill of Tara] in the form of a gigantic harp with five strings of different wire lengths so that it would be possible to broadcast ... to the five continents, so that Irishmen in Australia, Africa, America, can listen-in'.[145] Having been advised by Seán Lester, Director of Publicity at the Ministry of External Affairs (and soon to be appointed Irish representative to the League of Nations), that Lowe had cut a very ridiculous figure when in Dublin a few months previously (which included asking Lord Mayor Alfie Byrne to pay his hotel bill), and that he had alleged that he had the Postmaster-General's approval for this scheme, the matter was dropped.[146]

Another applicant, the Irish and Foreign Trading Corporation, was to be told that 'when conditions in the country again admit to the use of wireless telephony' the issuing of licences could be considered.[147] On 19 March 1923, towards the end of the civil war, Walsh's internal memorandum to O'Hegarty had read: 'On the assumption that peace will materialize within the next couple of months, we are likely to find ourselves unprepared for the Broadcasting scheme. For this reason we should now get a move on'.[148] Three weeks later, O'Hegarty replied: 'The time has now come when we may look forward to an early removal of the military ban on broadcasting and wireless'[149] and attached a draft letter for the PMG to send to the Minister for Defence (Richard Mulcahy):

> With reference to the military regulation prohibiting the holding by civilians of wireless or broadcasting apparatus, it seems to me that the time is now approaching when the use of wireless, etc., may be permitted without endangering the public interest. I shall be glad to know whether you see any objection to a public announcement being made to the effect that we hope shortly to be in a position to license broadcasting; and inviting persons and firms interested in the manufacture and supply of broadcasting apparatus to apply now, so that preparations may be made in good time. There is considerable public interest in broadcasting, and I should like to be in a position to give facilities as soon as it is safe to do so.[150]

145 Ibid. doc. 127.   146 Ibid. docs. 132–4.   147 Ibid. doc. 43, O'Hegarty to PMG 5 April 1923.
148 Ibid. doc. 38.   149 Ibid. doc. 56, O'Hegarty to PMG 9 April 1923.   150 Ibid. doc. 58, sent 11 April 1923.

As indicated in the departmental note quoted above, by August the military prohibition had been only partially lifted, but already in May, 'on the cessation of the war',[151] it had been considered sufficiently peaceful for the PMG to advertise for interested parties to apply for the broadcasting licence. It was this action that precipitated the telling of the 'secret history'.

151 Ibid. doc. 170, Memorandum from O'Hegarty forwarded by PMG to the President of the Executive Council 29 September 1923.

CHAPTER 3

The White Paper and the Wireless Report

THE WHITE PAPER

Broadcasting 'in the public interest' or 'in the public service' did not spring fully fledged from the head of anyone, either in Ireland or in Britain. As I have intimated, the emergence of the Irish radio service as an integral part of the civil service was not initially envisaged by the Postmaster-General, whose response to the overtures made to him by English and Irish interests was analogous to that of the British authorities in the establishment of the British Broadcasting Company. The eventual creation of 2RN as the incipient Radio Éireann was in fact a default model in the sense that it was entirely contrary to that envisaged in the PMG's White Paper, which in itself was only written after detailed negotiations had taken place and in response to questions in the Dáil.

In Britain, 'public service broadcasting' emerged as an explicit concept only four years after broadcasting had begun. At that point (at the end of 1926), as the Company, recognised as a public utility, was being transformed into a corporation, J.C.W. Reith, its managing director, could say 'We have tried to found a tradition of public service and to dedicate the service of Broadcasting to the service of humanity in its fullest sense' as a 'fundamental policy'. On the same occasion, and in the presence of Marconi and the Prime Minister (Stanley Baldwin), a letter from the previous Prime Minister, Ramsay MacDonald, referred to Marconi's work as having 'revolutionary significance of an elevating kind ... the wonderful discoveries of physics which have brought the BBC into being'.[1] But in Ireland, without a single-minded and far-sighted Reith to guide it, Marconi's work would be employed haphazardly and, due to Walsh's reservations, his own Company would be effectively excluded from participating in the project as principals.

---

1 A. Briggs, *The Birth of Broadcasting*, pp. 364–5.

A representative Committee appointed by the British PMG sitting in 1923 had responsibility for reporting on the status and the future organisation of broadcasting. As Asa Briggs has commented:

> It is not altogether fanciful to discern in [the Committee's] vague and tentative answers and in the often equally vague and tentative questions that elicited them the birth of the idea of a broadcasting system free from the direct control both of the manufacturers and of the Post Office.[2]

Reith's basic tenets were: that the organisation should not be profit-oriented; that it should provide national coverage; that it should exercise, or exhibit, 'unified control' – the institution being effectively a monopoly in order to ensure that there was no sectional pressure; and that it should maintain high standards.[3] These criteria are self-evident. If one accepts the principle of 'unified control' as being essential to the orderly conduct of broadcasting (but not necessarily exclusive of the possibility of more than one source of output) these criteria amount to nothing more or less than facilitating the best service possible in the national or public interest. But it is only in practice that they can be tested and confirmed: for example, the question of 'high standards' is purely subjective until it is applied to actual programming, while that of coverage depends on technical and engineering capacity as well as political will.

However, for historical reasons, the concept of this new form of communication coming within the ambit of the ministry traditionally responsible for other forms of communication was adopted in many European countries, regardless of size or age,[4] and, because the British were first in the field, their precedent provided a model which was amenable and acceptable to the Irish as it was to the Finns.[5] Thus, as in Britain, the Irish model would require that programmes should be to the 'reasonable satisfaction' of the Postmaster-General as arbiter and guarantor of public taste.

In the Irish debate, all of Reith's tenets were discussed with considerable disagreement among the parties as to their meaning and implementation. P.S. O'Hegarty, for example, when pressed to agree that radio was 'a public service demanded by the citizens of the State precisely like the telephone service', maintained contrariwise that it was 'merely a luxury'.[6] What he meant by the

---

2 Ibid. p. 160. 3 Ibid. pp. 214–7. 4 Of the smaller European states, with which Ireland might be considered comparable, the following established a privately-run service: Austria (1923–4), Belgium (1923), Luxembourg (1924), Norway (1924), while the following had established government-controlled or –sponsored stations: Denmark (1925), Greece (1928), Iceland (1930), Sweden (1924), Switzerland (1922); in Holland (1923) the station was jointly owned by the state and the operators. As we have seen, in Finland the service, initially started by amateurs in 1924, passed into state control in 1926.
5 R. Endén, *Yleisradio* pp. 19–20. 6 *Report* paras. 425–6.

term is debatable, since it is hard to understand his commitment to providing the service if he regarded it as something extra to people's real needs and therefore not strictly a utility. However, it indicates that while it is a common-place that the role of a public service broadcaster has been to *inform, educate* and *entertain*, there was no such agreement at the outset in the case of the Wireless Committee. Indeed, one member, Richard Beamish, refused to sign the final Report on the grounds that 'I totally dissent ... from any proposal to expend public monies on the supply of mere amusement'.[7]

Shortly after the Wireless Committee delivered its report, Reith, the archi-tect of British public service broadcasting, was to write, in his account of the BBC's first two years, that

> entertainment, in the accepted (but erroneous) sense of the term, may at one time have been considered the sole function of the service. It may still be, in the full sense, the primary function ... I think it will be admitted by all, that to have exploited so great a scientific invention for the purpose and pursuit of 'entertainment' alone would have been a prostitution of its powers and an insult to the character and intelligence of the people ... A closer inspection of the word 'entertainment' is sufficient to show how incomplete is the ordinarily accepted meaning ... It may be part of a systematic and sustained endeavour to re-create, to build up knowledge, experience and character, perhaps even in the face of obstacles ... Entertainment was the stated function of the Company, and many apparently considered that all its operations and the whole of the time available should be confined to purposes of entertainment alone ... It is impossible to occupy all the available hours in transmissions which would normally be described as of an entertain-ing nature. Entertainment, pure and simple, quickly grows tame; dissat-isfaction and boredom result.[8]

As with the BBC (as noted in Asa Briggs' observation), there are tentative suggestions on the Irish departmental file that the question of *policy* had to be discussed before the intended negotiations with interested parties could begin: 'The PMG thinks it would be better not to call a Conference ... until the Department has first formed some opinion as to what policy should be adopt-ed. His idea is that it would be useless meeting outsiders until we had first come to some agreed view amongst ourselves'.[9] This may seem rather inept until we reflect that not only were politicians, most of whom had been involved in both the war of independence and the civil war, finding their way

7 Ibid. p. xlv. 8 J.C.W. Reith, *Broadcast over Britain*, pp. 17–18, 147. 9 *Report*, doc. 61: PMG's private secretary to O'Hegarty, 11 May 1923.

to the experience and expression of freedom, but also, as a new administration, the civil service was establishing modes of procedure in which the question of policy was fraught with possible ambiguities.

Although there were 'vague and tentative' approaches to the question of policy, the general impression is that the Committee (and those whose actions had caused it to be established) put to the fore matters of detail such as copyright, wavelengths, and the licence fee and relegated the 'why' of broadcasting to the margins of the discussion. Time and again, the members would refer to the need to discuss fundamental issues and yet allow themselves to be sidetracked once more into relatively minor ones. This can be attributed partly to political and administrative immaturity and even to the unfamiliarity of the participants with the language of interrogation and elucidation and with the terminology of the infant science of broadcasting. But it also suggests that, despite the need for an appraisal – and eventual rejection – of the PMG's proposals, there was an urgency about the minutiae of their task which obscured the larger picture, as if a morning's debate with an expert witness on the use of radio as an educational medium was more compelling than a debate on the nature of radio *per se* or on its place within the national infrastructure.

In addition, much of this confusion and prevarication over the main issue can be attributed to the circumstances in which the Committee itself came into existence. To the Committee, Walsh would say 'Before we let this question of wireless loose upon the country we want to know where we stand'[10] but he had in fact been in the process of letting it loose without recourse to the country's elected representatives.

Nevertheless, as the work of the Wireless Committee proceeded, a picture was built up of the type of broadcasting which could be both useful and entertaining to an Irish audience, and thus, by a combination of serendipity and earnestness, its members were able to form (with the exception of Beamish) a consensus on what was needed and how it was to be provided.

As in Britain, so in Ireland, the fortunes of broadcasting lay in the hands of a small number of figures: firstly, the Postmaster-General (soon to be re-titled Minister for Posts and Telegraphs) and the Secretary of the Post Office; and secondly the members of the Dáil Special Committee. The Postmaster-General, James Joseph Walsh [Seumas Breathnach] (1880–1955), from Bandon in west Cork, had worked in the Post Office as a telegraphist until dismissed for his republican sympathies. 'From childhood I had hated England and everything English', he recorded in his memoirs, *Recollections of a Rebel*.[11] He was in the vanguard of several political and cultural initiatives in

---

10 Ibid. para. 2139.   **11** J.J. Walsh, *Recollections of a Rebel* (Tralee: Kerryman, 1944) p. 16.

Cork, including the establishment of the Cork City Corps of the Volunteers in 1913, and the development of the GAA, of whose Cork County Board he was President in 1906 and which he recognised 'as a training ground for Physical Force'[12] – a proclivity which found expression in his admiration for Mussolini and, later, Hitler.[13] The peak of this achievement was the occasion on which he and Colonel Maurice Moore[14] had reviewed 20,000 Volunteers outside Cork City. He went to Dublin in 1915, setting up a tobacconist's shop in Blessington Street, and was in the GPO during the 1916 Rising, where he could employ his experience as a telegraphist:

> Soon after entering the Post Office I discovered that Crown Alley,[15] with its nationwide network of telephonic communications, had not been occupied. The next morning, and without instructions, I proceeded to exploit the possibilities of Telegraphic contacts. Representing myself as Superintendent X, I had no difficulty in getting in touch with overseers in Cork, Limerick, Galway and Wexford ... In this way Connolly, Pearse, and their associates, knew how matters stood in the country.[16]

As a result of his participation in the Rising, Walsh was tried alongside Willie Pearse and Seán McGarry, his death sentence being commuted to penal servitude, during six months of which he refused to wear prison dress and was clad only in a blanket.[17] No doubt his first-hand experience of wartime telegraphy heightened Walsh's own sense of vulnerability when he became the minister responsible for such affairs. A tireless promoter of all things Irish, he was the chief organiser of the Tailteann Games, designed as a vehicle of Gaelic resuscitation in 1924 – a point which would be used ironically against him in the Wireless Committee and the Dáil. Walsh was elected an Alderman of Cork Corporation 1918–22 and MP for Cork City in 1918, working with Seán T. O'Kelly, Piaras Béaslaí and others in planning the inauguration of the 'first Dáil'.[18] In 1924 he became chairman of the Cumann na nGaedheal organising

12 Ibid. 13 Cf. J. Regan, op. cit. p. 94. 14 Moore (the younger brother of the novelist George Moore) was a County Mayo landowner who became a nationalist; in 1913 he was one of the first to join the Volunteers of which he became Inspector General in 1915. It was Moore who persuaded Darrell Figgis to return to Ireland from London in 1914 to become honorary Inspecting Officer of the Volunteers in County Mayo (Figgis, *Recollections*, p. 62). Moore was later to save Figgis' life at Carrick-on-Shannon when he intervened after Figgis had been arrested by British troops who were about to execute him (ibid. pp. 303–7). He was a Senator during both the Cumann na nGaedheal and Fianna Fáil governments, having become a member of Fianna Fáil when it entered the Seanad in 1928. In 1925 he urged that Ireland should cease payment to Britain of the land annuities due under the terms of the Treaty. 15 The 'National Telephone Company' had its Dublin exchange premises at nos. 6–7 Crown Alley, the street connecting Cope Street with Temple Bar. 16 Walsh, *Recollections* p. 37. 17 Ibid. p. 52. 18 As we have seen, he prepared the motion which put a rein on the Government's 'dictator' tendency. In 1920, in support of Ernest Blythe's proposal to encourage Irish manufacture, he had

committee and subsequently (1926–7) of the party itself. In debate he was a 'loose cannon', outspoken to the extent that he could both embarrass and contradict himself; he was never allowed to forget that he had declared 'the day an Irish Republic was formed, the landlords would be put against the wall and there would be an end to landlordism once and for all'.[19]

When appointed Postmaster-General, Walsh records that 'I at once selected my old school and college mate, P.S. O'Hegarty, to fill the post of Secretary'.[20] Together, they embarked on an ambitious programme of departmental reform which was interrupted by a strike of the Postal Workers' Organisation over pay and conditions, which Walsh claimed that they succeeded in breaking.[21] A series of symbolic changes in the areas for which they had responsibility saw red British post boxes being painted green, the Irish language taking the predominant place in post offices and on post office print material, and the over-printing of British postage stamps.[22] Furthermore:

> We determined to instal a telephone system. The word *instal* is not an exaggeration, for until then the British had neglected this medium of communication in Ireland. Inside the country, only the cities and larger towns had had a service and a limited one at that. Communications with Great Britain were hopelessly inadequate. For all practical purposes we started from scratch, because the exchanges and switchboards, such as they were, were practically useless in a nation-wide scheme. Within three or four years, every town and village from Donegal to Cork was furnished with an excellent service and, additionally, all main lines were provided with spare wires in anticipation of further developments … The automatic system was introduced in Dublin. This was long before it had been known in English cities, other than London.[23]

The experience of the Wireless Committee and its consequences in 1923–5 were a source of profound disillusion to Walsh, to which he gave scant space in his memoirs,[24] and although he left Dáil Éireann in 1927, principally in disagreement over the government's economic policy,[25] it is also likely that his defeat over the radio proposals – and the way he had been outmanoeuvred in internal Cumann na nGaedheal affairs[26] – was a major contributing factor.

suggested a 'buy Irish campaign', as 'the Irish people were asleep as regards their duty to support Irish manufacture' – quoted in A. Mitchell, op. cit. p. 163.   **19** *Anglo-Celt* 14 July 1917, quoted in M. Laffan, *The Resurrection of Ireland: the Sinn Féin Party 1916–1923* (Cambridge: Cambridge University Press, 1999) p. 257.   **20** Walsh, *Recollections* p. 61.   **21** Ibid. p. 62–3. But cf. A. Gaughan (ed.), *Memoirs of Senator James G. Douglas (1887–1954): concerned citizen* (Dublin: UCD Press, 1998) p. 88 where Douglas recalled that, as chairman of the commission of inquiry into the Post Office, he had persuaded the Government to take his view of how to bring the strike to a close rather than Walsh's – an early example of Walsh experiencing defeat.   **22** Ibid. pp. 63–4.   **23** Ibid. p. 64.   **24** With the exception of a rueful retrospect which is quoted in Chapter 5.   **25** J.J. Lee op. cit. pp. 119–20.   **26** As an Extern

Walsh's letter of resignation is ambiguous as to his real motives for resignation: 'The party itself has gone bodily over to the most reactionary characters of the state ... [who] subordinate their life-long convictions to the dictates of people whose only concern appears to be the welfare of England'.[27] When, in the wake of the Boundary Commission crisis, Cumann na nGaedheal urged him to form a government, Walsh with characteristic fairness suggested in turn that Thomas Johnson, one of his fiercest opponents over the wireless investigation, would be more appropriate.[28] In retirement from politics he spread his commercial wings, setting up a bus company in Dublin which he operated until 1933; in 1935 he established the Federation of Industries which in turn set up the Industrial Credit Corporation. He became President of the Federation of Irish Manufacturers and Chairman and Managing Director, 1938–44, of Clondalkin Paper Mills, in which he was a major shareholder.

As we have noted, one of those responsible for creating stability and dispelling confusion in the fledgling Free State was P[atrick] S[arsfield] O'Hegarty (1879–1955), a Corkman who, like many of Michael Collins' associates, had worked from 1902 to 1913 in the British Post Office in London and had become involved in the Irish independence movement, being a member of the Supreme Council of the IRB from 1908 to 1914, and editing the Gaelic League monthly An tÉireannach and (1911–14) Irish Freedom. He was deeply involved, with Arthur Griffith, in the establishment of Sinn Féin and its evolution into Cumann na nGaedheal, of whose executive he was a member. In 1918 when an oath of allegiance became obligatory for civil servants he resigned and helped to found the Irish Book Shop in Dublin's Dawson Street; as its manager he made it 'the centre of literary Dublin'.[29] He was a member of a private dining club known as 'The Twelve Apostles' which included Lennox Robinson, W.B. Yeats, Thomas McGreevy, Brinsley MacNamara, Desmond FitzGerald and the economist George O'Brien, and he was also closely associated with the Belfast republicans Robert Lynd and Bulmer Hobson. After the Treaty he also edited a short-lived periodical, The Separatist, which attempted to contain the split between the pro- and anti-Treaty parties. In addition to The Victory of Sinn Féin he wrote The Indestructible Nation: a survey of Irish history from the English invasion (1918), and contributed to many periodicals including the Irish Book Lover, The Bell, the Irish Review and the Irish Statesman (under the editorship of George Russell). His personal library[30] was enormous, and he compiled many bibliographies,

Minister, Walsh had often been at odds with the Executive Council, and his inclusion within it from 1927 was somewhat ironic; the power-play within the government and its relationship with the Cumann na nGaedheal party at grass-roots, in which Walsh and Séamus Hughes (see below pp. 140–1) were deeply implicated is a recurring theme in J. Regan's The Irish Counter-Revolution.   27 SPO S 5470 (National Archives).   28 Walsh, Recollections, p. 70.   29 James Meenan, George O'Brien: a biographical memoir (Dublin: Gill and Macmillan, 1980) p. 96.   30 Now mostly in the University of Kansas.

including one of Darrell Figgis, as well as of Standish O'Grady, Thomas McDonagh, Joseph Mary Plunkett, Patrick Pearse, Douglas Hyde, Joseph Campbell, James Clarence Mangan, James Joyce and Roger Casement. In retirement he wrote *A History of Ireland under the Union 1801–1922*.[31] He described his recreations as journalism, controversy and telling the truth.[32]

In *The Victory of Sinn Féin* he wrote: 'I belong to that small minority of people who founded the modern separatist movement, and fostered it, and educated it, and slaved for it, and beggared themselves for it ... The Sinn Féin movement was essentially a constructive, educational, intellectual movement. Its philosophy was the philosophy of Thomas Davis. Its sustaining force was love for Ireland and desire to serve her'.[33] When Griffith died in 1922 O'Hegarty wrote in *The Separatist*: 'By the death of Arthur Griffith we have lost not only the most constructive and political intelligence in Ireland, but the man upon whom for the last twenty and odd years has lain the whole burden of the travail of this nation ... perhaps the most gifted all-round nationalist since Tone'.[34]

Appointed to the Post Office [Department of Posts and Telegraphs] in 1922, he held the position until 1944. Although he may have appeared a natural choice, in the opinion of Lawrence W. McBride 'the appointment alarmed the British Treasury officials and, no doubt, many Irish civil servants who feared that men without meaningful experience would be rewarded for their political activities rather than for their administrative talents and professional achievements'.[35] More surprising, perhaps, is the fact that a senior civil servant should have published such an outspoken work as *The Victory of Sinn Féin*, containing not only a vicious and explicit attack on de Valera ('Devil Era') and the 'Irregulars', but also the statement 'the average level of ability and intelligence in the present Dáil is appallingly low'[36] – and even more surprising still that in 1932, when de Valera gained power, O'Hegarty should have remained in his post.[37]

---

31 Published by Methuen in 1952: it had the subtitle '*with an epilogue carrying the story down to the acceptance in 1927 by de Valera of the Anglo-Irish Treaty of 1921*'. **32** Close similarities between O'Hegarty's *Victory* and the writings of Kevin O'Higgins have been detected by John Regan: 'the idea of moral collapse, the perception of an attack on the social fabric and above all the reaction to militarist-republicanism' – op. cit. pp. 180–1. **33** P.S. O'Hegarty, op. cit. pp. 117–18. **34** Quoted in León Ó Broin, *Just Like Yesterday: an autobiography* (Dublin: Gill and Macmillan, 1985) p. 159. **35** L.W. McBride, *The Greening of Dublin Castle: the Transformation of Bureaucratic and Judicial Personnel in Ireland 1892–1922* (Washington: Catholic University of America Press, 1991) p. 308. As John McColgan (*British Policy and the Irish Administration 1920–22* [London: George Allen and Unwin, 1983] pp. 97–8) notes, O'Hegarty was the only departmental head who had not previously been a civil servant. **36** P.S. O'Hegarty, op. cit. p. 55. **37** This is partly explained by León Ó Broin in his autobiography *Just Like Yesterday* p. 161: 'I was not ... very surprised to hear in the Post Office ... that there had been no personal contact between O'Hegarty and his Minister, Gerry Boland, for years [1933–6]. Boland, who had lost a brother in the Civil War, could not tolerate P.S., and I'm sure that that was P.S.'s mutual sentiment ... Some people would wonder why P.S. hadn't been sacked or moved to some other office. I'm sure this was discussed among politicians, but if it was the decision was to avoid making a bad situation worse'.

Like one of his successors, León Ó Broin, O'Hegarty was able, especially in the pre-Fianna Fáil years, to exercise enormous power within his Department and, one suspects, at inter-departmental level. The 'networking' – as it would be called today – of the close association of higher civil servants and politicians emanating from the western and southern counties[38] suggests that there was a shared understanding among such men as to the meaning of terms such as 'culture' and 'nationality' which did not require explicit expression in order to be transmitted.

O'Hegarty's power and capacity for decision-making became legendary in the civil service. When the Post Office engineer, Patrick Mulligan, was examined by the Wireless Committee and was asked whether he was familiar with the White Paper, his response was: 'I am, in general terms. Of course that is all decided by the Secretary'.[39] It is small wonder that the White Paper earned the contempt of Thomas Johnson, leader of the opposition, since in *The Victory of Sinn Féin* O'Hegarty was scathing of the entire concept of parliamentary opposition at that time, describing it as 'opposition on principle, opposition to everything whether it is right or wrong ... ineffective because it is based neither on principle nor policy nor conviction. It is the most rigid and selfish of Party or personal opposition ... It has no more thought for the good of the country as a whole, no more notion of real patriotism, than have the mass of the people themselves'.[40]

The first official announcement concerning broadcasting came on 19 April 1923, when the newspapers carried a Post Office communique to the effect that the PMG intended to issue broadcasting licences and was inviting applications from interested parties. This attracted a disparate number of applications, among them Isaac Bradlaw of the Pioneer Wireless Company and the Princess Cinema in Rathmines; the Irish Wireless Company; the Irish and Foreign Trading Corporation; and Irish Developments Ltd.[41] Having eliminated the first two companies on the grounds that they had no real interest in broadcasting, the latter two, represented respectively by E. C. Handcock and Andrew Belton, were invited to proceed with negotiations to see if they could co-ordinate their interests 'for the purpose of establishing one Broadcasting Station and for the manufacture of wireless sets and electrical goods'.[42] The firms were unable to reach a joint position and each instead submitted a

38 In addition to Walsh, among civil servants, O'Hegarty was also from West Cork, as was Joseph Brennan, Secretary of the Dept. of Finance 1923–27, whose successor, J. J. McElligott (1927–53), was from Kerry; the Secretary of the Executive Council, Diarmuid O'Hegarty, was from Cork.   39 *Report* para. 1769.   40 P.S. O'Hegarty op. cit. pp. 102, 129.   41 In addition to these companies, applications or expressions of interest were received from: Mr. A. Phillips (Suffolk St Dublin), The Scientific Electrical Works (Charlotte St Dublin), W. M. Engineering (Fleet St Dublin), Messrs Pathe Freres, Irish Wireless and Electrical Supplies Ltd (O'Connell St Dublin) and Uebersee Handel, Berlin. 42 *Report* doc. 72.

separate scheme, pointing out that broadcasting in itself was uneconomic and would require a government subsidy. (The Marconi Company had withdrawn its own application on similar grounds.) Belton's scheme was based on the assumption that 'other work will be available' in order to make the project profitable.[43] Subsequently a similar scheme was received from Messrs Dixon and Hempenstall, who announced their intention of setting up a wireless factory. The latter's potential involvement upset the progress of negotiations, however, since, as Thomas Hempenstall's letter put it, 'the proposals ... will only receive harmonious acceptance by the public if the concession is completely controlled by men known to and having the confidence of the public'.[44] He would co-operate with Handcock (Irish and Foreign Trading Corporation) but not with Belton.

The first occasion on which the idea of a radio service (as distinct from wireless telegraphy) was mentioned in the legislature of the Free State was 7 June 1923, when Thomas Johnson asked the PMG whether he had entered into any arrangements with British firms in respect of supplying wireless apparatus in the State. Walsh assured the deputy that he had not, and that 'before any privilege is conceded to anybody both the Government and the Dáil will have a full opportunity of discussing it'.[45] As it turned out, Walsh had in fact been in detailed discussion with these companies, which he believed to be Irish-owned, and was on the verge of publishing a scheme for the establishment of a radio station.

In July, two further companies, Irish International Trading Corproration (Cork) and the Cork Radio Company, announced their interest in the matter, and their connection with Irish Developments Ltd; Belton himself started to put pressure on the Post Office to exclude Irish and Foreign and Dixon and Hempenstall, while they in their turn tried to have Irish Developments ousted on the grounds that it was not an Irish company. As a result of this, negotiations broke down.

On 2 August 1923 two items appeared in the Dublin newspapers. The first was the text of a further Post Office communique:

> The Postmaster-General has had several conferences with the Irish firms interested in broadcasting, and has placed before them an outline of the scheme which he would be disposed to sanction. The firms in question have, however, failed to agree amongst themselves, and the Postmaster-General is therefore reconsidering the situation. In the meantime applications from any genuine manufacturing firms, who have not hitherto applied, will be received.[46]

43 Ibid. doc. 94. **44** Ibid. doc. 107. **45** DD 3, 7 June 1923, cols. 1585–6. **46** *Irish Times*, *Freeman's Journal*, 2 August 1923.

The second was an advertisement inviting applications 'from Irish persons or firms who are prepared under licence ... to undertake the establishment and operation of a "Broadcasting" Station in Dublin for the supply to the public, by means of wireless telephony, of concerts, lectures, theatrical entertainments, speeches, weather reports, etc.' These headings under which broadcasting might be conducted are indicative of the Post Office mind.

This was not the first occasion, however, on which the PMG had sought interested parties, but it was the first time that it was brought to the attention of the Dáil, when, on the next day, Seán McGarry asked why such an advertisement had appeared *subsequent* to discussions which the PMG had already held with some potential licensees.[47] McGarry's intervention was crucial, as it revealed a situation which was potentially disastrous for the PMG, insofar as he and his officials had embarked on a process of extreme uncertainty in a haphazard and indeterminate fashion. McGarry was not far off the mark when he said: 'I think I may be pardoned for assuming that if those firms with whom he had conference had not failed to agree ... the Dáil would have been presented with what Mr De Valera would call a *fait accompli* without having one word of hint as to what his intentions were'.[48]

Leaving aside McGarry's mixed motives for raising the matter, his intervention indicates the delicate nature of the project. McGarry told the Dáil that he had been approached by two parties who were interested in getting involved in radio, had approached the PMG privately and had been told that he would be informed when arrangements were being put in place. 'When the British broadcasting company was being established ... the British Postmaster-General kept the British House of Commons informed step by step as the negotiations proceeded. It was a very necessary thing in view of the fact that the Government were involved in agreements, licences and concessions in every single step ... I do not think', McGarry continued, 'business of such magnitude as broadcasting, which is going to involve the expenditure of a large amount of capital, is going to be dealt with in a hole and corner manner'.[49]

McGarry also drew attention to what he considered muddled thinking: 'The last sentence in the paragraph [of the advertisement] is "In the meantime applications from any genuine manufacturing firms, who have not hitherto applied will be received". That paragraph', McGarry told the Dáil,

> is probably the result of confusion in the mind of the person who dictated it as to the difference between broadcasting and listening-in,

---

47 DD 4, 3 August 1923, cols. 1950–51.   48 Ibid. The remark by de Valera derives from Dáil (Private) Debates 15 December 1921 p. 150, on the introduction of 'Document no. 2' relating to the Treaty: I am indebted to Dr Michael Laffan for this information.   49 Ibid. cols. 1951–2.

or reception. I think everybody knows that broadcasting is the sending out of the messages, and listening-in is the reception of the messages. So far as manufacturing is concerned it does not enter broadcasting to any great extent, but the manufacturing of the instruments for the reception and listening-in is a very big industry. It would seem that there is an attempt to make the firm who gets the concession for the manufacture of the broadcasting instruments, the manufacturer also for the reception or listening-in apparatus. If that is so there are two dangers. The Postmaster-General, if that is his idea, is creating or endeavouring to create a monopoly. I do not think that is his intention. I rather think that is a matter of confusion.[50]

The word 'monopoly' was also to cause confusion (as it did in Britain),[51] as the notion of 'unified control' (the British model) became entangled with the idea of a single company or individual having the sole right to exploit the broadcasting 'concession'. In both Britain and Ireland, the need for control and the elimination of confusion or even anarchy was of greater importance than the freedom of expression and enterprise that deregulation would endow.

McGarry asked that the PMG publish his 'scheme' and that a Committee of the Dáil should 'go into and report upon how the Broadcasting business is to be started here'.[52] (The question of whether or not the manufacture of radios could contribute to the growth of the Irish electrical industry would in fact occupy a considerable amount of the Committee's time – see below pp. 73 and 105–6.)

In the absence of the PMG it fell to Cosgrave, as President of the Executive Council, to read into the record of the Dáil a memorandum from Walsh in which he detailed his negotiations to date. McGarry, as an interested party who might be in a position himself to import wireless sets for sale,[53] disputed the scheme which, he said, by creating a monopoly, would allow the broadcasting company to control the importation and sale of radios (thus implicitly preventing the existing wireless trade from reaping any of the benefits of this new industry).[54] At this point Darrell Figgis intervened to ask that the matter be deferred until after the impending General Election.[55] On a typically cryptic note, indicative of his own ambivalence in the matter, he said 'I urge that very strongly and for reasons which I say frankly I do not want to bring in here now'.[56]

After the election, on 3 October 1923, Figgis asked the PMG if 'he will now lay his proposals ... before the Dáil for discussion and sanction', to which

---

50 Ibid. **51** Cf. A. Briggs, *The Birth of Broadcasting* pp. 166, 300. **52** DD 4, 3 August 1923, col. 1953. **53** He was an electrical engineer by trade, with offices at 14 St Andrew Street, Dublin, and intended to deal in wireless sets once the situation was resolved. **54** DD 4, 3 August 1923, col. 1955. **55** The election took place on 27 August and the new Dáil met on 19 September. **56** Ibid. col. 1956.

Walsh replied that negotiations were still in progress and that he was 'not yet in a position to lay the proposals in the matter before the Dáil'.[57] It is extraordinary to us today that Walsh would have taken the matter so far before indicating to the Dáil what was being transacted.

The White Paper (see Appendix 1) was eventually published in November 1923 over the signature of 'Seumas Breathnach, Aire an Phuist', and had six main points. Firstly, the Post Office itself was not competent to operate an entertainment service. Secondly, it was necessary to give the licence to one organisation in order to avoid chaos and inefficiency. Thirdly, the service would be financed from a combination of licence fees and importation duties on radio sets. Fourthly, the service would be provided by an 'Irish Broadcasting Company' (IBC) formed initially by five named individual companies (with which Walsh had already agreed a Memorandum and Articles of Association). Fifthly, regulations were set down for the hours of broadcasting (11a.m.–12 noon, 5–11p.m.) and for the times and duration of news and advertisements, the suitability of programmes being 'to the reasonable satisfaction of the Postmaster-General'. Sixthly, the broadcasting station was to be situated in Dublin 'so that ... broadcasting can be brought within the reach of the greatest number of people'.

The constituent companies of the proposed IBC were to be: the Cork Radio Company; the Irish International Trading Corporation (Cork); Dixon and Hempenstall (Dublin); Philip Sayers (Dublin) and Irish Developments Ltd.

One is immediately struck by the bluntness of the opening statement of the White Paper: 'The first question which the Post Office had to consider in regard to wireless broadcasting was whether it should be worked as a Post Office monopoly ...' This suggests that no consideration was given to the question of whether or not wireless broadcasting was a desirable activity or in the public interest. Either it had not been considered at all – the decision to proceed having been taken as a reaction to perceived public demand – or it had been assumed that broadcasting *was* a necessary activity, in which case we have no evidence as to the bases for such an assumption. As we shall see, Walsh did urge the Wireless Committee to discuss the matter of policy, but since this happened after the publication of the White Paper we are entitled to question Walsh's political judgement on this point.

The most positive view that can be taken is that the proposed model offered a mixture of public and private enterprise based on the then situation in Britain. It was no doubt influenced by the thinking of Reith, who later that year would pen the *apologia* of the BBC:

---

57 DD 5, 3 October 1923, col. 145.

> The Company operates as a public utility service … In this business, the interests of the public and the interests of the trade happen to be identical, even though this may not be apparent at first sight. The greater the extent to which, as a public service, the Company is able to give satisfaction, the greater the benefit to the new British industry.[58]

Since Reith was to transform the Company into a Corporation within two years, it is difficult to accept this claim at face value except insofar as he was attempting to vindicate the establishment of the Company in the public interest. The fact that there was a genuinely large and developing industry for wireless manufacture in Britain made the situation qualitatively different from that in Ireland. In Britain, the concept of what radio actually was had evolved from the concept of what might be made of it by vested interests in the radio industry.[59] In Ireland, no such industry existed. Only in the most general terms, therefore – such as Reith's simplistic statement 'The policy of the Company [is] to bring the best of everything into the greatest number of homes'[60] – were the Irish and British circumstances 'analogous' as Walsh was to claim.

There the matter rested[61] until 14 December when Figgis, with the agreement of the PMG, moved:

> That a Committee of this Dáil be appointed to consider the circular addressed to Deputies entitled 'Wireless Broadcasting', especially in regard to the proposal by which it is intended that the State should pass over the right to licence and tax incoming wireless apparatus to a Clearing House under the control of a private company, the Committee to consist of nine Deputies to be nominated by the Committee of Selection and to be reported to the Dáil before January 16th, 1924.[62]

Walsh not only offered no opposition to this motion: in fact he seconded it, saying 'I desire the fullest possible investigation' but urging 'that no unnecessary time would be lost in coming to business'[63] – his anxiety being that wireless sets were being imported of which his department would lose track if a scheme were not put in place to control and licence the trade.

The Committee of Selection met on 10 January and nominated the Special Committee to undertake the examination of the 'Circular' – which was of course the White Paper.[64]

---

58 J.C.W. Reith, *Broadcast over Britain* p. 57.   **59** In Britain in 1926 there were 1,600 manufacturing enterprises associated with the BBC: ibid. p. 210.   **60** Ibid. p. 147.   **61** With the exception of a further attempt by Figgis to bring the matter to a head on 7 December (DD 5, col. 1585).   **62** DD 5, 14 December 1923, col. 1984–5.   **63** Ibid.   **64** DD 6, 10 January 1924, col. 17.

THE WIRELESS COMMITTEE

Who were the men appointed to make decisions affecting the future of broad-casting in Ireland? As we have already seen, they clearly all had a vivid memory of recent events, and in most cases had been directly and deeply affected by them. They were a cross-section of Dáil Éireann, which, Lennox Robinson reminds us, was composed of 'doctors of medicine ... a doctor of letters, professors of universities, a novelist-poet [Figgis] and a captain in the British army'...[65] as well as a strong representation of farmers.

The chairman of the Committee was Pádraic Ó Máille (1883–1946), the Leas-Ceann Comhairle [deputy Speaker] of the Dáil, a TD for the West Galway (Connemara) constituency who had been wounded in 1922 in the attack[66] which killed Seán Hayes, TD.[67] He was at the centre of the attempts to prevent a split between pro- and anti-treaty factions within Cumann na nGaedheal.[68] During the Army crisis in 1925, the year in which (with Thomas Johnson) he tried unsuccessfully to persuade the anti-Treaty side to enter the Dáil, he was expelled from Cumann na nGaedheal and joined the National Party founded by Joseph McGrath. He was a Senator 1932–6 and 1938–45.

We have already noted that Thomas Johnson (1872–1963) was Leader of the Labour TDs since his election for South Dublin in 1922, and Secretary of the Irish Trade Union Congress 1920–28. He had been a member of the Resources Commission of which Darrell Figgis was Secretary and Maurice Moore chairman, and in the attempt to induce the anti-Treaty deputies to enter the Dáil he was joint chairman with de Valera of a committee which included William Magennis and Pádraic Ó Máille. In 1927 he negotiated an electoral pact with Fianna Fáil which narrowly failed to dislodge Cumann na nGaedheal from power.[69] He lost his seat in the October 1927 election in a pincer movement by Cosgrave and the Larkin-led Irish Workers' League and was elected to the Senate the following year, remaining a member for ten years. He was general secretary of the ITUC 1938–45 and from 1946 to 1955 he was head of the newly established Labour Court. Much of his concern with the Army crisis and with Cosgrave's centralist tendencies was relevant to the work of the Wireless Committee. Cosgrave delivered a damning indictment of Johnson in 1927 when he said 'In no crisis that I know of during the last

65 L. Robinson op. cit. p. 153. 66 As they emerged from lunch in Dublin's Ormond Hotel the day after the Irish Free State came into existence. 67 In reprisal for which the government had executed four anti-Treaty prisoners. In 1920 Ó Máille had proposed legitimising poitín by taxing it. 68 Cf. J. Regan op. cit. p. 237. 69 In August 1927 Johnson also agreed a scenario for an alternative coalition government between Labour and the Independents with himself as President and Minister for Justice, and Bryan Cooper as Minister for Fisheries: the scheme was discovered by the *Irish Times* which published it on 15 August, commenting 'the list ... is distinctly interesting as indicating the Labour leader's desire that his cabinet should be broadly representative of those who did not actively participate in the recent strife and who have inherited no share of the legacy of political bitterness'.

five years did Mr Johnson ever exhibit the qualities of statesmanship'.[70] Joseph Lee has said that his 'personal integrity and political ineffectuality did much to consolidate the Free State as a conservative regime'[71] and it may be that his style as leader of the opposition (until the entry into the Dáil of Fianna Fáil) contributed to the consensus discussed by Jeffrey Prager.

William Magennis (1869–1946), born in Belfast, was Professor of English at Carysfort Training College 1889–1945 and Professor of Metaphysics at UCD 1908–45. He was elected a TD representing the National University in 1922, but largely supported the Government. He was later appointed chairman of the Censorship of Films Appeal Board and chairman of the Censorship of Publications Board from 1942 until his death. Like Johnson, he was to criticise the Government over the Boundary Commission crisis in 1925, founding the short-lived Clann Éireann in 1926 which brought about his electoral defeat in 1927, although he sat in the Senate 1938–46.[72]

W.E. Thrift (1871–1942) was to be Provost of TCD from 1937 to 1942 and was also a member of the Censorship of Publications Board 1930–36. At this time he was one of the four Dublin University representatives, and taught physics with the title Erasmus Smith's Professor of Natural and Experimental Philosophy.

Seán Milroy (1877–1946) had been born in England. A journalist, he was a close associate of Arthur Griffith and was one of the founders of the Irish Self-Determination League of Great Britain and had been a leader of the IRA in Cork. He was one of the deportees to England in the wake of 1916 and subsequently became Sinn Féin's organisational director. In the 1921 General Election he had been elected MP for Fermanagh-Tyrone and the same year became TD for Cavan, holding his seat until 1924. He was a Senator 1928–36. In 1917 he had declared 'Ireland is not going to let Ulster go. Ireland cannot do without Ulster; and Ulster cannot do without Ireland'.[73] He had written a book on the subject: *The Case of Ulster: an analysis of four partition arguments* (1922). His conversion from a strong Irish-Ireland standpoint to the pro-Treaty view (he was one of the architects of the Cumann na nGaedheal organisation) is indicative of the transition of a decisive section of Sinn Féin to create a viable State under Collins and later Cosgrave.

Seán McGarry (dates unknown) had been with Figgis at Howth on the day of the *Asgard* gun-running; in 1919, with de Valera and Milroy, he had been 'sprung' from Lincoln Jail by Harry Boland and Michael Collins. In 1922 –

70 *Irish Independent* 10 September 1927.   **71** J.J. Lee, op. cit., p. 172.   **72** When the question of divorce was raised in the Dáil, Magennis told Ó Máille, who was sympathetic to the retention of divorce for Protestants, 'you cannot be a good Catholic if you allow divorce even between Protestants': J.A. Gaughan (ed.), *Memoirs of Senator James G. Douglas* p. 114.   **73** *Irishman* 16 June 1917, quoted in M. Laffan, op. cit. p. 226.

the year in which he was elected a TD for Mid-Dublin – his son had been killed when their home was the subject of a fire attack. He was a contributor to *Bean na hÉireann*, the organ of Inghinidhe na hÉireann [Daughters of Ireland]. McGarry's putative involvement in the radio trade led to some colourful intervention in the committee room. Both McGarry and Milroy resigned from the Dáil on 30 October 1924, in disillusionment at the way politics was being conducted – again, Walsh had been intimately concerned with the Cumann na nGaedheal internal wranglings which led to these resignations.

Patrick Hogan (1886–1969) was a Labour TD for Clare. As TD and Senator he was a member of the Oireachtas for 44 years, holding the position of Ceann Comhairle [Speaker] 1951–67.[74]

Donal (Dan) McCarthy (1883/1957) had been a Sinn Féin organiser in his native Leitrim from 1907, and Director of Elections in 1921–22 in succession to Milroy; later a Cumann na nGaedheal activist, he was elected TD for Dublin South in 1922, becoming an unofficial Parliamentary Secretary the following year. He had been instrumental in proposing that the Cumann na nGaedheal organisation should control the government – a notion that was in fact reversed in practice.[75] In 1921 he was elected President of the GAA.

Richard Henrik Beamish (1861–1938) is an example of the transitional Ireland which saw many from the traditional establishment background and persuasion recognising – and acknowledging – not only the reality of the new State but also their potential role within it. As Lennox Robinson wrote of Bryan Cooper, 'two changes are taking place: the passing of power and ... the realisation by a few sensitive and intelligent landowners ... that their life and interests are inseparably woven in with the Irish people'.[76] Beamish, who was chairman of the brewing firm of Beamish and Crawford from 1901 until 1930, had been deputy Lord Lieutenant for County Cork. High Sheriff of Cork City in 1906 and 1911, he was elected an Alderman in 1906, the year he became Lord Mayor, and remained at the top of the poll until his retirement in 1931. He had been a member of a delegation to Lloyd George in 1920 which had initiated the slow progress towards the Treaty,[77] and represented Cork City in the Dáil from 1923 to 1927. Andrew Belton stated that it was through Beamish that he began to get involved in the Cobh harbour developments.[78]

The composition of the Committee indicates two significant factors: the first, self-evident, point is that the party which had opposed the Treaty and which might be expected to argue in such a Committee for a different view of

---

74 Hogan was not the first choice of the Committee of Selection: on 10 January it had nominated Nicholas Wall, a member of the Farmers' Party, but in his absence and apparent unwillingness to serve, Hogan was selected in his place on the proposal of Thomas Johnson: DD 6, 10 January 1924, cols. 18, 82. **75** Cf. M. Laffan, op. cit. p. 421. **76** L. Robinson, *Bryan Cooper*, p. 49. **77** Cf. J.A. Gaughan (ed.), *Memoirs of Senator James G. Douglas* pp. 17–18. **78** *Report* doc. 239.

what constituted national culture and national identity was not there to do so. The noted hostility and suspicion with which successive Fianna Fáil governments would regard Radio Éireann and later RTÉ is, I believe, directly attributable to the fact that it was unable to play a part in its establishment.[79]

The second factor is that, arising from this absence of opposition, the Committee at its outset ostensibly consisted of four Government deputies, two Labour, two independents and two University representatives. Thus (with the exception of the Farmers) it could be said to have been reasonably representative of the spread of deputies, not least since McGarry's inclusion, in theory at least, meant that the embryonic wireless trade was present. However, Figgis' resignation, and the virtual withdrawal of Beamish, McGarry and Hogan (and to a lesser extent Milroy), meant that the core attendance for most of the meetings was: four government, one labour and two University deputies, one of whom was a government supporter. It was the tenacity of Johnson, Magennis and Thrift which ensured that the discussion was as thorough as the subject merited.

The Committee met on thirty-seven occasions from 10 January to 25 March 1924. Attendance was as follows:

Ó Máille (chair)	37
Beamish	16
Figgis	11 out of 15 to the time of his resignation on 25 January
Hogan	16
Johnson	37
McCarthy	25
McGarry	13[80]
Magennis	35
Milroy	24
Thrift	36

It is perhaps not surprising that in the Committee the main emphasis on the nature of public service broadcasting should have come from Thomas Johnson, who referred to 'the necessity for co-ordination in giving a common

79 In 1966 Seán Lemass, then Taoiseach, told Dáil Éireann 'Radio Telefís Éireann was set up by legislation as an instrument of public policy, and as such is responsible to the government. The government have overall responsibility for its conduct, and especially the obligation to ensure that its programmes do not offend the public interest or conflict with national policy as defined in legislation. To this extent the government rejected the view that Radio Telefís Éireann should be ... completely independent of government supervision' (DD 224, 12 October 1966, cols. 1045–6).   80 McGarry attended 11 out of 16 meetings before he withdrew temporarily from the Committee on 28 January, and 2 subsequent meetings at the Final Report stage.

service and to ensure that it would be available to the poor and the rich, the distant and the near'.[81] Johnson also had reservations about control of the medium: observing that 'the possibility of [the influence of] wireless on the minds of a nation is so great and may be far greater than the influence of the Press' he also asserted that 'you must give as great freedom as it is possible to give for the communications that may be made, and not to control these communications in any way'.[82] 'I realise' he continued, 'that we are entering upon an entirely new field, which may ultimately alter our whole conception of human relations and ethical considerations'.[83]

On eighteen of these occasions the Committee heard evidence from, and examined, witnesses. The principal witness was the Postmaster-General (six occasions); the Secretary, P.S. O'Hegarty gave evidence only once, as did the Solicitor to the Post Office, while the Post Office engineers, Patrick Mulligan (Engineer-in-Chief) and T.J. Monaghan were interviewed once and twice respectively. Various members of the companies which intended to set up the Irish Broadcasting Company, who ostensibly had an interest in the wireless trade, were called on six occasions,[84] plus a deputation from the Marconi Company. Scientific or technical advice was received from three witnesses and finally a meeting was held with representatives of the Dublin newspapers regarding the impact which broadcasting might have on their business. In addition, the crucial matter of the relationship of Darrell Figgis and Andrew Belton, and of the nature of Belton's interest in the proposed Irish Broadcasting Company, was the subject of two lengthy meetings with each of these protagonists.

DELIBERATIONS OF THE WIRELESS COMMITTEE

The Committee met on the first evening following its appointment, and agreed initially to examine the Postmaster-General. Having held extensive discussions with Walsh[85] on the following Monday 14th and Tuesday 15th, and subsequently on that day with Andrew Belton (the principal promoter of the proposed Irish Broadcasting Company), it decided to issue an interim report to the effect that it was unable to reach any conclusions in the time available and therefore requested an extension of that time to 31 January.

81 *Report* para. 2062. 82 Ibid. para. 467. 83 Ibid. para. 469. 84 These were Philip Sayers, who was trading from 16 St Andrew St, Dublin, and who proposed to establish Sayers Broadcasting Ltd for the purpose of selling radios; Thomas Hempenstall of Messrs Dixon and Hempenstall; E. C. Handcock, representing the Irish and Foreign Trading Corporation; and T.P. Dowdall and Hugo Flinn representing Cork Radio Company – Flinn being chairman of the projected IBC. 85 At which O'Hegarty, P.J. Keawell (a Post Office official and a former associate of Pearse in the Gaelic League) and the Engineer-in-Chief, Mulligan, were also present.

At the end of the first day, the PMG delivered a bombshell by putting into the hands of the Committee a document signed by Andrew Belton which had been in his possession since September 1923 (but which was dated September 1922), setting out Belton's view of the acquaintance and business relationship which had existed between himself and Darrell Figgis from January to August 1922 (part of which is quoted at the beginning of Chapter 1).

The first session found Walsh expanding on his reasons for stating in the White Paper that the Post Office was not competent to run a radio service.

> In casting our eyes around to other countries – and one is well advised to take experience from elsewhere – we found that ... generally, broadcasting was and is being worked by private companies ... We discussed the possibility of running it ourselves, notwithstanding. I might say I have fairly strong views with regard to nationalisation. I feel that nationalisation is capable of accomplishing more than most people are prepared to admit. Generally speaking, I regard the Post Office – not this particular Post Office in this particular time – but the Post Office as such in these countries as being a very strong plank in favour of State control in certain directions. For that reason, we would have been very pleased to run broadcasting if we thought it were at all feasible. But on thinking the matter over, we came to the conclusion that to take responsibility for the employment of artists, and the production of programmes to the satisfaction of a very critical public in a matter of this kind, particularly in view of the raging criticism in other countries, would be really inviting disaster. We may conceivably find ourselves endeavouring to decide whether an Irish artist or an English artist should be employed, or whether an Irish song or an English song should be sung, or whether a particular speech, made in a particular way, was one which could be endorsed by a Government Department. On the whole, we are satisfied that the handling of this subject by the State is beyond our powers. We have no doubt at all about that, and we are satisfied that if we attempted to do it, much as we desire it, that we would produce the one and only and the greatest demonstration which the people have had of the inability of the State to handle enterprises of this kind.[86]

This may surprise us, since Walsh appears to be disavowing his department's capacity to formulate policy – a point which is reinforced by the lack of any

---

86 *Report* para. 2. The British PMG had held the same views, stating that 'I do not regard it as desirable that the work should be done by the Government and I do not contemplate a condition of things under which the Post Office will be doing this work', quoted in A. Briggs *The Birth of Broadcasting* p. 93.

sense of purpose or cohesion in the proposals. The turn of phrase 'On the whole ... we have no doubt' is indicative of uncertainty rather than conviction. However, Walsh would later explain that it was more the question of artistic judgement in contracting one artist in preference to another that had led his department to believe this.[87] (Although it became clear that the Post Office had made enquiries, through the Department of External Relations, as to how broadcasting was organised in Belgium, France and Italy, it also became clear that it was the British model which had been uppermost in mind throughout.)

Within Walsh's testimony there were startling inconsistencies. At one stage he admitted that he had originally believed that State operation, and State control, was essential, but that he had been in a minority of one within his own department and had been persuaded by O'Hegarty and Mulligan to reverse his view – 'under no circumstances should we touch broadcasting'.[88] He also clearly found it difficult to conceive of the nature and function of radio, recognising it at one point as 'an essential service',[89] and at another as 'a medium for the amusement and elevation of the people';[90] still later, as 'an entertainment'.[91]

The rest of the first day's discussions rambled back and forth over such subjects as whether the licensee should enjoy a monopoly; which were the constituent companies of the proposed Irish Broadcasting Company; the Marconi Company's position regarding patents; and the issuing of receiving licenses in advance of the radio station starting up.

On two occasions the PMG attempted to introduce the question of policy – an issue he might well have raised at the start of his own evidence – but to little avail:

> *PMG* — There is a point nobody has raised, and that I considered would be the first question an assembly of this kind would introduce, and that is what is the necessity for an Irish broadcasting station?
> *Deputy McGarry* — None.
> *Deputy Magennis* — We have asked that in half-a-dozen different ways.
> *PMG* — Admitting you have, it has not been put as a direct question.
> *Deputy McGarry* — We will put it now. I put it.[92]

Whereupon, characteristic of the proceedings in general, he was interrupted by Milroy and the question was not in fact put. At the close of the session on the first day the subject was raised again:

> *Deputy Magennis* — What we want to satisfy ourselves about is the policy of doing what is proposed here.

87 Ibid. para. 2059. **88** Ibid. **89** Ibid. para. 96. **90** Ibid. para. 389. **91** Ibid. para. 2075. **92** Ibid. para. 93.

Mr O'Hegarty—— You have no alternative.

PMG — … That is the point you will have to face the country upon in any decision you will take, just as we have had to. That is the one point above all. Ignoring petty points … if you never put up a Committee, you must face that question of policy. The question of whether Irish broadcasting is to be controlled at home, or externally, that is the question you have to decide.

Deputy Johnson — Or whether there is to be any broadcasting.

PMG — These are the points. I would like it if you would defer that whole matter until to-morrow.[93]

In the outcome, the deferral was to a 'tomorrow' more distant than merely the following day, not least because the two areas of policy identified in these exchanges – whether there was to be any broadcasting at all, and, if so, what form it would take – had already become confused by the nature of both question and answer. O'Hegarty's 'you have no alternative' is, once again, indicative of the administration's certainty that the need for a private entrepreneur was self-evident.

The question of policy, which had thus been mentioned – and neglected twice – was again reiterated when Magennis tried to raise it a third time, suggesting that the PMG should 'give us a justification for what he holds to be the need for a Broadcasting Company':

> There are two alternatives – no Broadcasting Company, or a Broadcasting Company. The Postmaster-General decided that it is advisable that there should be an Irish Broadcasting Company, and we ought to be satisfied by the Postmaster-General in the same way as he is satisfied.[94]

The documents produced by Walsh that evening meant that on the following day (16 January) the matter of policy would have to compete for attention with that of crisis management.

However, when Walsh came to expand on his reasons for believing in the need for broadcasting in Ireland, he again allowed his thoughts to be dictated by the perceived incapacity of the Post Office for running the service. His thinking ran along the lines: the Post Office cannot run it, the Marconi Company should not be allowed to run it (in case 'this country found itself in the helpless grip of a foreign combine'), therefore it must be 'reserved exclusively to the Irish people'.[95] But such thinking presupposed the point on which

---

93 Ibid. para. 122.   94 Ibid. para. 373.   95 Ibid. para. 389.

Magennis had asked for clarification – whether or not there should be such a service at all. There is considerable ambivalence in Walsh's reply to Milroy's question – 'You consider this an essential national service?':

> — Well, the community does.
> — Didn't you say at a previous meeting that you looked upon it as an essential national service?
> — Well, I do, too.[96]

As we noted in the Introduction, Walsh spoke very passionately of the sacrifices which had been made for Irish freedom and culture, and he would do so again when addressing the issue of Irish language broadcasting. Yet it is precisely the absence of a focussed view of how radio could serve the needs of social reconstruction, and of an explicit expression of that view, that surprises us today as we look for the mind of the practical patriot. The nearest that Walsh came to this was his statement that

> we claim to be – some people say we are not – at any rate those of us who are participating in the present Parliament claim that this nation has set out on a separate existence. That existence not only covers its political life, but also its social and cultural life, and I take it to be part of the fight which this nation has made during the last six or seven years that this separate entity should not only be gripped but developed to the utmost until this country is properly set on its feet as an independent, self-thinking, self-acting, self-supporting nation in every respect.[97]

It is, however, clear that, much as Walsh claimed to hate everything English, he was prepared to look to England for his broadcasting model and, when Séamus Clandillon had been appointed as Director, to send him to the BBC for acclimatisation. 'I think nobody will ever accuse me of being pro-English, even now, but I must confess ... that I have a very deep respect for the judgment of the English Government in the conduct of its public affairs'.[98] Walsh stated that 'we have followed very closely on the present position' in England as regards whether or not the service should be a monopoly. 'While broadcasting is becoming more and more popular in England, it is becoming less and less popular in the United States ... [where] there are rival companies and the system is more or less uncontrolled and confusion reigns'.[99] Walsh was perhaps in touch with Reith, who was at that point about to write his *apologia*

96 Ibid. paras. 2072–3.   **97** Ibid. para. 389.   **98** Ibid. para. 2059.   **99** Ibid. para. 3.

for the fledgling BBC, since the term employed to describe the monopoly, 'unified control', was in fact a Reithian expression which had been current in Britain during the previous twelve months.[100]

The main point for the British in making their decision had been to avoid the creation of a plethora of unregulated radio activity such as existed in the United States, which by 1924 had reached over five hundred stations. In Ireland, a much smaller country than Britain in terms of area and population, the argument was much less compelling, whereas the issue of security would have been much more relevant. Walsh displayed himself as a naïve figure in many aspects of his evidence, but nowhere more so than in that of the envisaged IBC. When Magennis pointed out that the Post Office 'was attempting to set up in Ireland something upon the lines on which the BBC had been set up' and asked 'Is this an exact counterpart?', Walsh replied 'Not an exact counterpart, but it follows as closely as circumstances will permit on the English model'.[101] This was patently misleading, since the BBC was a consortium of radio manufacturers, whereas the members of the IBC were to be merely importers who were not as yet in the radio trade. When Prof. Thrift came into the discussion with the question 'Does not the White Paper indicate the differences' in the two models, Walsh could only answer 'It does, but only roughly'[102] – a response which was both unsatisfactory and unhelpful. To follow this immediately with the statement 'The shrewdest course for us was to take a model which had proved by a test to be a sound model. For that reason we kept as close as possible to the English model'[103] exhibits Walsh at his worst. For someone who openly expressed his hatred of England, to take the English model was an act of blindness as well as one of laziness. Within seconds, Walsh had been challenged as to whether or not the White Paper fully disclosed the difference between the two models, and was forced to answer 'There is only this vital difference' – that in the IBC the participants were not manufacturers.[104] Quite apart from the issue of Andrew Belton himself, it is not surprising that the Committee formed the view that the IBC was ill-conceived when the PMG could utter a statement of such naïvety as 'There is only this vital difference'.

A further point which was compelling in the Irish context but had little or no significance in Britain was the need to use radio in the interests of the Irish language. On this, again, Walsh was passionate, far-sighted and, unfortunately, ahead of his time:

> The Dáil has decided ... on spending a considerable sum of money, and I believe it has the support of the Irish people in that expenditure, on the development of the Irish language. It has decided that this language

---

100 Cf A. Briggs, *The Birth of Broadcasting*, pp. 91–4. **101** *Report* para. 343. **102** Ibid. **103** Ibid. para. 344. **104** Ibid. para. 345.

is the official language of the State, and its desire naturally is that that language would not only percolate into every home in the country but that eventually it ought to be the language of the Irish people.[105]

That year, as we noted, O'Hegarty was to write:

> If we do not revive and develop Irish, we must inevitably be assimilated ... and in that case our name and tradition and history will vanish out of human ken, and our national individuality will be lost. There is no disputing that, and no use in refusing to look it in the face. There is no case known to history where a nation retained its individuality, its separateness, once its language had been lost.[106]

Yet León Ó Broin recalled that O'Hegarty had said in 1915 that Irish offered a young man no avenue to professional or vocational advancement – 'it has practically no modern literature save school text books, it has practically no translations, its vocabulary is centuries out of date, it is not habitually used anywhere in Ireland for official, church, business or professional purposes nor is it possible so to use it. It has no international value outside philology'.[107] Clearly the problem of reinstating Irish as a vernacular medium, as well as creating a mandarin status for it, was a major task, and it is almost certain that the Minister and his Secretary were *ad idem* on this point, whatever differences they may have had on other aspects of broadcasting. The fact that Cosgrave, a Dubliner, had insufficient Irish to make a speech in Irish, in his capacity as head of government, without the aid of a phonetic transcription, was to prove a salutary indication of the vulnerability of such a passionately argued facet of the national plan, and Walsh, who two years later would announce his intention of establishing a radio service for the Gaeltacht, must have wondered if he was capable of persuading the Dáil to 'put its money where its mouth was'.

Yet, Walsh felt, broadcasting was likely to be predominantly in 'a foreign tongue, to the entire exclusion of our native language', and went on to emphasise that part of reconstruction and the restoration of Irish included the development of a sense of Irishness:

> We desire naturally to cultivate Irish music and Irish songs. I am not one of those people who believe that our people are not capable of producing some music and some songs worth listening to.[108]

And, as we have seen, Walsh went on to speak of the 'Gaelic future' in which broadcasting would be a 'potent element'. Yet the fact that he was more

---

105 Ibid. para. 390.   **106** P.S. O'Hegarty, op. cit. p. 127; very similar sentiments had been expressed by Darrell Figgis (*The Gaelic State* pp. 83–4).   **107** L.Ó Broin, op. cit. p. 66.   **108** *Report* para. 391.

concerned with ensuring that no outside influences were involved than he was in designing a structure and a *modus operandi* speaks volumes for the inherent naïvety of the inchoate mindset in the transition from servant to master: the assumption that, without a word being said, '*sinn féin*' could achieve an 'Irish-Ireland'.

A great deal of confusion was exhibited over the question of the assembly of wireless sets in Ireland, and the importation both of fully assembled sets and of their constituent parts. Since the White Paper envisaged that the IBC would be given a vested interest in controlling this importation, as was the BBC in Britain, it became a matter of considerable debate, and occupied what transpired to have been a disproportionate amount of the Committee's time; although the time was largely wasted, since the IBC scheme was shot down by the Committee, it has a certain relevance because it indicates the contribution which the radio trade might have made to the development of Irish manufacture and the Irish electrical industry generally. In these exchanges Seán McGarry became a thorn in the side of the PMG, not, however, without some humorous aspect:

> *Deputy McGarry* — I heard Spain on a set manufactured in Ireland. I was on the run at the time and that is a long time ago – before the Truce … As a matter of fact I have a set at the present time. I do not mind the PMG knowing it. He will not raid it.
> *PMG* — as a matter of fact I will.
> *Deputy McGarry* — You will have to find it first[109]…
> *PMG* — We are considering prosecution. We are going to make a demand for a very heavy fine. Deputy McGarry is one of the people we have on our list.
> *Deputy McGarry* — You will not get his set.[110]

There is a neat irony in the mention of being 'on the run'[111] coupled with that of a concealed wireless apparatus, which must have brought a collective *frisson* to the eleven men in the room, of whom seven had in the recent past been either 'on the run', under police surveillance, or deported to English prisons.[112]

Despite McGarry's assertions to the contrary, Walsh was adamant in his belief that no sets were being manufactured in Ireland – it still being illegal to possess (or at least to use) an unlicensed set or parts thereof.[113]

---

109 Ibid. para. 33.   110 Ibid. para. 37.   111 The expression occurred again during the proceedings, when Figgis told the Committee that Belton said 'he had been of service to Colonel Moore when the Colonel had been "on the run" in London' – ibid. para. 534.   112 For a sympathetic account of these experiences, cf. M. Laffan, op. cit. pp. 64–8.   113 *Report* para. 30.

Deputy McGarry — There are sets manufactured in Dublin by two or three people. The PMG says that he is not aware that that is so ... I know one factory turning out six a week for farmers and others ...

PMG — I may say in that connection that it is illegal for anybody to make an instrument at the moment ... I have asked the Deputy on a previous occasion to let me have the name of such a person. The information of my Engineering Department is, and my own instinct tells me, that there is not one essential part of an instrument made in this country notwithstanding anything to the contrary. They are assembled and the people who have an interest in this matter insist on confusing the word 'assemble' with the word 'manufacture'. There is a distinct difference ...

Deputy McGarry — I am not going to give the information. I know it is being done and it is being done by one member at least of the Broadcasting Committee. I know one manufacturer turning out sets as quickly as he can turn them out and the Postmaster-General says that as far as he is aware that is not so. We are told that it is premature to raise the question of manufacture in Ireland. How can it be premature when sets are being manufactured in Ireland for months?[114]

(Whether McGarry really meant a 'member ... of the Broadcasting *Committee*' is questionable: it is more likely that he had in mind one of the representatives of the Irish Broadcasting *Company*. If it was an error, it went uncorrected. If it was deliberate, it went unchallenged.)

It became clear in the course of the PMG's evidence that he had formed the view that the Marconi Company was a menace to Irish security and that its attempt to secure the broadcasting concession represented not only a tough commercial interest but also some intangible threat:

It is quite obvious it is not for financial reasons Marconi is after this. What is it? Is it that the control of what would be an essential service, wireless, in this country, shall be under the control of an outside body? If that is so it raises a matter of special consideration, and one that should be very seriously considered, whether or not that the State should allow anything like that to an outsider, or even a private body to have that control. We want to know the object behind Marconi's desire to control.[115]

There had, indeed, been a 'Marconi Scandal' in Britain in 1912–13, when the Company had tendered for the installation of stations for the planned

114 Ibid. paras. 29–33.   115 Ibid. para. 96.

Imperial Wireless Scheme. The managing director of Marconi was Godfrey Isaacs, brother of the Attorney General, who, it was alleged, had speculated in Marconi shares together with Lloyd George (Chancellor of the Exchequer). A Committee of Inquiry cleared them, and the Marconi Company won the contract. (Plans for the worldwide network were deferred by the First World War.) Although Guglielmo Marconi was not himself implicated, there was sufficient resonance within the acoustic of government for suspicion to be attached to the name of someone so dogged in his pursuit of fame and fortune.

Walsh was quite convinced that two members of the Committee, McGarry and Figgis, were potential agents of Marconi and said so, and apparently used a secret service detective, Moynihan, to observe them.[116] He also believed that Marconi was using its ownership of the patents to manoeuvre itself into the concession.

> What we are up against in the very start of this business is a campaign by shareholders of the Marconi Co., and by touts of the Marconi Co., and from the very start we have had to fight against these people insisting on our handing them over the exploitation of broadcasting in this country unconditionally, or on their own conditions. One of the things they say is: 'You cannot get on with an Irish Company for the reason that we hold all the patents' ... During the time that the military controlled the wireless... the Marconi people came along here to a man named Kelly – Alderman J.J. Kelly. He dogged me until I kicked him out, and he then haunted the Secretary. He tried to get some kind of guarantee that this business would be handed over to Marconi.[117]

Walsh also stated that the Marconi Company had demanded £300,000 in compensation for the damage to the Clifden station, which it would then apply to the construction of a broadcasting station.[118]

All of this appears, at least on the surface, to be quite at odds with the straightforward application which the Post Office had received from Marconi. However, Walsh would have been aware of the situation in Britain, where the Secretary of the Post Office had said in 1912, during the proceedings of the Select Committee investigating the 'Marconi Scandal', 'for years we have been fighting the Marconi Company. We have had years of struggle with them'.[119] This was part of the hard-nosed commercialism through which Marconi himself and his executives had achieved what Asa Briggs has called 'a commanding

---

116 Ibid. paras. 862–5.   **117** Ibid. paras. 88–88a.   **118** Ibid. para. 89.   **119** *Report of the Select Committee on Marconi's Wireless Telegraph Company Ltd.* (1913) quoted in A. Briggs, *The Birth of Broadcasting* p. 31.

position in international business, including a virtual monopoly in Great Britain, Italy and Canada'.[120] In 1922, when the constituent companies of the BBC were being assessed, Godfrey Isaacs told *them* that, since the Marconi Company owned 152 patents, its command of the situation was decisive.[121]

At some stage in his preparations for what Belton assumed would be the concession of the Irish radio to the IBC, he was in communication with the chairman of the BBC, Sir William Noble, a former engineer in the British Post Office and employee of GEC, in respect of the possible supply and installation of equipment. This appeared to Walsh to have been of some significance, but when Walsh discussed it with the Committee he stated bluntly that 'Sir William Noble and Marconi are all one in this matter'[122] – he was completely wrong in fact, but giving voice to a widely held perception of the Marconi Company as synonymous with the BBC as far as its commercial and technological reach was concerned.

It was perhaps due to the fear of the power of international capital such as Marconi's that the PMG insisted that it was 'fundamental' that the IBC should be Irish-controlled. (It even reached the point where the Committee discussed whether a ban on Sunday broadcasting was intended to protect Irish listeners from 'British sermons'.)[123] 'The object of the Irish Broadcasting Company and our desire is to get Irishmen to invest capital in their own country rather than to encourage business with another country'.[124] If the Post Office was not going to operate the station, there were two alternative options:

> one, that the application received from the Marconi Company for the exploitation of wireless in this country should be accepted, and the other, that the control and exploitation of this very vital and important medium of communication should be reserved exclusively to the Irish people.[125]

When he stated that the members of the Cork Radio Company were 'men of outstanding business capability' Thomas Johnson challenged him:

> — But there are very many outstanding men of business in this country who have relations with the Marconi and other big industrial trusts …
> — *Mr O'Hegarty* [intervened] – Capital is international.
> — *Deputy Johnson* — Capital is undoubtedly international, and the people who control it may have international views.[126]

120 Ibid. p. 29.   **121** Cf. ibid. p. 97.   **122** *Report* para. 533.   **123** Ibid. para. 115.   **124** Ibid. para. 388.   **125** Ibid. para. 389.   **126** Ibid. para. 104.

When asked if the names of those associated with the five constituents of the IBC were Irish, Walsh replied: 'As far as we know, they are'.[127] Thomas Johnson then pressed him:

> — You presumably know all about these companies and you know that some of them have no records as business concerns.
> — No, I would not say that. As far as I know, these companies have records which would be considered good.[128]

At this point P.S. O'Hegarty intervened again, and there is in his brief remark a naïvety that betrays his political master:

> — They are all good names. We have not inquired into everything.[129]

When Johnson pressed again about the *bona fides* of the five proposed companies, O'Hegarty again intervened:

> *Deputy Johnson* — I take it that the Postmaster-General ... had at least some knowledge of their respectability and antecedents.
> *Mr O'Hegarty* — We had not. They were the only people we could get to come into the thing at all.[130]

In these exchanges there is revealed a discrepancy between Walsh's assumption that all was well and above board and O'Hegarty's knowledge that not everything had been done to satisfy the Department that the men with whom they had been preparing to do business were suitable candidates for operating a broadcasting service. Later, one of these men, Philip Sayers, would give evidence that he had been partly coaxed, partly press-ganged into the arrangement and that at that stage he was not in fact a party to the IBC.[131] At the time of the publication of the White Paper, which stated that Sayers was a member of the IBC, Sayers was in fact still trying to decide whether he would join it or not, and was being pestered by the Post Office because Walsh and O'Hegarty were, as far as their conduct suggests, desperate to have a fifth constituent – one who had actually, independent of Belton's initiative, announced his intention of setting up in the radio trade – even though, as he said in evidence, 'I know nothing about broadcasting or electricity'.[132] For its part, the IBC resented the PMG's attempt to impose Sayers on the venture.[133] The Committee, in turn, suggested that Sayers was unfit to be involved because, it

127 Ibid. para. 98   128 Ibid. para. 103.   129 Ibid. para. 104.   130 Ibid. para. 104.   131 Ibid. paras. 727–39 and docs. 196, 200, 203, 205–6.   132 Ibid. para. 761. He was, in fact, in the business of wholesale woollens.   133 Ibid. paras. 662–685.

was alleged, he was not Irish but Ruthenian,[134] to which Sayers retorted that he was a Peace Commissioner, and had lived all his life in Ireland.[135] Commenting on the difficulty of attracting suitable applicants, during a Dáil debate Walsh was to say that

> anything in the nature of a Government concession is pretty sure to bring trouble. The same question has caused serious trouble in other countries. We do not stand alone in respect to it. People rush to the conclusion that a concession of this kind is something in the nature of the presentation of a gift on the part of the Government. As a matter of fact, in our own experience, we found it extremely difficult to get anybody to accept the gift. We found it necessary to advertise on four successive occasions, and beg of our countrymen to chance their money in what, I think, may be reasonably regarded as a risky speculation.[136]

THE FIGGIS-BELTON AFFAIR

It is a reasonable speculation that the presence of the document handed in by Walsh at the end of the first day's proceedings fundamentally altered the way in which the Committee sought to do its work, and indeed that it flawed the entire process of reporting on the White Paper and the committee's conception of what its role really was. It is also reasonable to accept at face value Figgis' statement that he did not know of this document's existence and that its arrival in the committee room was completely unexpected. As it is so central to the transactions of the Wireless Committee and to the 'secret history' of modern Ireland it is necessary that this narrative is interrupted at this point in order to give an account of what had been transacted between Belton and Figgis during that short period.

Belton's formal association with Figgis began in March 1922 and ended in August of the same year, when Figgis finally repudiated Belton's overt attempts to manipulate him. The intervening five months show Figgis to have

---

134 Ibid. para. 109: *Deputy McGarry* — 'He comes from the little Republic that was created by the late war, a little Republic that was created from Poland or somewhere. I think it is called Ruthenia'. **135** Ibid. para. 751. Another witness, Thomas Hempenstall, clearly wishing to deprecate Sayers as an unwanted member of the IBC, said (para. 1044) 'Mr Sayers gets wrong ideas of things sometimes, owing to his want of a complete knowledge of English'. Xenophobia was a feature of Irish-Ireland which applied even to the highest level of political leadership: when the 'Blueshirts' threatened briefly to destabilise politics after the accession of Fianna Fáil, Ned Cronin informed a meeting that they had no objection to de Valera (born in New York), Robert Briscoe (Jewish) or Hugo Flinn (Manx) but if they 'were going to live here and be tolerated they must become decent citizens' – Richard Mulcahy papers in UCD Archives, quoted by J. Regan, op. cit. p. 357. **136** DD 6, 14 February 1924, col. 1083.

been at best the dupe, at worst the accomplice, of Belton in a number of schemes, which included harbour developments in Cobh and Galway, the electrification of Kilkenny City, the supply of wireless equipment to the Army, the rebuilding of the Four Courts and Custom House in Dublin, and the raising of British finance for a loan to the Irish Free State. In these schemes the operating company would be Irish Developments Ltd, with Belton and Figgis as its joint shareholders.

Privately, Belton and Figgis were also looking at the possibilities of opening a casino, a factory for making concrete blocks, and – the only instance where Figgis actually used public funds in this connection – the agency for the 'Noiseless Typewriter', three of which Figgis authorised to be purchased for the Constitution Committee.

It had been agreed, on Figgis' insistence, that Belton would take no direct part in Irish negotiations. If Figgis is to be believed, Belton tried to break their agreement in order to exert direct influence in affairs, rather than acting through Figgis. If Belton is to be believed, Figgis' energies after his election as a TD in June 1922 had been directed to politics, to the exclusion of his work for Irish Developments. When the relationship turned sour, Belton wrote the memorandum which had been handed in by the PMG. In addition to the allegations which I quoted at the opening of Chapter 1 concerning Figgis' apparent willingness to act as a front and to use his influence with Collins, Griffith and later Cosgrave on behalf of Belton, Belton went in greater depth into Figgis' supposed political status:

> he had been offered a seat in the Senate, and thought that he might accept it, as it would mean an easier way to him ultimately becoming the Leader of the Government ... He was going to be Minister for Reconstruction in the next Cabinet ... He had been offered the Chairmanship of several Government Committees by Mr Griffith and Mr Collins, and ... he had declined these posts as acceptance would mean interference with his activities on our behalf.[137]

In rebuttal, Figgis was to tell the Committee that he had declined Griffith's offer of a Senate seat, and that he had not sought appointment to any chairmanships: 'there was rather a rush at the time for such things, and I have always had a distaste for crowds'.[138]

It seems that, when Figgis raised the matter of broadcasting in the Dáil on 3 August 1923, Belton took the precaution of sending the memorandum to Walsh in the hope that it would discredit Figgis, or at least prevent his own

---

137 *Report* p. 21b.   **138** Ibid. para. 2536.

profile from being damaged by anything Figgis might say in committee about his prior knowledge of Belton. In his own words,

> I saw that Mr Figgis had, towards the end of the last Dáil, spoke [*sic*] rather feelingly on the subject of broadcasting and said that he would at some later date speak more fully on this subject. There had been several instances from the time that Mr Figgis had severed his association with Irish Developments, which led me to infer that, as and when opportunity occurred, Mr Darrell Figgis would put his knife into Irish Developments.[139]

A few minutes later he repeated this:

> There were certain things said on which I did not place a great deal of stress, casual remarks made by people who said: – 'Figgis says you are no good, or Figgis says this, that or the other', one-twentieth of which … might have been true. I thought it wise … to be prepared to meet Mr Figgis in case he ever did try on a future occasion to do me an injury.[140]

Figgis was of course present, and, both Belton and he having put in their correspondence files as evidence, he stated:

> I traverse everything he has said, with a considerable amount of indignation. I traverse the whole substance, and every word of the dossier, in which there is a certain degree of truth and a large admixture of untruth.[141]

The fact that there was indeed a degree of ambiguous truth was to be Figgis' downfall as well as Belton's. When Belton was recalled on 28 January, he set out to modify the impression he had painted of Figgis, no doubt realising that in his previous statement he had done himself more harm than good. 'He is a very able man, a very eloquent man, a very intellectual man, and the way he presented the case was that the Treaty should be fought for, and that he was the only man with courage enough to go out and do it.'[142] The memorandum was 'really and truly to give the Postmaster-General an idea of how we had parted company, and that our relations were not cordial'.[143]

At this point William Magennis became extremely hostile to Belton, and a heated exchange ensued:

139 Ibid. para. 201.   140 Ibid. para. 328.   141 Ibid. para. 336.   142 Ibid. para. 2303.   143 Ibid. para. 2307.

Deputy Magennis — To show the Postmaster-General what manner of man this Deputy Figgis was, who was so anxious about clean-handed administration, public welfare and so on?

Witness — I do not know whether he advocated clean-handed administration.

— At any rate you put in this correspondence and the Postmaster-General could not fail to see that Mr Figgis was not the impeccable Figgis he would like to be believed to be?

— No: that was not the idea at all. There was no attempt made to impeach the integrity of Mr Figgis at all in the sense that he was corrupt.

— That is the position you take up to-day – that Mr Figgis is pure?

— No: I do not. Mr Figgis is, I think, sometimes not accurate in what he says.

— Pure, but careless of his truth?

— Do not put it that way, Professor.

— You did not put in this document with a view to showing up Mr Figgis? ...

— It was to put before the Postmaster-General what our relations had been. I do not know whether the Postmaster-General knew we had been associated in business.

— It was to put yourself right with the Postmaster-General?

— I do not know that I required to put myself right with the Postmaster-General or anybody else.

— Mr Figgis had been saying nasty things, and you did not like that, and you wanted to clear the air?

— It is very difficult to get a string on Mr Figgis. He seldom comes out in public. When he says things in private or in the darkness of a corridor, people are naturally reluctant to come and allow their names to be given as the persons to whom the statements were made.[144]

The Committee's proceedings on 15 January (interviewing Belton), 17 January (interviewing Figgis), 28 January (Belton in rebuttal) and 19 February (the final interview with Figgis, after his resignation from the Committee on 25 January) constitute an informal tribunal sitting in judgement in the matter of Belton *v.* Figgis, with the Postmaster-General caught in the crossfire between them. Not only were the chief protagonist of the IBC and his former associate implicated, but the PMG's suspicion of, and hostility to, the entire question of manufacture and importation of sets led him to make allegations

144 Ibid. paras. 2308–2313.

against Figgis, Seán McGarry and Dan McCarthy which were interpolated into the proceedings, thus making the meetings of 15 and 18 January a mêlée of accusation, counter-thrust and above all innuendo in which all became vulnerable to their own phobias and prejudices. And in addition to that, a point would soon be reached at which the PMG himself would be implicated in the scandal with the suspicion that he, too, had a personal interest in the radio trade – a point on which he would be exonerated by the Committee and the Dáil.

On 17 January the Committee recalled the PMG and another heated exchange took place between himself and Figgis, which implied that Walsh bore some animosity towards Figgis and had employed Belton's memorandum in a clandestine fashion. Figgis asked Walsh if he recalled a conversation between them in which he had asked 'what was being done in regard to the question of broadcasting' and to which Walsh allegedly replied 'that perhaps it would be better for me [that is, Figgis] if I left the whole question of broadcasting alone'[145] – a conversation which Walsh repeatedly failed to recall. (At his second interrogation, on 19 February, Figgis would state that he had been informed by Thomas Hempenstall that Walsh '"had a rod in pickle" for me if I pressed enquiry into wireless broadcasting … Mr Belton … said that he had seen to it that the PMG was ready to deal with me.')[146] Next Figgis asked why, when he received Belton's memorandum, Walsh had not acquainted Figgis with its contents, rather than sending it (as he had done) to Cosgrave – again, Walsh refused to comment.[147]

When it came to examine Figgis himself (on 17 January), Figgis pressed this point: the Belton memorandum should have been brought to his attention as soon as the PMG received it. 'Instead of this the document has been used with one obvious intention, namely, to intimidate me from pressing a matter that I thought right to raise in the public interest – to intimidate me because of the fear of the filth that must always cling when unclean matter is handled.'[148]

Figgis then agreed with an intervention by O'Hegarty, that he had said to the latter 'If the Postmaster-General's hands were as clean as mine I think he would be all right' – 'That is exactly what I said to him. I do not deny it'[149] – thus causing consternation and confusion to dominate the proceedings for the next two days.

> *Postmaster-General* — Did you say that my hands were not clean in this matter?
> *Figgis* — I never said anything of the sort.

145 Ibid. paras. 492–5. **146** Ibid. para. 2536. **147** Ibid. paras. 499–502. **148** Ibid. para. 534. **149** Ibid. para. 506.

— I want a clear answer, and I want to have this thing cleared up. This is the basis of the whole business, and I am here to see this matter through.[150]

Walsh's turn of phrase was unfortunate: 'this is the basis of the whole business' was one of his *motifs*, occurring often in his evidence and usually in different contexts. He had used the expression to explain the resistance to international capital, and he would use it again in contexts where it is clear that he was heated on a point which, at that moment, appeared to be the essential point under discussion. But in the cold light of analysis it strikes one as indicative of carelessness in formulating responses which ideally should have demonstrated ordered and prioritised thinking.

> ... I want to know if Deputy Figgis, outside the privileges [*sic*] of the Dáil, made a statement to the effect that my hands were not clean in this broadcasting matter, and I want 'Yes' or 'No' as an answer.
> — I am not here to be heckled by the Postmaster-General.[151]

On being pressed by the Chairman to withdraw the remark, Figgis went on:

> The statement that I made was that my own interest in the matter was attacked, and I said if his hands were as clean as mine it would be well for both of us. If these words can be construed as conveying a suggestion that the Postmaster-General's hands were not clean I withdraw them.[152]

If Figgis meant that, since his own hands were clean, then so were those of the PMG, he had chosen an unfortunate and convoluted way of saying so, and one which continued to rankle in Walsh's mind. Walsh went on to allege that at a Cumann na nGaedheal meeting the evening after Figgis had said this, Dan McCarthy had repeated Figgis' words to him:

> He said there were people in this room whose hands were not clean in this matter, and for this reason it was necessary to have an inquiry into broadcasting ... This ruffianly statement started in this House and was started by members of this House and, unfortunately, not to the credit of the House, started with a very definite purpose. It was initiated with a definite object to destroy a man who had the misfortune to be a little more outspoken than he should have been. He should, in other words,

---

150 Ibid. paras. 507–8.   **151** Ibid. para. 508.   **152** Ibid. para. 511.

have minded his own business and let bygones be bygones. I have had the foolhardiness occasionally in public life to strike out in matters ... which, in my opinion, are in the interest of the public generally and I have very often been made to feel that it had been better that I had left them alone. This is one of them. It is, I think, a monstrous thing that statements of that kind should have been initiated here and spread out to the public. In my opinion though the man who made it believed I was perfectly innocent, he acted on the principle that by throwing muck at least some of it would stick and that it would in future help as a medium for silencing me in doing what I consider best in the interests of the Irish people.[153]

Walsh himself was highly sensitive to the situation, since he too had been mentioned in connection with an interest in broadcasting – 'a malicious libel'[154] which he insisted was untrue:

I suppose every member here is cognisant of the fact that, at the outset of these proceedings, rumours went around that I was financially interested in this business and a phrase was being used at the time that my hands were not clean.[155]

When pressed by McCarthy, Walsh said that the rumours had emanated from Figgis and McGarry, and that McCarthy was also supposed to have been involved. As Figgis had alleged that Walsh had threatened not only himself but also McCarthy, there may be some truth in this, but the entire episode, with allegation and counter-allegation, seems almost unreal unless we read it in the context of the complexity of the claims and counter-claims of modern tribunals.

Figgis then went on to state that he had received a letter from Belton referring to his (Figgis') 'influence with the Provisional Government' to which Figgis objected. Although Belton had apologised for having used the expression, Figgis continued

he said that such methods of approach were quite usual in other countries, and that he could not understand why I should resent it. I replied that I hoped that they would never become usual in Ireland and that I personally did resent any such suggestion. I added that I did not possess any influence with the Government, and that if ever at any time the assistance of Government was required in any project suggested by me I would state precisely the nature of my interest in it.[156]

---

153 Ibid. para. 512.   154 Ibid. para. 850.   155 Ibid. para. 851. The rumours were said to do with Walsh's wife having a business interest in radio, which the Committee definitively rejected.   156 Ibid.

As a result of this exchange, Figgis related, Belton agreed that no approach would be made to any public body for the advance of capital except through Figgis himself[157] – Figgis urging always that he saw this as a necessary precaution if Irish projects were to remain in Irish hands. Whether or not with hindsight he realised that this could make him appear to be Belton's 'front' is hard to determine. Figgis further stated that it was at his suggestion, and with Belton's agreement, that a company, Irish Developments Ltd, was to be formed with five Irish directors: himself, George Nesbitt, T. Condren Flinn, Sir Edward Bellingham and Belton, with either Figgis or Bellingham as chairman. 'In this manner, it seemed to me I had fully protected myself as to all direction and control being in Irish hands'.[158] In the outcome, Belton objected that the others should only come into the company as and when they produced projects in which they could 'pull their weight', with the result that the company remained with only two directors, Figgis and Belton.[159] Figgis was to draw a director's fee of £25 per month [£500 per month at 2000 values; €625].[160]

As we shall see, Belton would hedge very cleverly when asked to define 'influence', and here, too, Figgis was ambivalent: when charged by Belton with not 'pulling his weight', Figgis denied that it meant 'dealing with the Government'.[161]

The General Election of 1922 was imminent, and, Figgis said, he accepted Belton's offer of a contribution to his election expenses 'with all alacrity' – the amount, £150 [£3000 at 2000 values; €3,750], to be drawn from the company by Figgis and reimbursed to the company by Belton.[162] Then Figgis informed the Committee:

> Shortly after the election[163] I, while in Mr Belton's company, passed President Griffith … At lunch that day President Griffith asked me what my relations were with my companion. I told him. I also, later, showed him my agreement with Mr Belton. Mr Griffith said the agreement was fair enough and he believed that outside capital should be attracted to Ireland for development purposes. He added, however, that he had met Mr Belton before, and he warned me against him. He said that Mr Belton had gone to see him while the Treaty Negotiations were in progress, purporting to speak on behalf of Lord Midleton and the Southern Unionists,[164] and that he had behaved with great rudeness

157 Ibid. paras. 535–6. **158** Ibid. para. 536. **159** Ibid. **160** Ibid. **161** Ibid. paras. 624–5. **162** Ibid. para. 537. In the outcome, Figgis drew only one month's fees and only £100 of the £150 allocated for his election expenses. Later in the interview (para. 553) he stated that the total cost of his election had been £800 [£16,000 at 2000 values; €20k], to which Richard Beamish had contributed. **163** The election was on 16 June; later (para. 598) Figgis said that this meeting with Cosgrave took place 'three or four days before the attack on the Four Courts' which was on 28 June. **164** Viscount

and insolence. He added that he believed Mr Belton to be in touch with undesirable political influences in London, and he thought that, while the agreement between us was well and good so far as it went, I should need to be careful with the man himself.[165]

One of these 'political influences', Griffith had said, was Lord Beaverbrook, the 'press baron' who was closely associated with Winston Churchill as well as with Bonar Law, who had been Prime Minister 1922–3.[166] It was remarkably naïve of Figgis to put this information in such a way, given that, at the time of this conversation with Griffith, he was about to implicate himself in the very political débâcle against which he had been warned.

Thus warned, Figgis said he 'should … have then and there severed relations with Mr Belton', but that since their articles of association were being drawn up, he continued to go forward with the formation of Irish Developments 'but went warily and carefully, holding Mr Belton always firmly to the terms of our agreement'.[167] Following 'the attack on the Four Courts' (that is, the start of the civil war on 28 June 1922) 'for nearly a month I was imprisoned in Government Buildings' (at that stage located in City Hall), during which time Figgis proceeded with the Irish Developments proposal 'for a loan to the Provisional Government', to be financed by the London banking house of Bernhardt Scholle, which was discussed first with Michael Collins and, after Collins' appointment as Commander-in-Chief of the Army, with Cosgrave.[168] 'After I had broken with Mr Belton', Figgis said he was aware that Belton and the managing director of Scholle & Co. had had an interview with Cosgrave, which had been arranged by Cosgrave's brother-in-law, Frank Flanagan (who had been appointed a director of Irish Developments in Figgis' place).[169]

> It was during this time [July 1922] that the relations between Mr Belton and myself became strained … During this time I could not give much time or attention to the affairs of Irish Developments. To that extent Mr Belton had a legitimate grievance, but, while fighting was on, it was obvious that no work of the kind we projected could be accomplished in the country. Yet it was apparent to me that the true cause of grievance in Mr Belton's mind was that he desired to be free to make direct approach to public bodies in Ireland, whereas he was debarred

(later Earl) Midleton had been MP for West Surrey and Guildford and held several government posts including Secretary of State for War (1900–3) and for India (1903–5); he became the leader of the southern unionists, and was one of the negotiators of the Truce in 1921 and subsequently developed good relations with Michael Collins. **165** *Report* para. 537. **166** Ibid. para. 538. **167** Ibid. **168** Ibid. paras. 538–9. **169** Ibid. paras. 539–40.

from such approach by the terms of our agreement. On several occasions he demanded, somewhat peremptorily, to be freed from that stipulation; but I was not susceptible to his peremptory manners, and held him to his agreement. I did this deliberately because of what Mr Griffith had said to me.[170]

Matters were brought to a head on 14 August 1922, when Figgis became aware that Belton had had direct contact with members of the Galway Harbour Board, and attempted to enforce their agreement 'which I was advised was binding in law. His [Belton's] answer was remarkable. It was that I, as a public man, could not afford legal proceedings: that in all such proceedings much unpleasantness could be raised that could be made the worse for me, whereas he could always return to London'[171] – a scenario for which Belton's prediction was accurate. Although Figgis' instinct was, he said, to remain in the company in order to control Belton, he obtained counsel's opinion that he should resign, and he followed this advice on 30 August. 'It only remains for me to add that during the whole period of my association the question of a Wireless Concession was never mentioned between us'.[172]

Figgis' naïvety was brought out during the grilling he received from Magennis:

> — When a man makes a proposition to you that you were to take payments from him as a consideration for influencing the Government, would you not instinctively distrust this man as regards any further proffers, on his part, of moneys to you?
> — Now I do see that that incident should have scored more deeply on me than it did at the time.[173]

When asked about Belton's proposal to sell wireless equipment to the Army at a cost of £10,000, in which Figgis would have enjoyed 50% of the profits, Figgis said that he did not refer the proposal to the Government because he would have had to declare his interest in it. Yet he was unable to acknowledge that this indicated that Belton was 'trying to use you because of what he believed to be your influence with the Government'.[174]

Asked by Johnson whether he thought it was consistent for the vice-Chairman of the Constitution Committee 'to be making arrangements for deals with the Government' Figgis said 'I would not describe them as deals with the Government. Only in one of them was there any suggestion of the

170 Ibid. para. 540. **171** Ibid. **172** Ibid. **173** Ibid. para. 564. **174** Ibid. paras. 616–21.

Government coming in'.[175] He then gave an extraordinarily truthful but damning answer to Johnson's next question:

> — I think you said in the course of your statement that you did not introduce Mr Belton to any member of the Government?
> — Yes.
> — Did that cover an attempt to introduce him to any member of the Government?
> — No.[176]

In other words, Figgis was prepared to admit that he had attempted such an introduction, and in fact he had set up a meeting with Cosgrave which had then been deferred. He was adamant that Belton's actual meeting with Cosgrave had been arranged by Flanagan.

Questioned as to his putative involvement with the southern unionists, Figgis insisted that the initiative had been taken by Belton, but had to admit that he knew that Belton 'was mixing himself up in politics'.[177] 'Mr Belton said he was acting as messenger for Lord Midleton and that he saw Mr. [Senator Andrew] Jameson on one or two occasions'.[178] Figgis was then asked by William Thrift:

> — I am afraid this is a very direct question, and I do not know whether you care to answer it or not. But when you came to accept this subscription from Mr Belton did you suppose that the reason was generosity?
> — I did not suppose it was through generosity....
> — Knowing at the time that he was anxious to be mixed up with political things was it not strange that you did not connect in some way the offer of his subscription to your election funds with that?
> — Well, in order that there might be some kind of connection, such as you suggest, it should exist in two minds...
> — Did you think you could accept subscriptions of that kind and be perfectly free of obligations to the donor?
> — Certainly.[179]

Magennis then returned to the discussion:

> — Deputy Figgis will remember that he [Belton] said that Deputy Figgis knew well at the time what the nature of the transaction was. He

175 Ibid. paras. 604–5. 176 Ibid. paras. 606–7. 177 Ibid. para. 615. 178 Ibid. para. 638.
179 Ibid. para. 642.

said you knew very well ... what the money was for.

— I did not know very well what it was for.[180]

Nevertheless, he was prepared again to admit, with hindsight, that it had been 'an indiscretion'.[181] On his second interrogation on 19 February he would say 'It is easy to be wise after the event; and a great deal that has been said in this matter is simply wisdom after the event ... I progressed forward, with ripening knowledge; I did not progress backward with full knowledge'.[182] One wonders why 'mature reflection' took so long to enter the Irish political phrasebook.[183]

By the time that the Committee met Belton again, on 28 January, it had formed the view that, however misguided Figgis may have been, he was, relatively speaking, the innocent party, and that Belton was a rogue. This view had been formed largely through the interrogation of Hugo Flinn, an electrical engineer who had formed the Cork Radio Company and was the chairman of the proposed IBC.[184] Thomas Johnson, in particular, had become suspicious of the combination of companies forming the consortium, which, as the situation emerged, appeared to be a number of paper enterprises set up to give the impression of critical mass but in fact having nothing of substance except their relationship with Belton.

Johnson had 'led' the witness by asking Flinn:

> — I want to be careful. Do you think it within the province of probity for this group of men to be associated in such a Company as this applying for a Government concession, when the chief spokesman admittedly had engaged in an attempt to bring undue influence to bear upon members of the Government with a view to obtaining concessions in other Companies?
> — Well, I have listened to you very carefully, but quite honestly you have been rather too careful.
> — I have, perhaps.
> — Put it quite bluntly.

---

180 Ibid. para. 648. **181** Ibid. para. 650. **182** Ibid. para. 2536. **183** During the Presidential election campaign in 1990 one candidate, Brian Lenihan TD, having denied that he had acted improperly in an alleged interference in the relationship between the government and the office of President, subsequently admitted such an attempted interference: his explanation for his change of statement was 'mature recollection [*sic*]' by which he intended 'mature reflection'. **184** Hugo Flinn (1880–1943), who became an electrical engineer in 1901 and was Chief Engineer of Liverpool Electricity Supply Board, was to become a Fianna Fáil TD for Cork in 1927, and Parliamentary Secretary, first at Finance (1932–9) and later the Board of Works. He was chairman of the Civil Service Economy Committee set up at the outset of world war 2 to stabilise the economy. He died suddenly in 1943. His brother, T. Condren Flinn, was a putative director of Irish Developments, and his father, a fishmonger, had given Thomas Johnson one of his first jobs in 1892.

— If it is alleged that the chief spokesman in all these arrangements admits having endeavoured to obtain concessions from Government, and to have entered into financial arrangements with other persons with a view to bringing undue influence to bear upon the Government with a view to obtaining these concessions, would you think it was good policy, sound public policy, to give a concession to a body of this kind, who had chosen as their chief spokesman a man who self-confessedly had taken the course which I have indicated?

— … If a man has done a thing that is corrupt, he is not certainly speaking for us; but, mind, I do not accept it as a fact that he has confessed, nor do I believe he has.[185]

Having heard of this exchange, in which Johnson (with the support of Magennis) had clearly manipulated the situation so as to oblige Flinn to use the word 'corrupt', Belton wrote to the Committee, asking for the opportunity to rebut the inference. Given that the Committee was now heavily against him, it was a brave move, understandable perhaps if we realise that he was in a desperate situation but still with everything to play for if he wanted to keep the Irish pot of gold in sight.

When Johnson repeated the question which had been put to Flinn, Belton's response was 'The whole question is based on what is meant by the word "influence" '.[186] Johnson's rejoinder was to confront Belton with his own record of his relations with Figgis as contained in his memorandum:

Do you say that they do not warrant the interpretation that you used undue and unfair influence, that you paid money to Mr Figgis because of the influence that he could bring to bear upon the Government?[187]

Belton's reply is remarkably adroit:

No. The position is in the three phases which you have just read out. The first, influence, the second knowledge of the resources of the country, and third, ability to secure contracts.[188]

Belton in fact almost succeeded in gaining the moral high ground by setting out what appeared to be a very reasonable (if Machiavellian) exposition:

where he could be useful was that he might have a better approach to a Minister than a stranger. His influence was based on the fact that he

185 *Report* paras. 1468–73. 186 Ibid. para. 2260. 187 Ibid. para. 2261. 188 Ibid.

was taken to be a man of repute, and a man of repute and well-known has a much better chance of getting a hearing than a man who is an absolute stranger … The only occasion on which he did come in direct contact with the Government on our behalf was in introducing me to a Minister, and his influence ended with that introduction.[189]

(It will be recalled that Figgis denied ever having made such an introduction.) Johnson then turned to the original remark attributed to Figgis:

— Do you remember him suggesting to you that some members of the Government were not above making money commercially?
— Commercially, but he did not say corruptly.
— Do you remember him saying that to you?
— Yes, he did not define what 'commercial' was.[190]

A few minutes later, when Magennis came to question Belton, they returned to this topic:

— The word in this sentence that you would emphasise is 'commercially'. You wrote that. 'It had come to his knowledge that some members of the Government were not above making money commercially'. The words *I* select to emphasise are 'not above'. Why should the Minister be above an innocent transaction?
— Is a commercial transaction necessarily a dishonest transaction? …
— What meaning did you put of the words 'not above making money commercially'?
— That they were associated in business enterprises, and that he also, doing business for the Government, could also be associated with business enterprises …
— Did it not strike you as being a peculiar phrase that Ministers are 'not above making money commercially'? Did not that mean 'I might just as well follow their example'? In other words, 'They dare not impugn my action because they are tarred with the same brush'?
— Well, you are probably putting an interpretation on it now that I did not put on it …
— You did not think, when you transcribed that for the Postmaster-General, that it would make the Postmaster-General feel that Mr Figgis was a queer person?
— There was no desire, when that was written, to show that Mr Figgis

189 Ibid. para. 2263.   **190** Ibid. paras. 2269–70.

meant corruption in any shape or form. It was to show that he could while doing work for the Government take an active part in a business undertaking.[191]

Belton was at all times quite open about his commercial interest in reconstruction:

> *Deputy Johnson* — What was your reason for attending that Commission?[192]
> *Belton* — To see if at some subsequent time I could do anything which would assist in the development of the country, and to see if, in any possible way at all, I could get engaged in commercial undertakings in this country.[193]

Moreover, although he maintained that there were few politicians involved in his schemes, he was quite prepared to name them where they came to light: thus Andrew O'Shaughnessy, TD for Cork Borough, and Liam de Roiste, former TD (1922–3) for the same constituency, were revealed as directors of the Irish International Trading Corporation – one of Belton's cover companies,[194] while a member of the Wireless Committee, Richard Beamish, was mentioned as 'one gentleman with whom I discussed business … [who] was not then a member of the Dáil',[195] and whose name occurred in correspondence between Belton and Figgis as a likely (and in fact an actual) candidate for the Independent Party.

When the discussion turned to the scheme for a casino, which would require not only the permission of the Government but also the tacit agreement of the Catholic Church, it was put to Belton that the minuted decision of the consortium, that Figgis would be the go-between with the Government, was an example of employing his services to exercise influence, to which Belton answered:

> Yes; but the placing of a proposal before the Government by anyone, even a brother of a Minister in a position to grant it, does not necessarily mean that there is anything corrupt, as someone must submit a proposal. It is obvious that a proposal must be submitted by someone well known to the person in authority. If one man in a group has more influence than any other member of it, I do not think that there is anything corrupt in asking him to submit a proposal.[196]

191 Ibid. paras. 2333–43.   **192** The Commission of Inquiry into the Resources of Ireland of which Figgis was secretary and Col. Maurice Moore was chairman and at which, Belton claimed, Moore had introduced him to Figgis.   **193** Ibid. para. 207.   **194** Ibid. para. 246.   **195** Ibid. paras. 322–3.   **196** Ibid. para. 2281.

Belton did, however, admit that Figgis had been paid for 'services rendered' which included making introductions, and continuing to 'keep the thing alive' once a project had been initiated.[197]

> *Deputy Magennis* — So that what Mr Figgis set out to you as his espe-
> cial value, was that he was close at the elbow of President Griffith, and
> that he could keep things from falling into the Limbo of forgotten
> things?
> — Something like that.
> — So it was his persistent, pertinacious advocacy of your projects, and
> the possibility of being of use, that rendered him of especial value?
> — Yes; that advocacy and that persistence were legitimate.
> — Because you interpret 'commercial' so as to include that. Whatever
> is done in the advancement of a commercial enterprize for dividends is
> legitimate?
> — No ...
> — The Figgis goldmine did not pan out as expected; the lode or vein
> was soon exhausted, and it was a bad speculation?
> — He posed as being a man who was universally and generally respect-
> ed, and I do not think that was quite accurate.
> — Would you say, apropos of that, that he was a decided handicap?
> — Unfortunately, that was the case.[198]

Later, Figgis himself was to agree ruefully that 'I do not think I have exactly proved myself to be a marketable commodity'.[199] There was, howev-er, a surprise twist to this issue. We have seen that, according to Figgis, Belton had been introduced to Cosgrave by Cosgrave's brother-in-law, Frank Flanagan, after an earlier meeting which had been set up by Figgis failed to take place. We have also seen that Figgis denied he had ever introduced Belton to any Minister and that Belton had referred to at least one occasion on which, he alleged, Figgis had in fact done so. Now, Belton spoke of a meeting he had with Cosgrave which had been arranged by Figgis and at which Figgis was present.[200] He was adamant that this was so, and it appears that the Committee accepted this, as none of its members continued to pursue the issue.

However, on 19 February Figgis was recalled to answer the allegations against him made by Belton during his second interview. On that day, the Committee received copies of letters Figgis had sent to Cosgrave concerning

---

197 Ibid. paras. 2286–9, 2354. 198 Ibid. paras. 2355–60. 199 Ibid. para. 2536. 200 Ibid. paras. 2446–56.

Belton, in one of which Figgis mentioned having introduced Belton to Cosgrave. Even if this were merely a casual and passing introduction, it seems extremely remiss of Figgis not to have mentioned it in his evidence, especially since (presumably ignorant of the letters having been received from Cosgrave by the Committee) he was to re-state unequivocally on that day 'Belton never once met a public man by my introduction and in my presence'.[201] Nevertheless, it was another point either not noticed by the Committee or considered too slight to pursue.

Figgis also vehemently denied having had any expectation of political influence, or of having used any such influence. He was challenged on this point by Thomas Johnson, who read from the minutes of the meeting attended by Figgis and Belton (among others) to discuss the establishment of a hotel-casino:[202]

> After the scheme has been prepared Mr Darrell Figgis should be asked to pave the way and sound whatever members of the Provisional Government he thinks it advisable to approach confidentially on this matter.[203]

Figgis' reaction was to repudiate the minute and to state that he had told Belton immediately that he would take no such steps. However, when confronted with an ambiguous reference in one of his letters to Belton, which could be construed as meaning that he had spoken to both Collins and Griffith on the subject, Figgis said that, while he had no recollection of such a meeting, he would no longer be prepared to say so on oath: 'It would appear I had met both Mr Collins and Mr Griffith with regard to it. I have no recollection of it ... I may have met and spoken to them, but I do not remember having done so ... I may have gone to Mr Griffith and asked him if he had heard anything about it. What I would say is I do not remember doing so.'[204] Yet within a few moments we find Figgis reiterating 'All I can say to you is that Mr Collins and I never discussed the matter'.[205]

It would later be suggested that, because of the seriousness of the Figgis-Belton affair, and the way in which questions were put, answered and recorded during the Committee's proceedings, a new, judicial, inquiry should be held. It is certainly true that if any of the Committee had been able to turn a forensic mind to the evidence, as distinct from the political and patriotic energy which its members brought to the subject, witnesses such as Figgis and Belton, as well as Walsh, would have emerged far more injured than they did.

---

201 Ibid. para. 2536. 202 It was intended to purchase Sir Stanley Cochrane's property at Woodbrook, near Bray, Co. Wicklow, at which Cochrane had already built an opera house (still extant) where the London Symphony Orchestra was to perform in the 1910s and in 1930. 203 *Report* para. 2788. 204 Ibid. paras. 2809–16. 205 Ibid. para. 2824.

One of the more serious aspects of the partnership between Figgis and Belton was the raising of a loan to the Free State from British sources. The resistance to international capital which we have noted was necessarily tempered by the recognition that Irish reconstruction could not be financed entirely from Irish sources – a point on which we have Figgis' assertion that Griffith concurred.

Belton's apparent qualification for acting on behalf of Messrs Bernhardt Scholle, an international banking house, was that he had previously raised a similar loan to British Guiana. It caused considerable alarm within the Wireless Committee because Figgis, in promoting the project to Collins, had used the term 'ruse' to describe the strategy to be employed in floating the loan.

When asked what had been meant by this, Belton explained:

> At that time the state of the country was so troubled that if it had been necessary to raise a loan outside of the country it would have needed a little more than ordinary support to maintain it, and to get the public to come in … It would have … required a great deal of boosting. When you hear of one-half of the country being in revolt and places going up into the sky every other day, if at the same moment you are to ask the public to invest money you certainly would require some boosting.[206]

The proposal which was forwarded to Collins on 12 July 1922 over Figgis' name pointed out both the difficulties of obtaining a loan in such circumstances and a 'ruse' to overcome them:

> This would be the first public loan issued by a national Irish Government on the money markets of the world, and it would be issued at a time, or immediately after a time, of considerable home disturbance and unrest. Both these considerations combine to make a loan of this kind a matter requiring some delicate handling, for it is of the first importance, in spite of the uncertain circumstances, that the first public loan of the Irish Government should have a good reception. If this could be assured, subsequent loans could start off under the best auspices. In order to get this result I have adopted a certain financial ruse which I think will commend itself to you. I have taken the sum of £6,000,000 as the basis of such a loan, and I have divided this into two

---

206 Ibid. para. 2386. Belton's and Figgis' correspondence gives a realistic picture of civil war conditions, with references to fighting in Kilkenny City (doc. 337) and snipers in Dublin: 'I went round on Sunday [from his flat in Fitzwilliam Street] to the Shelbourne and was sniped at from the houses in Ely Place' (doc. 361).

parts, (a) £1,000,000 and (b) £5,000,000. By issuing (a) on terms which would be generous to the general public it could, not being for a large sum, and in good hands, be over-subscribed, and so pushed up to a high premium. When it stood at about par (b) could then be issued at, say, 99.[207]

Belton pointed out that, although the scheme did not originate with Figgis, the word 'ruse' did. He supported the 'ruse', however, to the extent that he regarded it as justifiable for an Issuing House (i.e. Scholle) to create a sense of security among the lending public: 'very often that is necessary for an absolutely good sound enterprise ... It is commercial'.[208] Magennis did not agree:

> — This is a proposition to the head of Government to play a trick ... The British Government, standing at its very highest, issued War Loan at 95, now bearing 5 per cent., but this new State, in all these perilous circumstances on which you have just now dilated, would be in a position to issue at 99. In other words, this firm would make it appear a far better thing than the British War Loan at the best and highest of the British credit.
> — No. I always had faith in the country: but it was very difficult in those days to get anyone to have any other view but that the country was going to the deuce ... It was a question of panic then, when everyone thought that the country was going to disappear, and funds were, I was given to understand, required probably to carry on in order to save the State: but you must remember that during the crisis there were many reverses, and there was a great deal of uncertainty even amongst some of the best people connected with the national movement.
> — But you will forgive me if I remind you that while much might be said in favour of what you say about saving from disaster, what is put up in that letter to Mr Michael Collins is quite the reverse. It is a proposal to use a device in order to have a successful flotation on terms more favourable to the Government than might otherwise be made.
> — No, the Banking House itself would never under any circumstances perpetrate a fraud on the public ...
> — The advantage to you, however, was that Mr Figgis was in the peculiar position that he could dare to write a letter like that to Mr Michael Collins ... Did you ever write a letter in which you repudiated that

207 Ibid. doc. 365.   **208** Ibid. paras. 2408–9.

transaction? ... There is no letter on the file to say 'Dear Darrell ... I and the firm behind me could not countenance such a ruse'.
— A move of supporting a loan on the market is not a dishonourable move...
— This trick was to inspire confidence which could not otherwise be secured?
— Where was the harm in inspiring confidence in the Free State at the time?
— Not in the Free State, but in the loan.[209]

Figgis, too, defended the 'ruse' during his re-examination on 19 February.

> The procedure is an ordinary financial one, and any Finance Minister who neglected to take it would be neglectful of the national interests he was entrusted with ... It is rather an elementary precaution which, if a Finance Minister did not take, he would admit himself unaware of the technical operations of money markets.[210]

He pointed out that the same strategy had been employed in the current National Loan:

> Directly the present loan was over-subscribed it went up to 98, 98½ and 99 ... And the Government Stockbrokers have been buying in these to keep the price up. That is always done, and then the next loan will certainly not be issued at 95.[211]

Having declared his interest in the matter by informing Collins of his agreement with Belton, Figgis made the offer without, he said somewhat disingenuously, entering into any discussion of whether it should be accepted. When Collins passed the matter to Cosgrave, Belton became anxious to meet Cosgrave personally to pursue it, contributing to the breach with Figgis. Belton, Figgis alleged, displayed 'violent repugnance' to Figgis' intention of adopting the same procedure with Cosgrave, 'saying that such a course was unnecessary and impolitic'.[212] In the course of the fall-out, Figgis had writtten to Cosgrave denouncing Belton:

> I have every reason now to believe that persons highly connected with English political affairs are associated in this particular matter and other similar matters that are being pushed forward in Ireland. This is

---

209 Ibid. paras. 2417–36. **210** Ibid. para. 2536. **211** Ibid. para. 2833. **212** Ibid. para. 2536.

particularly the case in respect of port development, where it will be obvious to you that any work undertaken or any control exercised by the very people to whom we could be potential rivals would be a prime disaster for this country ... If it ultimately becomes necessary to go outside Ireland I suggest that it would be better to go direct (without London intermediaries) to the States, with whom we could co-operate, rather than to England, against whom we must compete.[213]

Nevertheless, Magennis could not be shaken free of his belief that something unethical had been attempted: 'there is a radical difference between a scheme which is intended to prevent disaster to National credit and a scheme which is intended first of all to create a fictitious credit and then on the crest of a wave of that fictitious credit to float a further bigger loan'.[214]

Mention of 'persons highly connected with English political affairs' brings us to the point raised by Griffith when warning Figgis against Belton. Again, this final area of their involvement shows Belton to have been unscrupulous and Figgis to have been incautious and unwise.

Following his initial letter to Cosgrave concerning the loan, Figgis wrote once more on 27 September 1922:

> I now learn, on what I know to be very good authority, that he [Belton] is apparently the agent in this country of a certain political-financial group of which Beaverbrook is either the head, or of which he is largely representative. It would appear to be the purpose of this group to get a certain hold over affairs in this country particularly in the vital matter of port development.[215]

At his re-examination of Belton on 28 January Belton was asked:

> — Not only did you advance money to promote his success as a candidate, but you contributed to Mr Winston Churchill passages for use in his election campaign provided by Mr Figgis.
> — Yes, for the good of the Free State ...
> — Mr Figgis sent you a speech to hand to Mr Winston Churchill which the latter was to deliver at Dundee?
> — No, Mr Figgis suggested that it would be a good thing if Mr Churchill stated in some public address that it was the intention of England to stand honourably by the Treaty and that Mr Churchill should come out very definitely in favour of the Treaty.[216]

---

213 Figgis to Cosgrave, 29 August 1922, ibid. para. 2533.   **214** Ibid. para. 2822.   **215** Figgis to Cosgrave, 27 September 1922, ibid. para. 2532.   **216** Ibid. paras. 2457, 2462.

Belton cannot have been insensitive to the mention of Churchill's name in the context of the election of 1922: Churchill, as the British Cabinet member responsible for Irish affairs, was bullying the Provisional Government into effecting the Treaty,[217] which was imperilled by the existence of an electoral agreement, commonly known as the Collins-de Valera pact, which would have resulted in the unchallenged election of anti-Treaty candidates and the subsequent formation of a coalition government. Figgis was one of those pro-Treaty figures who saw the promotion of independent candidates in key constituencies as a means of excluding the anti-Treaty people. As such, he was in communication with Griffith and Midleton, treading a dangerous middle ground between those who wished to see a sustainable Irish state leading ultimately to a Republic, those who would settle for nothing less than a full Republic, and those who, like Churchill would, if the anti-Treaty side prevailed, tear up the Anglo-Irish agreement and take steps to castrate the emergent Irish state.

Beaverbrook's name, also, would ring warning bells with members of the Wireless Committee, since it was his *Daily Express* whose early application to the PMG for the radio franchise had been resisted along with that of Marconi.

Although in this Figgis was once more manipulated by Belton, this is the only aspect of their relationship in which he himself had taken the initiative, inasmuch as he had not been prompted to do Belton's bidding but to allow himself to be taken over by Belton who, it appears, was already in discussions with people like Midleton to attempt to stabilise the political situation so that commercial activities could be initiated.

On one occasion, Belton wrote to Figgis that he had asked Churchill 'to embody your suggestion in his next speech'.[218] On another, he told him that he had crossed to Dublin on the mailboat and had been spoken to by Alfred Cope, Churchill's man in Dublin Castle, who 'said he would be glad to see independent candidates go forward and that he would help all he could'.[219]

The day after he received that information, Figgis prepared a memorandum to which the title 'Memorandum for Lord Midleton on the present Irish situation', was applied, presumably by Belton. He claimed that it had been written 'as a matter of public interest' and that Belton had asked him for a

---

217 The British Cabinet papers record that on 5 April 1922 Churchill pointed out to the Cabinet 'that Mr Arthur Griffith and Mr Michael Collins considered it vital and indispensable to the success of the policy of the Treaty to avoid striking the first blow against the republicans, or any preparatory step which might be regarded as provocative' The Cabinet papers continue: 'There was general approval of the Prime Minister's proposition that the British Government could not allow the republican flag to fly in Ireland. A point might come when it would be necessary to tell Mr Collins that if he was unable to deal with the situation the British Government would have to do so' – Martin Gilbert, *Winston S. Churchill* (London: Heinemann 1977) vol. 4, Companion pt. 3, *Documents April 1921–November 1922*, pp. 1852–3. **218** Belton to Figgis, 1 April 1922, *Report* para. 2462. **219** Belton to Figgis, 26 May 1922, ibid. para. 2465.

copy, which he gave him, since they often spoke together of public matters. The memorandum summarised the developments regarding the Collins-de Valera pact in the run-up to the elections, to be held in three weeks' time. It is the first occasion on which Figgis displayed any of the dislike which mutually existed between himself and Collins.[220] It suggested that, with the pact endangering the Treaty, and with the Provisional Government divided over the isssue, Collins 'should be compelled' to go to London:

> He has only one card to play, and that is 'bluff'. There should not be any friendly greetings, but he should be told quietly and firmly that he has dishonoured his signature to the Treaty. It is possible to break him down in London; his banging the table and vulgar language can be ignored ... Independent candidates ... will all be pro-Treaty men who will take the form of oath outlined in the Treaty ... If the independent candidates are carefully-chosen business men they will be returned without any difficulty ... With the pact broken, Griffith would be first [in the Cabinet], but at a subsequent election the Independent Group should be in the majority, with their own leader.[221]

To this memorandum Belton attached his own viewpoint:

> If Independent candidates are put up two results are achieved: (1) The Treaty is ensured and stable government also is ensured and (2) Strong independent interests, representing business, commerce and farming are brought into an assembly that has hitherto not heeded such interests but has occupied itself with political wrangling ... The candidates standing on such a platform would be responsible men, chosen not for political reasons but because of business capacity and knowledge.[222]

Figgis did not expect that Belton would put his memorandum to use as he did:[223] Belton in fact sent both documents to Midleton, asking for £10,000 to fund the election campaigns of 40–60 candidates. The next day he told Figgis that 'Lord Midleton ... agrees with practically everything you said in your memo. to me, copy of which I gave him so that he could show it to Mr Churchill' and adding that Midleton did not think the funding would be forthcoming 'unless a public statement can be made that Mr Griffith favours this development'.[224]

---

220 Collins had objected to Figgis being appointed secretary of the Constitution Committee, but had been over-ruled by Griffith. Figgis subsequently told the Wireless Committee of this mutual dislike (ibid. para. 2824). **221** Ibid. para. 2469. **222** Ibid. para. 2470. **223** Ibid. para. 2536. **224** Belton to Figgis, 27 May 1922, ibid. para. 2472.

Figgis declared himself as being 'horrified' that the paper had been shown to Churchill, but recognised that they were still pursuing the best course of action: 'I am still convinced it is the only thing to give the country the chance it wants'.[225] Belton's precipitate action in a matter affecting the internal workings of the Irish government was beginning to alarm him:

> I am bound to say that I am disturbed about these connections of yours. Do not misunderstand me. I am sure business can be done in this country, for the advantage of this country. But if that business is to come off at all, much less if it is to be successful, it must have nothing to do with what we in our jealousy consider to be political meddling. I am bound to say that I share that jealousy myself to the full.[226]

Belton claimed that he had never received this letter, and that it had been written subsequently and inserted into the file. Partly as a result of this development, Figgis, realising for the first time (as he claimed) that Belton was involved politically at a far deeper level than he had previously thought, and partly alarmed by Belton's clear interest in backing a 'Business Party', declined to be further involved with the business faction and ran his own campaign – albeit with money from Belton and other business interests, including Beamish. It was only after the election, when Griffith spoke to Figgis about Belton, that Figgis showed him the memoranda to Midleton, wherewith Griffith told him that Belton had spoken to him personally 'purporting to speak on behalf of Midleton'.[227]

In examination by Dan McCarthy, Belton stated that 'it was common knowledge, and you must have known it at the time, that people were getting tired of what Figgis called continual wrangling', and that a settled, businesslike situation was needed.[228] When charged with having 'show[n] an anxiety to depose Griffith and Collins and set up a Figgis-co-Unionist combination and having done that you would call the tune' Belton retorted 'You know that is Utopian',[229] yet it is quite possible to place such a construction on the matter. In fact, Figgis' role in the election, and particularly in opposing the 'Collins-de Valera pact', was to earn him in his turn the epithet 'the Figgis Plot' for his involvement with the Independents and the unionists.[230]

---

225 Figgis to Belton, 29 May 1922, ibid. para. 2473. **226** Ibid. **227** Ibid. para. 2536. **228** Ibid. para. 2500. **229** Ibid. para. 2507. **230** Cf. J. A. Gaughan, *Thomas Johnson* p. 204.

THE COMMITTEE'S REPORT

The period (16–30 January 1924) between the curt first interim report and the much more detailed second interim report saw the committee pressing on with the analysis of the situation while all the time trying to assess the damage caused to the Postmaster-General's proposals by the Figgis-Belton scandal. In that period they interviewed Walsh a further three times, O'Hegarty once, Figgis himself once, and, on 28 January, recalled Belton. As noted above, they also interviewed the other members of the proposed consortium of the IBC, the Post Office engineers, representatives of the Marconi Company, and the Post Office solicitor. On 23 January they considered a motion not to admit the Press to their proceedings, tabled by Dan McCarthy, which was agreed by five votes to two.[231]

On 25 January the Committee received a letter of resignation from Figgis. On the face of it, his decision was obvious and reasonable, but in later evidence, during his second examination, it transpired that it had been 'very strongly against my own wishes and desires in the matter, and only because it was put so powerfully by the Chairman and one or two others. I am never one to run away from a field, and that was the first time I have gone, and I only went because I felt my colleagues desired me not to be present'.[232]

At this stage the Committee had before it two quite different, but equally disturbing, facts. The first was Walsh's – and O'Hegarty's – unwavering determination that the Post Office was unsuitable and indeed incompetent as far as the administration of an 'entertainment' channel was concerned. This in itself would not perhaps have presented such a problem were it not for the continued display of muddled thinking on Walsh's part in respect of the distinction between 'entertainment' and the other possible functions of radio in the public service and in the public interest – a confusion which, to be fair, several other contributors also displayed.

The second fact was the revelation by Andrew Belton of his previous business relationship with Darrell Figgis. That this revelation threw an unpleasant light on Figgis and also showed Belton himself to be a grasping adventurer is, again, only part of the disturbance. That the PMG and O'Hegarty, aware of this relationship and of Belton's motivation in getting involved in 'reconstruction', should have continued to view Belton as a suitable principal in the matter of an Irish broadcasting station is inexplicable unless we surmise that a lapse of judgement of such magnitude was due to their sense of urgency in

---

231 *Report* p. xxiii: Hogan, Magennis, McGarry, Beamish and McCarthy voted in favour, Thrift and Johnson against. No request had been received from the Press to be allowed to attend the Committee's sessions: if such a request had been received at the outset, it is likely that the matter would have been raised in the Dáil. 232 Ibid. para. 2551.

setting up a service which would be cost-free to the State, involving minimal administrative supervision, and with a profit incentive to its promoters sufficient to carry the whole business successfully.

Although their understanding of the problem was incomplete, it is in fact possible to appreciate their choice of solution: if they truly felt that radio programming would be principally 'entertainment', and if they therefore had serious doubts as to the capacity of a Post Office department to act as impresario, then it becomes obvious that their insistence that such a service should be provided by an entrepreneur, subject to the approval of the PMG, was reasonable, not least in the light of Walsh's own recall of the determination with which he and O'Hegarty had set about the reform of the Post Office and the implementation of improved services.

The fact that the country was in a financially precarious state meant also that there was a very strong incentive to ensure that the service would not be a burden on the exchequer – and with Blythe as Minister for Finance there was, in Joseph Lee's words, a policy of 'rigorous retrenchment'.[233] Beside that, however, is the curious view that, rather than harness the forces of development, 'the state should do as little as possible' – a view which Lee attributes in part at least to partition: 'nation-building would have occurred only had the state embraced all Ireland ... No new nation had to be created in 1922, only a new state'.[234] This is supported by deputy William Hewat's observation that 'As far as I can see, a broad programme of broadcasting on national or other lines would not be very well handled by any Government Department. Government Departments, we know, are not particularly prone to exhibiting a large amount of initiative'.[235]

While Walsh and O'Hegarty were aware of the pact, and then the rift, between Figgis and Belton, and had been in possession of Belton's memorandum for some time – a fact of which Figgis was unaware when he stood up in the Dáil on 14 December to propose the setting up of a Special Committee – we can also add the fact that Figgis was in many ways his own worst enemy: he was in fact widely regarded as being very talented but at the same time a contradictory figure who had few friends and an inflated sense of his own importance. In the year after his death, the critic Laurence Patrick Byrne (who wrote under the pseudonym 'Andrew E. Malone') said of him: 'as a politician he merely wasted his energy and his talent. The members of the Dáil treated him as a joke in which they soon lost interest; they demonstrated their lack of interest by trooping out of the House when he rose to speak.'[236] He has been described by Michael Laffan as 'anathema to most radicals and disliked even by some moderates'.[237] In his memoirs, published posthumously, Figgis

233 J. J. Lee, op. cit. p.108.   **234** Ibid. pp. 92–3.   **235** DD 6, 3 April 1924, col. 2870.   **236** A.E. Malone, 'Darrell Figgis', *The Dublin Magazine* vol. 1, April–June 1926.   **237** M. Laffan, op. cit. p. 363.

constantly records his frustration at the incursions which the imperatives of politics had made on his life of art and scholarship, and conversely there may have been many who wished that, after the war phase of Irish history had closed, he had returned to that life. Without the encouragement of his English paymaster, Andrew Belton, he might have done so.

But it remains inexplicable how, firstly, Walsh and O'Hegarty can have been taken in by Belton; secondly, how the IBC associates such as Hugo Flinn and T.P. Dowdall, and Irish Developments associates such as Sir Edward Bellingham could have agreed to work with him; and thirdly how, after Figgis' revelations, the Post Office could have continued to regard Belton as a reliable concessionaire.

We turn now to the remaining evidence given to the Wireless Committee, principally by the members of the proposed IBC; and the Post Office engineers who, besides upholding the Department line on the IBC, spoke mainly about the technicalities of transmission and reception. It was only after the second interim report was issued that the Committee heard the opinion of independent scientists and the case of the newspaper industry. It should be recalled that at this stage, apart from the Postmaster-General's statements in favour of the Post Office-IBC scheme, little had been heard about the concept of introducing radio into the Free State. It must be said that, since little was understood of the nature of radio or its technical requirements, there was in fact a vacuum in which both the Committee and later the Dáil and Seanad had little space or opportunity for anything other than speculation. One point of speculation which we have already noted was the prevision of the mobility of radio receivers (the 'transistor' which affected outdoor behaviour so significantly in the 1960s). Another was E.C. Handcock's suggestion that 'you could eliminate the telephone. I can imagine such a possibility ... as reaching the point where one with a receiving set could telephone to other people'[238] – a prediction of both citizen band radio and the mobile phone. He also foresaw a radio equivalent of television's pay-per-view in a system wherein 'the proprietors of the station should let out so much per hour or per minute to the various people requiring to use the instrument'.[239]

One of the most important points to arise was promoted by Professor J.J. Dowling of UCD, who observed that city and country are quantitatively different, and that therefore 'very useful applications of radio that might be of very little use in a city would be of great interest in country districts'.[240] One of these would be information such as weather forecasts and market reports; another would simply be what he called 'modified amusement' to relieve 'the

238 *Report* para. 1181.   239 Ibid. para. 1173.   240 Ibid. para. 2954.

monotony particularly in the winter nights' – a point of considerable significance at that time which was mentioned by several contributors to the debate.
Stating bluntly that 'there is no form of amusement in the country home-
stead', Dowling said that if this were the principal motive for introducing
radio, then on technical grounds the transmitter should be located in the
Midlands in order to reach as many of these homesteads as possible.

Throughout the inquiry one is astonished to find Walsh, O'Hegarty and
other officials taking the view that, because more artists were available in
Dublin, Dublin was inevitably 'central' to the country – in which they were
encouraged by one witness, Professor F.E. Hackett, who thought that a self-
supporting Dublin station should be set up, with gradual penetration into the
south and west of the country by means of licensed amateur organisations;
Connemara and Roscommon he considered 'too sparsely populated'.[241] (At
one point one of the commercial parties referred to consideration of these
regions as 'broadcasting to sheep'.) When we consider that in the field of folk
music, in which Radio Éireann eventually came to excel, the vast majority of
potential broadcasters were outside the Dublin area, this view of Dublin's
centrality becomes somewhat untenable. In fact, the decision, in 1927, to place
a high-power transmitter at Athlone, which was physically at the centre of the
country, coming as soon as it did after the start-up of 2RN, implicitly confirms
Dowling's viewpoint and criticises the original siting of the station in Dublin.

The red herring relating to manufacture was raised continually, and on each
occasion was seen as such. Although Seán McGarry might know of radio manufacture taking place in Ireland, it transpired that in effect the main part of the
radio trade would be importation of built-up sets, with a limited amount of
assembly of imported parts. When Belton stated, apparently unequivocally, 'it is
as manufacturers of wireless that we are interested',[242] he may not have intended to mislead the Committee, and may simply have used the term loosely.
However, another witness, Dr J. O'Doyle, who stated that he had been invited
by Belton to become chief engineer of the IBC,[243] also stated that Belton had
been emphatic that the IBC would not be engaged in manufacture, but that its
constituent companies would function as agents of imported goods.[244]

Thomas Hempenstall, in whose workshop some radio parts were already
being made, argued that to start Irish manufacturing of radios would give
employment to the many students of the technical schools, and might attract

---

241 Ibid. para. 2989. Both J. J. Dowling and F. E. Hackett had been students of the professor of Physics
at UCD, John McClelland, who had himself been a student at the Cavendish Laboratory at Cambridge.
Dowling was successively lecturer and Professor of Technical Physics at UCD 1937–58. He objected to
2RN's interference with his reception of radio from Britain and Europe, and obtained a licence to 'cut
out' the Dublin signals (M. Gorham, *Forty Years* p.38). Hackett was Professor of Physics at the Royal
College of Science of Ireland 1921–6, after which he held the same position at UCD until 1952; he was
treasurer of the RIA 1930–62.   **242** Ibid. para. 249.   **243** Ibid. para. 2861.   **244** Ibid. para. 2867.

manufacturers elsewhere to relocate in Ireland.[245] However, it was also unclear from his evidence whether he in fact meant 'assembly' rather than 'manufacture', or whether he thought the broadcasting initiative would be commercially successful: he expected that 'the only really good scheme would be if you could get the newspapers to take it up' and that he would probably lose his money.[246] Another contributor, E.C. Handcock, who was chairman of the Irish Radio Traders Association and who represented the Irish and Foreign Trading Company, thought that radios might be manufactured as part of a larger electrical industry, with the same machines being used for different types of output, which had been investigated by the latter company, and had been incorporated into its proposal to the Post Office for broadcasting.[247] One of the scientists approached, O'Doyle, who had studied with Hertz and had extensive experience of the radio industry in Germany, considered that an electrical industry would require supplementary input from the glass industry in order to be viable, but that the engineering personnel were already available in Ireland to train a workforce – 'but there is no scope for them'.[248]

Nevertheless, we should not take too seriously this type of aspiration. Although Walsh told the Committee that 'we have been striving from the very outset to get some company to come in here to manufacture not only broadcasting sets but electrical appliances as well',[249] there was no evidence to substantiate him. Unlike Russia or Sweden, where accelerated industrialisation was under way, in Ireland the issue was divisive since it separated those who saw the future in terms of the past from those whose pragmatism made them look forward; Joseph Lee again suggests that, rather than encouraging manufacture, the Department of Industry and Commerce actually discouraged it.[250]

The only point on which most of the IBC constituents agreed (the exception being Hempenstall) was their interest in making a commercial success of the station. Sayers' contribution was typical:

— I was going into this business because I thought it was a good business transaction.
— A money-making transaction?
— Of course.[251]

---

245 Ibid. para. 994. **246** Ibid. para. 1038. **247** Ibid. para. 1061. The directors of this company were Lord ffrench, Senator Edward MacLysaght (later a noted genealogist and Chairman of the Irish Manuscripts Commission), James Douglas (a member of the Constitution Committee and at this time vice-chairman of the Senate) and Lionel Smith Gordon, who was a member of the Apostles dining club (see above p. 54), a shareholder in the *Irish Statesman* and managing director of the National Land Bank which had been set up to encourage co-operative work and which owned 50% of the company. **248** Ibid. paras. 2845–8. **249** Ibid. para. 2130. **250** J. J. Lee, op. cit. p. 120. **251** *Report* para. 93.

On the subject of whether or not the IBC was a front for Belton, and whether its members trusted Belton, there was divided opinion. Hugo Flinn, soon to enter the Dáil himself, said 'every member of the Company, my fellow-directors, and every shareholder of the Company have absolutely the highest confidence and respect for Mr Belton ... confidence in his personal character, and in everything that we know about him'.[252] When challenged as to whether Flinn really knew anything of Belton, other than hearsay, Flinn replied 'We go through life following our judgements in the confidence of the knowledge of one's personal character that comes to us'[253] – thus implicitly agreeing that the basis of his judgement in this case *was* hearsay. Another point on which Flinn was grilled consistently was the issue of whether the IBC really was composed of genuine, separate constituent companies, such as the Cork Radio Company of which Flinn was a director, or had been put together to appear as such to replicate the BBC model in this respect. Professor Magennis who, as we have seen, had already succeeded with metaphysical skill in putting words ('corrupt influence') into Flinn's mouth, now scored a similar point by getting Flinn to agree hypothetically that a number of companies with identical directors was really the same company – thus creating the ground on which the IBC could be seen as a solo undertaking by Belton with a number of business associates. The fact that Richard Beamish, with whom Belton had had some tangential dealings, was present but tacit throughout this session, is suggestive of his timidity in this regard. (He was also silent during the next session, at which T.P. Dowdall[254] attended and revealed that he had contributed to Beamish's election expenses, although claiming to have been unaware of Belton's involvement with Figgis and the Independent Commercial party.)

On the other hand, there is a transparent honesty about the commercial interest of the Cork-based members, Flinn and T. P. Dowdall. The latter, who was also harried by the Committee regarding his and Belton's *bona fides*, was quite blunt:

— The position is this so far as I know. There is to be a licence from the Government for five years. We anticipate that after five years if it is a success the Government will take jolly good care to get hold of it, and we think that that being so, we should be permitted to take any of the plums that are going in that five years.

— To make hay while the sun shines?

---

252 Ibid. paras. 1261–2. 253 Ibid. para. 1264. 254 His brother, J. C. Dowdall, a Senator and founder-President of the Cork Industrial Development Association, was also a director of Cork Radio Company. Both T.P. and J.C. Dowdall left Cumann na nGaedheal to join Fianna Fáil in 1927, one week after the announcement of J.J. Walsh's resignation.

— Yes. Frankly I am in this for what I can get out of it.[255]

When pressed by Magennis on the same tack as he had pressed Flinn, Dowdall was equally insistent, and succeeded in avoiding the same trap:[256]

> — You would not think it good public policy to grant a concession to a Company if the leading spirit in it was a man who sought to exercise, by the influence of money, influence upon members of the Government ...?
> — No, I would not. I do not think that anything in the nature of bribery would be advisable.
> — If we were to have it in this country you would not agree to be associated with it?
> — No I would not. At the same time I would like to make it clear that I do not wish anything I say now to be taken as agreeing that Mr Belton has attempted to do that.[257]

It is probable that, if it were not for the fact that Belton had shown himself to be unscrupulous in the matter of 'influence', and if he had not given the Committee reason to doubt his word, his associates would not have been subjected so persistently to attempts to tar them with the same brush. It was, for example, ludicrous for Thomas Johnson to try to implicate Dowdall in the matter of the morality or otherwise of operating a casino when it was clear that Dowdall knew nothing of that aspect of Irish Developments Ltd; and when, for example, Dowdall said 'I think Mr Belton is a very competent and straight man'[258] there was no reason to suppose that he was speaking anything but the truth. Guilty though Flinn, Dowdall and others may have been of an error of judgement, none of them, as far as we are aware, was, up to this time, in possession of the inside knowledge available to Figgis. On the other hand, one can only wonder at the ability of Belton to harness the goodwill and the good names of reputable men, several of whom were about to enter the legislature, but who had no suspicion either that they were being used or that the leader in these endeavours was untrustworthy.

On 31 January 1924 the Committee submitted its second interim report to the Dáil. It referred to two matters which had taken its work outside its original scope – the 'widespread publication of rumours affecting the honour and integrity of the Postmaster-General' which 'were found to be wholly baseless',[259] and the Figgis-Belton matter. Pointing out that its work was incomplete, the Committee (with the exception of Figgis who had resigned and

---

255 Ibid. paras. 1676–7.   256 It is of course possible that between this and the previous session he had spoken to Flinn and thus been put on his guard.   257 *Report* paras. 1750–1.   258 Ibid. para. 1706.
259 Ibid. p. iv.

McGarry who had stood down temporarily 'because of his connection with the electrical trade')[260] stated that 'the main questions raised by the Official White Paper are these':[261]

> (a) Is it desirable to have a broadcasting station set up and a transmission service provided in Ireland?

– to which the answer was

> The Committee ... is ... convinced that the control of broadcasting in Ireland must be rigorously preserved a National control [*sic*] ... It is desirable to have at least one broadcasting station set up, and that provision be made for the transmission of messages helpful to Agriculture and business generally – for example, weather reports, market reports as to prices and supply; of lectures, educative or entertaining; and of communications of national interest and importance.[262]

To the next three questions the Committee was not yet in a position to give an answer:

> (b) should broadcasting be a State service purely, the installation of apparatus and the entire working of it in the hands of the Postal Ministry?
>
> (c) If not reserved as a State monopoly, should it be at least partially so, and in which case to what extent?
>
> (d) If on the other hand the provision of broadcasting service for Ireland to be made over to private enterprise, should the concession be given to an individual business firm, or to a group of otherwise separate companies associated as constituent units of an Irish Broadcasting Company? And further, how should such Irish Broadcasting Company obtain its revenue?[263]

The Committee had yet to hear from experts as to the viability of the scheme, but it was tending to the belief that 'the station and its equipment should be retained in State ownership', that the staff should be under State control, 'while the provision of concerts, lectures and other entertainments to be broadcasted [*sic*] might well be left to cultural associations, and to business enterprise'.[264]

---

260 Ibid.   **261** The questions conform very closely to those of the 'Sykes' Committee which had preceded the establishment of the BBC: cf. A. Briggs, *The Birth of Broadcasting*, pp. 8–9.   **262** *Report* pp. iv–v.   **263** Ibid. p. iv.   **264** Ibid. p. v.

This latter point might be regarded as a missed opportunity. In concept, it comes close to the practice of 'pillarisation', or the sharing out of airtime to representative sectors of the community, which was to be a feature of early radio in countries such as Holland and Finland.[265] It was a subject which the Committee had visited on several occasions without drawing out the potential. Given the various interests which might have made use of such a structure – religious denominations, farmers, educational groups, as well as 'cultural associations' – all supplying responsible programming at *nil* cost, it is perhaps surprising that it was not pursued.

The fifth point (e) was:

> Should the public interest require that the concession be given to a composite company, is the Irish Broadcasting Company as set out in the White Paper such in its inception, formation, and composition, as to warrant the grant to it of the broadcasting concession?[266]

To this, the Committee responded 'No': firstly, because the IBC bore only 'superficial resemblance' to the BBC 'but there is no real analogy' since the companies in the IBC were not engaged in the radio trade; secondly, however, the Committee had become acquainted with the details of the Figgis-Belton affair and the various schemes in which they had been involved, and had had to 'form a clear judgment as to the suitability of Mr Belton to be a State concessionaire'. They had realised that the entire enterprise rested on their judgement of Belton (and by implication also Figgis and Walsh): 'We have to substantiate Mr Belton or otherwise …We cannot avoid it now … We must also see that the thing is clean'.[267] They had 'summon[ed] Mr Belton for examination regarding these schemes, as they seemed to savour of corrupt practice', and had decided that in a matter which bore 'so closely upon national cultural development and national safety alike … it would be altogether unwise and unjustifiable to grant a State concession' to a company in which Belton was 'if not the prime mover, certainly the most active agent'.[268] As a result, a parliamentary debate ensued which foreshadowed many of the developments of the 1980s and 1990s.

The Committee's final point – whether the PMG should proceed at this stage to issue licences – was affirmative, thus defeating Walsh yet again on an issue on which he had taken such a determinedly contrary stand. Walsh would in fact attempt to have this recommendation set aside when the Dáil met to consider the Report, arguing that the issuing of licences depended on 'the

---

265 Whereby recognised cultural, religious or social associations would enjoy guaranteed access to the airwaves in agreed proportions. **266** *Report*. p. iv. **267** Ibid. para. 364. **268** Ibid. p. vi.

Dáil's decision to have a broadcasting station set up in this country'[269] –
precisely the argument he had put forward to the Committee and which the
Report rejected.

As a result of the Committee's decision regarding his trustworthiness, Belton
precipitately left the country, no doubt recognising that he was *persona non
grata* and fearing that to stay in Ireland would expose him to legal action by
Figgis.

The Committee then turned to the question of the press which, as in
Britain, was perturbed by the prospect of radio being able to broadcast news
and advertisements and thus damage the appeal of newspapers. A conference
had already been held between the Post Office, the IBC and representatives
of the Irish newspapers on 23 November 1923, to examine the possibilities of
co-operation between the radio service and the press, 'having regard to each
other's legitimate interests' as O'Hegarty put it.[270] The press asked that, as in
Britain, there should be no broadcasting of news before 7p.m.,[271] and no
broadcasting at all of 'news of a descriptive nature'; that the broadcasting
station should pay for a news service through an agency; and that there should
be a complete ban on broadcasting advertisements. Agreement was reached on
all points with the exception of advertising, which the Post Office considered
could not be regarded as a legitimate monopoly of the press (since there
already existed the practice of poster advertising), but which would be limited
to 15 minutes between 7p.m. and midnight.

This agreement could reasonably be regarded as having been overtaken by
the decision not to proceed with the IBC, and therefore some similar conditions had to be re-negotiated and incorporated into the Committee's report.
The newspaper representatives[272] returned unsuccessfully to the fray on the
question of advertising. Of greater interest was their statement that, if licences
were available, they would wish to provide a broadcast news service on a
commercial basis,[273] but the Committee unaccountably overlooked this attractive proposal.

The Committee then proceeded to write its final report, which turned once
more to the question of whether or not the service should be under State
control, and if so, to what extent; if not, how it should be organised under
private enterprise. Given the increasing value of radio to the public in the form
of lectures, concerts, operas, financial and meteorological information, it

269 DD 6, 31 January 1924, cols. 781–2. **270** *Report* doc. 223a. **271** Cf. A. Briggs, *The Birth of
Broadcasting* pp. 121–3, 158, 240–4. **272** *The Irish Times* was represented by its general manager J.J.
Simington, the *Irish Independent* by T.A. Grehan and the *Evening Mail* by J.H. Whitehead. *The Freeman's
Journal*, which had been represented previously and was to cease publication in December, sent no-one
to this meeting on 29 February. **273** *Report* paras. 3265–8.

should be 'a State service purely' and should be set up by the Post Office at an estimated cost of £5,000 (£100,000 at 2000 values; €125,000) and with an annual running cost of £5,000 exclusive of the cost of buying in concerts. The estimated number of licences (based on British figures) would be one per cent. of the population – approximately 4,000 crystal-sets in the Dublin area and a further 1,000 valve sets. They suggested a licence fee of £1 (£20 at 2000 values; €25), and they identified advertising as an additional source of income.[274]

> The Committee has considered the Postmaster-General's objection to the establishment and working of a broadcasting station by the Post Office as a State Department and his reluctance to make the provision of entertainments to the public through broadcasting a function of the State; and it does not regard his objection as sound ... No new principle would be introduced. The State has for a long time subsidised national culture combined with entertainment through its National Library, National Gallery ... and National Museum, not to speak of the Tailteann Games, and in the enlightened municipalities on the Continent, the same principle has been applied more directly and extensively to the cultivation of operatic and dramatic art as well.[275]

The Committee considered that the PMG could run the service with a Director and an unpaid advisory board which 'would consist of chosen representatives from various scientific societies and other bodies interested in the diffusion of knowledge, from linguistic, musical and other cultural associations' and might also include representatives of the licence payers.[276]

If its chief recommendation were not acceptable to the Dáil, it recommended secondarily that a company should be set up in which the State had a controlling interest. Without naming it, it referred indirectly to the Irish and Foreign Trading Corporation as a likely candidate in those circumstances.

Like the Postmaster-General, the Committee had relied on the British experience for its awareness of radio's potential:

> Whereas at first only musical programmes specially provided for the purpose were broadcasted [*sic*], to-day actual theatrical performances and operas, concerts in concert halls, lectures and speeches are regularly broadcasted; and in more practical matters meteorological information, weather forecasts, market and trade reports, financial news, and lessons in languages, form items in the normal programmes of the principal stations.[277]

274 Ibid. p. x. **275** Ibid. p. xi. **276** Ibid. p. xi. **277** Ibid. p. ix.

The Committee further considered that

> the use of wireless telephony for entertainment, however desirable, [is] of vastly less importance than its use as ministering alike to commercial and cultural progress. It would be difficult to over-emphasise its value as an instrument of popular education. In connection with the spread of the national language and of the phonetic teaching of modern languages, so necessary to commerce, there is no agency which lends itself so readily to the wide and cheap propagation of knowledge.[278]

In a paragraph which was to elicit a scornful response from the PMG, the Committee suggested that lectures on 'the elementary principles of hygiene, of gardening, of fruit-growing, bee-keeping, poultry-raising and the like direct from men of recognised authority in the subjects', talks on new legislation, 'the institutions of government and civics generally', as well as adult education, could feature in the schedules.[279]

278 Ibid.   **279** Ibid. p. x.

CHAPTER 4

The Dáil and Seanad debates and public reaction

The Dáil debated the matter of broadcasting only three times during this period. The first was on 31 January and 14–15 February 1924, when the second interim report was presented by Pádraic Ó Máille. This, because of the major impact on deputies of the Figgis-Belton revelations, overshadowed the second, the debate on the Report proper, which took place on 28 March, 3 April and 7 May of that year. There was no further discussion of the radio issue until after 2RN had come on air, since the approval for its start-up depended simply on the sanction of the Minister for Finance, given on 1 June 1925. The third debate – again, not nearly as far-ranging or as intense – came two years later with the introduction of the Wireless Telegraphy Bill, 1926. By this stage, 2RN had been up-and-running for almost a year.

The Seanad naturally did not discuss the Report of the lower house, although on 24 January 1924 Sir John Keane attempted to raise the subject of 'the policy of the Government in the matter of wireless broadcasting'. Suggesting that he thought the Government was pursuing a BBC-type model and that as an Extern Minister J.J. Walsh might be taking action without consulting the Executive Council, he said 'I do not know that that would be altogether wise ... In order that the two houses should exercise their sovereign powers' he asked that nothing should be set in train without recourse to the Oireachtas.[1] The Seanad debate on the Wireless Telegraphy Bill, following that of the Dáil, was short and pointless.

Given that the introduction of radio had been perceived as a divisive issue and a topic of considerable national and cultural significance, it is astonishing that its future centrality in Irish life was not debated more thoroughly, and that the service could have been started without a thorough examination of its form and content. Instead, the period between the publication of the *Report*

---

1 Seanad Éireann Debates (hereafter cited as SD) 2, 24 January 1924, cols. 541–2.

and the start of 2RN was occupied with harrying of the Minister by various deputies and by special interests such as the Dublin Wireless Club and the electrical trade.

As we have seen, Figgis and Walsh made personal statements regarding the attacks on their integrity, and, as the members of the Dáil had not had time to consider the implications of the interim report, very little else was transacted on 31 January, the debate being adjourned until 14 February. In the meanwhile, the Committee continued to meet, examining the scientific and technical evidence and meeting representatives of the press. It then deliberated from 4 March until its final Report was agreed on 25 March.

On 14 February the debate was renewed with Bryan Cooper's motion that the entire evidence and documents which the Committee had considered (the 'secret history') should be printed and circulated.[2] With a prescience which, with hindsight, one would hesitate to describe as remarkable, he said

> It may be, I hope it will not be, the case that charges of this kind – charges of graft, corruption, jobbery – whatever you like to call it – will become commonplace in our politics ... I believe it would be bad for the Dáil, and for public life in Ireland, if there remained the slightest suspicion in the mind of the general public at large that we were trying to hush up anything.[3]

In supporting this, Thomas Johnson, who revealed himself to have been strenuous within the Committee in opposing Belton's suitability for the concession, went further, proposing that 'a different kind of enquiry' was required to clear up the extra-broadcasting matters which had been raised, 'a smaller Committee [of the Dáil] composed of people who have not prejudged any question', the evidence to be taken 'in a strictly legal form' with witnesses entitled to legal representation.[4] A small number of deputies, half of them members of the Wireless Committee – Magennis, Thrift, Figgis, Milroy, Richard Wilson (Wicklow), Patrick Baxter (Cavan), Ernest Alton (Dublin University), and William Hewat (Dublin North) – discussed the implications of publication and of further enquiry (as alluded to in my Introduction), all of them agreeing with Cooper and Johnson that it was essential that 'the course of public life [be] made clean',[5] before leaving it to the discretion of the President, Cosgrave, to find a *via media* which would satisfy all parties.

The Dáil then proceeded to consider the interim report. In a speech which strove to argue that the allegedly 'extraneous' matter considered by the Committee was not in fact extraneous, that conversely everything they had

2 DD 6, 14 February 1924, col. 1054. 3 Ibid. col. 1055. 4 Ibid. col. 1059. 5 Ibid. col. 1075.

considered was germane to the issue of what model was the most appropriate for a broadcasting station, Magennis adverted to the purpose of establishing such a station. The Committee completely agreed with the Postmaster-General's aspirations to place a broadcasting station

> at the service of cultural agencies which would provide lectures, concerts, music and the like to develop and cultivate an Irish taste in the matter of the arts as practised in Ireland ... There are three things in which we confirm his judgment. One is that there ought to be an Irish Broadcasting Station, that Wireless Telephony should not be merely such for Irish listeners-in [*sic*] as would be provided by foreign stations; secondly, that it ought to be kept strictly under Irish national control; and thirdly, that the purposes to which that Irish station should be devoted, in addition to the strictly utilitarian purposes of giving meteorological information to farmers and fishermen, and reports about ruling prices to business men, that it should be utilisable for educative purposes of a higher type ... We confidently believe that when the Irish public begin to appreciate from experience what broadcasting can afford them in the way of education and cultural entertainment, they will demand the provision of further pabulum of a distinctive Irish character, and, with belief in Irish artistic capacity, they will demand that foreign listerners-in will have an opportunity of being acquainted with the development in Ireland of the civilised arts as exhibited in the matter of broadcasting.[6]

Walsh now began publicly fighting a rearguard action in defence of the Post Office model of an IBC:

> I am ... deeply concerned to see that the edifice built up by my Department ... will be displayed in its entirety to Deputies before they are called on to destroy that building and set up something else in its stead ... The Committee, while asking the Dáil to accept that demolition, has taken no steps whatever to ascertain whether a feasible substitute is possible.[7]

He urged that the Committee should get on with its work by 'presenting an alternative': 'I see no reason whatever for the presentation of this Interim Report, or at least for its adoption here'.[8] And Walsh attempted to route the discussion once more through the morass of morality by suggesting that, by

6 Ibid. cols. 1078–80. 7 Ibid. cols. 1073, 1081. 8 Ibid.

rejecting the IBC model, the Committee was casting aspersion on the suitability or capacity of named persons – he in fact named T.P. Dowdall – to be associated with such a venture.[9]

More serious, perhaps, is the fact that the PMG dragged in the role of both McGarry and Figgis in what he had already alleged to the Committee was their association with the Marconi Company: in doing so, he again raised the spectre of self-interest, suggesting that their move in the Dáil to set up the Wireless Committee was an attempt to have the IBC quashed in order to subsequently promote Marconi's suitability. Within Walsh's speech is the implication that he himself had introduced Belton's memorandum into the proceedings with the intention of discrediting Figgis, because he believed Figgis to be in Marconi's pocket. If the Dáil were to see the evidence, Walsh asserted,

> it would come to the conclusion that an extern company – a combine in a neighbouring country – is directly associated in an effort to prevent the control of broadcasting by the Irish people ... It is common talk here that this Company initiated the efforts to destroy this White Paper ... that they did it with the sole object of collaring and controlling wireless in Ireland ... that they have thrown the country open to free exploitation in regard to the sale of sets, and that in short Ireland, for their purposes, is simply a continuation of an English Shire.[10]

Even bearing in mind the genuine reservations which might be held about the commercial motivations of the Marconi Company, it was ludicrous of Walsh to suggest that the evidence might bear that interpretation. Johnson was quick to jump on Walsh's hysterical weakness:

> The Postmaster-General regrets the damage done to his own wee ewe lamb, and he feels sore that the Committee should have destroyed his hopes ... Because of the loss of that particular creation ... he thinks that the whole prospect of Ireland's cultural development through broadcasting is lost ... I wish he had been a little more frank in the matter, and stated bluntly what had been in his mind. He spoke of tactics within and without the Company[11] ... which he alleges took place on behalf of the Marconi Company. He did not mention Marconi, but no doubt it is Marconi he referred to –[12]

9 Ibid. col. 1082.   **10** Ibid. cols. 1083–4.   **11** Johnson clearly meant 'Committee'.   **12** Ibid. col. 1085.

to which Walsh lamely – and disingenuously – replied 'I intended to'. It was a point which he would retract the following day, stating unequivocally that he trusted fully in the complete integrity of the entire Committee.[13]

Johnson went on to ask the Dáil the same question which we considered in the previous chapter: how could Walsh and O'Hegarty have gone on trusting Belton implicitly after the Figgis revelations and his own self-damning evidence?

> It was the duty of the Postmaster-General, before recommending that a concession should be given to a company of this kind, to have assured himself, especially when the evidence had been put into his hand, of the character of the chief promoter of the company.[14]

The day ended with Walsh saying 'I leave the responsibility for providing the alternative to the Committee with a light heart. It is their funeral and not mine'[15] – a point on which he was mistaken – and the Dáil adjourned to the next day.

On the resumption, Figgis stated emphatically that he had no connection with the Marconi Company, and rounded on Walsh, asking 'if this process be not a process of blackmail, what else is it? On what basis was this suggestion made yesterday?'[16] But Figgis, too, showed himself to be – or to have been – less than forthright in what he chose to tell the Dáil. He now said that his reason for proposing the motion to establish a special committee was that he believed that the White Paper 'contravene[d] the Constitution' insofar as the PMG's proposals in respect of the tax on imported wireless sets were 'the special prerogative of the Minister for Finance' and had nothing to do with broadcasting.[17] Figgis had in fact implied or suggested nothing of the kind at the time and had said nothing of the kind in the Committee. His introduction of the issue at this stage is a remarkable example of the way that almost all the actors in this drama, reading from unseen and inconsistent scripts, were constantly improvising, as their unpredictable temperaments and sensitivities manifested themselves in the course of different scenarios.

Even more astonishing was Cosgrave's intervention in the debate to deliver a devastating series of observations on the PMG's mishandling of the affair. Having observed significantly and pointedly that the PMG, as an Extern Minister, was responsible to the Dáil rather than to the Executive Council, and stating bluntly that he was opposed to Walsh's attempted rebuttal of the interim report, Cosgrave dwelt on the instability of the IBC constituents: 'we

---

13 Ibid. 15 February 1924, col. 1106.   14 Ibid. 14 February 1924, col. 1088.   15 Ibid. col. 1091.
16 Ibid. 15 February 1924, col. 1100.   17 Ibid. cols. 1101–2.

appear to be dealing in this case with company-promoting rather than with companies that are in business. I do not think that the Dáil would subscribe to a proposition of that sort ... The proposition appears to me to be the most outlandish one that I ever heard of in my experience'.[18]

Cosgrave was in a difficult position, as was the Government, and he said so:

> It is the first time this question has arisen and I would like in consider-ing it that the utmost possible justice should be done to an Extern Minister. It is a constitutional position that we have scarcely had an opportunity of dealing with so far ... The Postmaster-General is responsible to the Dáil and, therefore, the weight of the Executive and of the Government should not be thrown into the scales one way or the other.[19]

Having on the one hand stated his own opinion as to the IBC scheme, and on the other having withdrawn Government support for the PMG, Cosgrave then made it clear that a vote of no confidence in the White Paper could not be construed as a vote against the Government. Furthermore, he observed that by voting against the White Paper the Dáil would not be committing itself to the alternative – namely, public expenditure to support broadcasting.

Once again, the central issue of radio *per se* had almost been ignored in the pursuit of questions of procedure and propriety. But one deputy, Denis Gorey (Carlow-Kilkenny),[20] observed that

> the subject [is] one of great national importance ... Broadcasting in the future may develop into one of the greatest elements in our national life. Perhaps in the very near future broadcasting may find its way into a good many homes, possibly into every home. When one realises the great educational influence that broadcasting will have in this and every other country where it is operating, to my mind it will be almost as important in a national and moral sense as our schools. Any Government or any representatives of the people who are careful of the national, as well as the moral, life of the nation will be anxious to see the system controlled in the same way as our national education. Who in this country, I ask, would think of handing over national education to a private company or to a foreign company? ... I believe that broad-casting should be controlled by the Government regardless of the

---

18 Ibid. cols. 1109–10. **19** Ibid. col. 1111. **20** A member of the Farmers' Party who, in 1927, attempted a merger of his party with Cumann na nGaedheal; when this failed, Gorey joined Cumann na nGaedheal himself (J. Regan, op. cit. p.265).

expense involved ... It has been stated that this is only a business proposition. It is much more: it is a national proposition ... It is only in its infancy and we want to be very careful as to who controls it and how it is used.[21]

Gorey was, in fact, voicing (albeit surreptitiously) the need for censorship and, sensing this, Bryan Cooper also expressed the need for State control, but voiced the opposite view – the need for inclusiveness:

A broadcasting service has certain tremendous factors in the development of a people, and is such a tremendous aid to education ... But if we are to have proper education, we are not going to obtain it by building a Chinese wall around our country ... The Minister, in his speech yesterday, dismissed all wireless which comes from outside this country as 'British muisc-hall dope and British propaganda'. I do not know if he has studied the programmes of the British Broadcasting Company. The last time I 'listened-in' in London, the propaganda, whatever it was, was not British ... To-night the principal feature ... is 'Hamlet'. Hamlet, I suppose, is 'music-hall dope' ... to be followed by the third act of 'Parsifal' ... I am afraid that if we are to have wireless established on an exclusively Irish-Ireland basis, the result will be 'Danny Boy' four times a week, with variations by way of camouflage. Every performer will be told: 'The Postmaster-General wishes you to sing something of an exclusively Irish character' ... and then of course we shall have the Postmaster-General's speeches about the Tailteann games to follow up. I am afraid that after a short time the people will begin to look for variety ... We cannot ... establish an exclusive civilisation. If we wish to do that, let there be no wireless broadcasting, let there be no telegraphic cables, no foreign postal service. If we are to pursue that policy let us pursue it to its logical conclusion. We are not a little island in the Atlantic between America and Europe. For good or evil we are a part of Europe.[22]

To which Walsh responded:

I have never for one instant suggested that foreign music and foreign propaganda should be excluded. As everybody knows, there is such a thing conveyed through wireless as dope that will not assist this country, and dope that the people of this country do not desire.

---

21 Ibid. cols. 1112–13.   **22** Ibid. cols. 1117–20.

Nevertheless, that is conveyed through wireless. Even if I tried to prevent its dissemination here, I could not succeed. It is my obvious duty to see that that material which is of the utmost importance to the life of this country, material concerning the country and concerning its culture, should not be quietly placed aside to leave the field free for this foreign material.[23]

And returning to the fiscal question, Walsh subtly threatened the Dáil by suggesting that if it were to vote in favour of a scheme involving State expenditure, he was sure that the Treasury would turn it down. But when the motion was put, the interim report was passed unanimously.

One week later, on 22 February 1924, Cosgrave returned to the problem with which he had been charged – the examination of the non-broadcasting issues by means of some kind of tribunal of the Dáil. It was to be one of the most illuminating as well as perplexing sessions of the Dáil's early years. One clause of Cosgrave's motion read that the proposed committee should investigate charges and imputations and

> report to the Dáil the evidence given in support of such charges and imputations, and to what extent the same are substantiated or established upon the face of the ... evidence, documents and statements.[24]

Professor John Marcus O'Sullivan (North Kerry)[25] objected that this was 'a dangerous precedent, and one that the Dáil should not readily drop into'.[26]

> If that is not a Court it goes very near being a Court. I ask, can you set up by resolution of one House of the Oireachtas a Court? As I understand the Constitution, if that is not a violation of the Constitution it is sailing pretty close to the wind.[27]

On the other hand, deputies recognised the need to clarify any issue or topic on which there could be any question of impropriety, lack of probity or concealment from the public on the part of the Dáil or members or committees thereof. As William Davin (Leix-Offaly) put it:

> If the State has got to be run on honest lines, and if Deputies are the people to see to that, I say that no Deputy has a right to come into the

---

23 Ibid. cols. 1122–3.　**24** Ibid. 22 February 1924, col. 1361.　**25** Parliamentary Secretary to the Minister for Finance 1924–6; Minister for Education 1926–32; succeeded J.J. Walsh as chairman of Cumann na nGaedheal in 1927.　**26** Ibid. col. 1365.　**27** Ibid.

Dáil and to use his position and his influence as a member, in order to promote his own selfish interests or ambitions. If there is anything in the evidence or in the charges brought before this particular Committee, so far, that would prove that any Deputy has abused his position in that direction, I say that it is in the interests of the purity of public life of this country that it should be exposed.[28]

Nevertheless, Davin also objected to the method:

In my opinion it sets up not what in effect is a court of inquiry but something in the nature of a judicial inquiry. That, I think, is a policy that should not be subscribed to by Deputies, especially when personal charges are made against members ... The people entitled to judge are the voters who were responsible for sending them into the Dáil. When those concerned appear before the electors next the electors will be given an opportunity of giving a final decision with regard to their conduct in public life.[29]

This was an opportunity of which the electors of County Dublin would be deprived by the suicide of Figgis.

Magennis forcefully put the point that another enquiry would do nothing to allay public suspicions that the Dáil was keeping something hidden. He felt that full publication of every document and every piece of evidence was required, as contained in the terms of Bryan Cooper's original motion, so that there could be no further occasion for gossip or innuendo. Anything less would be disastrous for the public perception of, and faith in, politics and politicians:

What will the public whose attitude of suspicion has been heightened by all these debates and by the articles that have been written on them, think? Simply that the Dáil has been informed secretly by members of the Committee that there are dreadful things, terrible scandals, and that if the evidence were to be published the Dáil might close its doors, and the Government might shut down and retire from business.[30]

The issue is still with us. Not only that, but there was one further serious consideration connected with the question of publication, or disclosure, of documents. As Ernest Blythe (Minister for Finance) pointed out:

---

28 Ibid. col. 1368. 29 Ibid. cols. 1368–9. 30 Ibid. col. 1397.

If the idea is once broadcasted in the Civil Service, that whatever one official writes to another official or to his Minister will be liable to appear in print and in the newspapers, there will not be the same confidence in Departments and you will not have advice or suggestions given with the same candour as would be the case if these things would not be published. It might lead to the setting up of a custom to give advice verbally and have no minutes written ... I think that the privilege of confidence in the Civil Service should be retained.[31]

Thus the Freedom of Information Act 1997 was anticipated and criticised.

The problem was to agree an acceptable mechanism for conducting an inquiry. Perhaps intuitively sensing that the problem was insoluble, the Dáil retreated from it, and instead passed Cooper's motion which had been in abeyance while Cosgrave's proposal had been under discussion. Thus Cooper, as his biographer related, was responsible for the publication of the 'secret history'.

The press reported the Dáil proceedings in considerable detail. The double column in the *Freeman's Journal* was headed 'Wireless Graft Rumours' and reported Cooper as saying

This was the first case of the kind that had come before the Dáil; it was a case in which they were charged with a very heavy responsibility, because the action they would now take would be a precedent for future actions. He hoped it would not be the case that charges of this kind – charges of graft, corruption, jobbery, or whatever they liked to call it – would become a commonplace in their politics.[32]

The newspaper also reported the PMG's strong criticism of the interim report 'which, he stated, meant that Ireland would have no Broadcasting Station, and nothing but British music hall dope and propaganda would be received by those listening-in throughout the Saorstat'.[33]

On 26 March the full Report of the Wireless Committee, together with all the evidence and documents, was published and was presented to the Dáil on 28 March. Its arguments and recommendations, as detailed above, rested on the basic premiss that broadcasting should be State-run and, therefore, State-funded. It thus ran counter to the proposals of the Postmaster-General, who had asked, during the debate on the interim report, that the Committee should devise an alternative *modus operandi*. This the Committee supplied in the form of a line of command by which the PMG, 'through the agency of a

31 Ibid. col. 1403.   **32** *Freeman's Journal* 15 February 1924.   **33** DD 6, 22 February 1924, col. 1403.

Director working in conjunction with a non-paid Board', would provide and control the programming.

Now in possession of the evidence, the press was eager to emphasise its exclusion from the Committee's proceedings. The *Freeman's Journal* (which devoted almost three pages of its issue of 29 March and a further page on 31 March) headed its coverage 'Public Men Mentioned in Remarkable Documents' and began with the full text of Andrew Belton's memorandum to the PMG detailing his relations with Darrell Figgis, and – with the exception of a summary of the Report's main recommendations – predictably it concentrated on the allegations and counter-allegations between Belton and Figgis and the fact that 'the names of prominent politicians, both in England and Ireland, are mentioned in the many documents put before the Committee'.[34]

Once again, Walsh did his best to stall proceedings, arguing rather obviously that 'the Committee's report is in direct conflict with the representations submitted by my Department'[35] and thus suggesting that there was another debate in the offing. In order to give deputies time to consider the huge tome of almost 650 pages (which Johnson, presumably in jocose mood, had suggested that Ó Máille should read to the Dáil), discussion was put back to 3 April.

On 3 April Ó Máille put forward and justified the main findings of the Committee: farmers would benefit from the State providing an information service; amusements would be more likely to be 'national in tone and in sentiment'.[36] With these two representative examples of the Committee's thinking, Ó Máille set the tone for the character of public service broadcasting. He continued:

> It is a hopeful sign of the times to see a Committee representative of all Parties in the Dáil quite ready to probe every question as regards any matter of undue influence to the bottom and have the matter made public ... Honesty and purity in Irish public life are well worth a good deal of expenditure and time.[37]

Initial opposition came not from the Postmaster-General but from Michael Heffernan, a Farmers' Party TD for Tipperary, who argued against State control on the grounds that the State should not be in the business of supplying amusements, although he acknowledged that the State might be partially involved in order to provide information for farmers. Even here, however, he felt that the Committee had over-emphasised the public benefit: 'It is a bit ridiculous, I think, to talk about giving lectures on bee-keeping and on agricultural subjects through wireless'.[38] Nevertheless,

---

34 *Freeman's Journal* 29 March 1924. **35** DD 6, 28 March 1924, col. 2618. **36** Ibid. 3 April 1924, col. 2861. **37** Ibid. col. 2862. The cost of printing the *Report* was £800 (£16,000 at 2000 values; €20k) and sold at 7s. 6d. per copy (£0.375 or £7.50 at 2000 values; €9.4). **38** Ibid. col. 2863.

one of the greatest curses in rural life is the useless way in which people spend their spare time. They really do nothing, and from the ethical point of view that, of course, is very bad. It would be a great thing if they could have the advantage of the entertainments placed at their disposal by wireless.[39]

He was supported in this view by Denis Gorey, who observed, as he had previously:

Wireless in the future is going to find its way into all the rural homes and villages of the country. Hitherto, our big towns and populous districts have had amusement; they have had almost everything that they could wish for, while our rural areas have been neglected. The only amusements the people in villages find are standing up against walls, playing pitch-and-toss, playing cards, or visiting public houses.[40]

However, unlike Heffernan, he wanted State control, because 'if you have a State concern control will lie directly with the people's representatives'.[41] But he was opposed to issuing licences for public houses:

that may be a wild doctrine, but I do not think it is right that houses licensed for the sale of drink should be allowed to instal sets and thereby draw custom that otherwise would never go to these houses. It would not make for good citizenship and it would not make for a sober country.[42]

Patrick Hogan gave a clear indication that in Committee he had accepted the PMG's arguments concerning the Irish language and culture:

I think you can find a very good reason for putting under the control of some national body, such as a State Department, the entire control of everything that appertains to the revival of Irish culture, and everything that is proper and distinctive in the life of the nation ... What we have got to ask ourselves is, whether any private body is going to take the same interest in the revival of the Irish language and of Irish music as the State would take?[43]

Joseph MacBride (South Mayo)[44] also criticised the concept of State control, arguing not only that broadcasting was a commercial undertaking and that it

39 Ibid. **40** Ibid. col. 2868. **41** Ibid. col. 2869. **42** Ibid. **43** Ibid. cols. 2864–5. **44** Brother of Major John MacBride.

should not be a cost to the State, but also that 'the Postmaster-General will not give me ... what I require, but, rather, what he thinks I should require ... I really object to the Postmaster-General setting himself up as an inquisitor of my estimate of the proper standard of tastes and morals'.[45]

At this point Ernest Blythe intervened to state that he would 'deprecate the adoption of the Report' until such time as the financial implications had been considered. The Committee had gone beyond its terms of reference, he argued, inasmuch as, in addition to considering the specific proposal in the White Paper, it had also recommended an 'actual course of action'.[46] Blythe continued:

> We have very heavy calls on the Exchequer. We have an unbalanced Budget, and we are carrying out the most drastic economies in order to effect a balance of the Budget.[47]

Blythe need hardly have laboured the point: only that afternoon, deputies had voted by 43 votes to 18 to reduce the old age pension by one shilling (£0.05 or £1 at 2000 values; €1.25) – one of the most controversial fiscal measures in the history of the State.[48] He went on to observe that the proper course of action would be for a Minister to submit a scheme to the Department of Finance for evaluation. It appeared to him that the Report was an attempt to pre-empt that evaluation:

> Whatever the Dáil adopts here it ought to take care to adopt a thing that would not prevent the fullest financial control and criticism of the enterprise henceforth. I think it would be undesirable that any enterprise should be given a sort of special blessing that would in any way free it or exempt it from criticism.[49]

Walsh smartly leapt onto this bandwagon, arguing that the Committee should have 'taken the necessary steps to ascertain whether the Minister for Finance was prepared to back this primary recommendation of theirs',[50] as he himself had done with his own proposal. The comparison was hardly fair, since Finance could not have exercised such a lien on the IBC project as it would now do in respect of a new initiative within the Post Office. Walsh continued in the same wounded and jeering tone that he had adopted throughout towards the Wireless Committee:

---

45 Ibid. col. 2865.   46 Ibid. col. 2866.   47 Ibid.   48 It was in the same spirit that Richard Corish (Wexford) had said on 5 March: 'The people have got absolutely sick of this discussion about wireless ... We ought to realise that this country, at the present moment, is practically in a state of chaos, and we ought to try and do something for the people who are suffering, and stop all this cant about wireless' – DD 6, cols. 1681–2.   49 Ibid. col. 2867.   50 Ibid. col. 2874.

I think we are more or less wasting time here in discussing the scheme ... because if we merely pass this pious resolution, we might find ourselves later on face to face with an adverse decision on the part of the Finance Ministry.[51]

Despite Blythe's assurance that 'if the Dáil passes the resolution, it is not a thing that can be turned down lightly by the Minister for Finance',[52] Walsh continued to embellish the fiscal situation in his own favour: referring to the vote on pensions, he once more twisted the argument against State control in a direction which he had hardly indicated either in the White Paper or in evidence to the Committee:

> This spirit of economy which has been in evidence on the part of the Government for a considerable time past, meets with my entire approval, and it had quite a lot to say in determining my decisions in regard to non-State control of this service ... I aimed at the elimination of any financial responsibility on the part of the State, and I maintained, on the other hand, all the necessary control which a State should require.[53]

At no previous point had Walsh exhibited such verbal dexterity in manipulating the political situation. Sensing a victory which had hardly been conceivable two months earlier, he adopted the tone: no deputy who has just voted to reduce the pension would vote in favour of a proposal which will place an additional burden on the Exchequer. Yet if this had been a primary consideration, it should, logically, have been the principal – and, indeed, sole – reason for proposing to harness private enterprise, whereas the principal stated reason for not operating the radio service within State control was the inability of the Post Office to administer a medium of entertainment.

In this debate Walsh also demonstrated to an alarming extent the capacity for outspokenness and acting as a wild card, for which his political career was noted. As if this were not argument enough, Walsh went on to make the additional point that

> we are discussing here a question which, to my view, has rather resolved itself into one of nationalisation versus private enterprise ... The Committee, in order to impress its desire for nationalisation, has accepted that financial responsibility ... In the White Paper [market reports, agricultural reports, weather reports, and educational matter]

51 Ibid.   52 Ibid.   53 Ibid. cols. 2874–5.

were provided free, in the case of the scheme before the Dáil the nation will pay for it … It is a very remarkable thing that this country should be made the stalking horse for what I consider a very peculiar form of nationalisation … I should not mind very much accepting the responsibility as the head of a State Department. I suppose there is nothing within limits that we cannot do when we try. I have no doubt myself, if this House determines that the Post Office must do the showman, must differentiate between rival organ-grinders, rival tenors and people of that kind, and even rival politicians who want to get control and preferential treatment, we will be able to do it; but we will do it at a price, and it will be a very dear price … The station is to cost £5,000, that is, £5,000 of the public money unnecessarily gone bang … Later on the State will be faced with a vote for a second £5,000 for engineering purposes … It must … vote at least £10,000 for the provision of concerts and for the maintenance of a Director and an Announcer, and all their hangers-on … For what? For the novelty of saying that we have introduced nationalisation into the control of wireless … It would be undoubtedly unfair on my part if I were to accede to unnecessary expenditure of public funds, considering that I have been screwing down the people through the medium of the Department … that I dismissed 475 postmen, men who had no other means of supporting their families and themselves, that I shut Post Offices, and deprived poor people of a living.[54]

Thus Walsh neatly said that he could do what he had previously said he could not do, while pulling the rug from under the concept of State expenditure on broadcasting – 'a forecast which is likely to rape the finance of the nation'.[55] Then in a *tour-de-force* of illogic he attacked the public service basis of the entire scheme:

If you believe in this station which you propose to put up in Dublin to cater for the citizens of Dublin, that you are going to get away with your agricultural reports, your fishery reports, and your education, and that the people will possess themselves with wireless sets and pay licences for the purpose, I am satisfied that you are assuming something that will not materialise. What, for instance, do the bulk of the people of Dublin city require to know about agriculture? They have not as much land as would sod a lark. What do they want to know about fishing? I believe it is all nonsense, and if you believe it is necessary to

54 Ibid. cols. 2875–80. 55 Ibid. col. 2877.

saturate them with education, I think they will very much disagree with you. Most of them think they know all that is to be known ... The fact is, and you cannot get away from it, much as one may sympathise with the idea of enlightening a community in the various ways suggested by the Committee, the people want amusement through broadcasting; they want nothing else, and they will have nothing else.[56]

Effectively, both the IBC and the Committee's recommendation were dead. William Thrift recognised this and pointed out that if the motion were adopted, the result would be for the PMG to take the concept back to the drawing-board and to devise a new *modus operandi* which he would have to submit to Finance before presenting it to the Dáil. That Walsh should have accepted this, stating that the Dáil 'can count on my whole-hearted, not halting, support' is indicative either of his naïvety or of his disingenuousness. In closing the debate, Pádraic Ó Máille made clear that whereas the PMG had stressed the importance of musical programming, 'we [the Committee] think that the national interests are far more important'.[57]

There, as far as the Dáil was concerned, the matter rested for two and a half years. But as soon as the *Report* was published, the newspapers began to comment. Rather unrealistically, the *Irish Independent* said:

We trust that the Deputies will give the matter serious thought, for we frankly confess that we are by no means enamoured of the chief recommendation ... We are not convinced that a good case has been produced in favour of making Broadcasting a state service ... Can the country afford this at a time when it cannot make its Budget balance?[58]

As far as the suggested lectures on hygiene and similar topics were concerned, the *Irish Independent* echoed the opinion of Heffernan and Walsh:

The reasons which the Committee argues in favour of a State service are in some respects ludicrous ... Is it seriously suggested that any ordinary citizen could buy a wireless set and pay a licence to learn elements of these subjects?[59]

The *Freeman's Journal* concurred and the April 1924 issue of the *Irish Radio Journal* also argued against State ownership of the system.

It thus appears that, rather than saving the day for public service broadcasting, in rejecting the PMG's proposals the Committee had acted with

56 Ibid. cols. 2878-9. 57 DD 7, 7 May 1924, col. 390. 58 *Irish Independent* 2 April 1924. 59 Ibid.

considerable courage in going against public feeling. That the budgetary problems were to the fore of everyone's consideration was natural; but that the country at large should prefer private to State ownership is surprising.

After the debate had concluded, and Walsh had been sent off to reconsider the scheme, the *Irish Times* commented:

> Presumably, the Postmaster-General will do his work faithfully, although it is well-known that his views are 'hostile' to State control of 'broadcasting', and that in this attitude he is supported by a large body of opinion in the Dáil and throughout the country.[60]

The paper hoped that Blythe would reject the scheme, which, like O'Hegarty, it viewed as a luxury.

The *Irish Radio Journal* returned to the subject in its issue of 15 May, opining:

> A service of this kind would, in the hands of Government officials, gradually get interwoven with red tape, and instead of being a solace to citizens would prove a source of annoyance and bring forth irritability from the most quiet and peaceful person.[61]

In the interim, Walsh was to be asked on three occasions[62] what progress had been made, while the 15 October issue of the *Irish Radio Journal* criticised him for procrastination. In fact Walsh's new scheme, in which he had proposed expenditure of £9,285 to erect and equip a station, with a relay station in Cork, and an annual budget of £20,000 (£400,000 at 2000 values; €500k) was rejected by Blythe in a 7-page critique in December 1924. Blythe's grounds were that the scheme would encourage widespread evasion of the licence fee as in Great Britain; that Walsh's intention of retaining total control of the scheme was contrary to the spirit and intention of the Civil Regulations Act, 1924; and that it did not provide for an Advisory Board as recommended by the Wireless Committee. He suggested that he might sanction a scheme which provided for broadcasting on two nights a week, one being a locally produced programme, the other a relay from the BBC.[63] This manoeuvre by Blythe was unknown to members of the Dáil at the time.

---

60 *Irish Times* 8 May 1924; it is indicative of attitudes to broadcasting that the *Irish Times* should have continued to employ inverted commas to frame the word itself, thus suggesting that it was something unknown or even suspect. **61** *Irish Radio Journal* 15 May 1924. **62** 17 June 1924 (Peadar Ó Dubhghaill, Dublin South) DD 7, col. 2390; 22 October (Peadar Ó Dubhghaill) DD 9, col. 117; 19 November 1924 Patrick Hogan (Limerick) DD 9, cols. 191–2. **63** SPO S 3532a (National Archives).

ALTERNATIVE PROPOSALS

On 19 December 1924 Tadhg Ó Dubhghaill (Carlow-Kilkenny) asked Blythe whether he had considered the PMG's scheme, to which Blythe replied that it had been sent to the Executive Council, without disclosing that he had damned it in his own memorandum;[64] asked on 10 March 1925 what was the position at that stage, Blythe replied that he had yet to assent to the PMG's proposals;[65] by 22 April he was in no better position to satisfy Thomas Johnson on the point: 'it has only recently become possible to examine them on their merits'.[66]

In such uncertain circumstances, with large sections of the public eagerly anticipating a radio service of some kind, provided by some source, frustration built up. In January 1925 the *Irish Radio Review* suggested granting the concession to the BBC – partly, one suspects, with a dash of sarcasm, especially since the notion of introducing foreign material was so anathema to Walsh himself.

Eleven months later, on the eve of the launch of 2RN, the *Irish Radio Journal* would be arguing that Irish listeners were apprehensive about the quality of its programmes which were expected to be 'much inferior to those of the BBC owing to the fact that there is very little local talent'.[67] Two weeks later, however, the *Journal* had inexplicably changed its tune: 'we feel confident that there is an extremely large amount of local talent ... that will again place this country in the forefront of the musical and dramatic world'.[68]

Much more serious, however, was the suggestion, contained in a letter to the *Irish Times*, that the Royal Dublin Society (RDS) be asked to administer the service. 'The Society has an efficient organisation, while its Council and committees include many men [sic] distinguished in science and art, no less in agriculture.'[69] This was supported two days later in the same paper by letters from the Dublin Wireless Club and the editor of the *Irish Radio Review* representing the electrical trade.[70] This must have seemed to Walsh and his officials to be an alarming development, since it was supported by an editorial in the *Irish Times* two days later, when the paper carried the text of a leaflet circulated by another trade organisation, the Wireless Retailers Association of Ireland, protesting at the effect of the delay in implementing the radio service:

> Hundreds of citizens, many of whom are young and enterprising men, who have committed themselves to a heavy investment of capital and energy in the hope of gaining a decent livelihood for themselves and

---

64 DD 9, 19 December 1924, col. 2701. **65** DD 10, 10 March 1925, col. 761. **66** DD 11, 22 April 1925, col. 3. **67** *Irish Radio Journal* 16 November 1925. **68** Ibid. 1 December 1925, quoted in Robert K. Savage, 'The Origins of Irish Radio', unpubl. MA thesis, UCD 1982. **69** *Irish Times* 20 April 1925. **70** Ibid. 22 April 1925.

establishing a new industry in the country for skilled workers, are faced with the prospect of ruin.[71]

On the previous day (23 April) the Council of the RDS had met to consider the situation. Its minute recorded that

> it was unanimously agreed that the subject is one of paramount importance in the Scientific, Agricultural and Educational life of the country, but in view of the official statements that schemes are at present under consideration by the Government it is considered inadvisable to take any definite step at the present juncture.[72]

This may have seemed as if the Council was merely acknowledging the significance of the subject and the level of public concern. But the RDS went on to make its position very clear: 'The Council would, however, be willing at any time to give the matter the special consideration it deserves should the government so desire'.

Two days later, the *Irish Times* correctly forecast that 'The Royal Dublin Society's announcement ... will probably induce the government to hasten an announcement of its decision on the subject'.[73] The situation must have seemed quite serious, since the RDS was a highly respected institution which had carried out cognate functions in areas such as art education, agricultural training and the establishment of cultural institutions such as the National Gallery of Ireland and the present-day National College of Art and Design.

The proposal was sufficiently strong and serious to concentrate the minds of both ministers: at their meeting in May, Blythe dropped his demand that broadcasting be restricted to two days per week, and accepted the principle of State control. In the Dáil on 27 May 1925 Walsh stated that Blythe had agreed the scheme (for two stations, erected at a cost of £9,000 and with an annual budget of £20,000).[74] It was anticipated that 10,000 licences would be issued in the first year, 15,000 in the second year, and by the third year the service would be paying its way. 'Within five years we believe the original loss will be wiped out'.[75]

One of the more surprising (and little-known) facts about Irish radio is that the service has consistently paid its way. The importation duty on radios in the early years may have been a tax additional to the licence fee, and, at the rate of $33\frac{1}{3}\%$ on which Blythe had insisted,[76] it was perhaps unnecessarily high. Nevertheless, the figures contained in a departmental memorandum of 1942 speak for themselves:[77]

71 Ibid. 24 April 1925.   **72** RDS Council Minutes vol. 6, p. 347.   **73** *Irish Times* 25 April 1925.
74 DD 11, 27 May 1925, col. 2336.   **75** Ibid.   **76** SPO S 3532A (National Archives).   **77** Ibid.

Year	Licence fee	Advertisements income	Customs Duty	Expenditure Voted	(Deficit)/ Surplus[†]	(Deficit)/ Surplus[‡]
1925–26	7,823	–	–	9,450	(1,627)	(1,627)
1926–27	9,684	204	20,019	23,471	(13,583)	6,436
1927–28	12,071	101	26,578	29,445	(17,273)	9,305
1928–29	13,411	50	27,178	30,111	(16,650)	10,528
1929–30	13,050	119	30,565	31,015	(17,846)	12,719
1930–31	13,408	509	34,663	30,069	(16,152)	18,511
1931–32	14,725	1,329	43,347	47,921	(31,867)	11,480
1932–33	17,296	220	64,682	78,214	(60,698)	3,984
1933–34	26,497	22,827	71,728	50,923	(1,599)	70,129
1934–35	33,847	13,225	88,248	47,849	(777)	87,471
1935–36	43,861	23,438	87,063	51,731	15,568	102,631
total	205,673	62,022	494,071	430,199	(162,504)	331,567

[†]not taking customs revenue into account
[‡]including customs revenue

The Exchequer thus benefited to the extent of £331,567 during this period from the income derived from radio activity and the radio trade.

In the economic climate of the time it was Blythe's turn for displaying courage in the face of reality. In his history of the Department of Finance, Ronan Fanning comments that 'the Wireless Telegraphy Act of 1926 illustrates the powerlessness of the Department of Finance successfully to resist new expenditure when political considerations affecting national prestige were adjudged paramount'.[78] However, there is plentiful recollection of the resistance on the part of the department to any substantial investment in or expansion of the radio service.[79]

It was not until 27 January 1926 – a month after 2RN had started transmission – that Walsh informed Bryan Cooper in the Dáil that he would introduce the Wireless Telegraphy Bill 'in the very near future',[80] and this he eventually did on 17 November; the second stage was reached on 30 November 1926 and passed on 16 December.

78 R. Fanning, *The Irish Department of Finance 1922-58* (Dublin: Institute of Public Administration, 1978) p. 112.   **79** See below pp. 157–8, 175.   **80** DD 14, 27 January 1926, col. 98.

THE DEBATES ON THE WIRELESS TELEGRAPHY BILL

In the interim, between the debate on the Wireless Report and the introduction of the Wireless Telegraphy Bill, Darrell Figgis had died by his own hand and 2RN had been established, the only recourse to the Dáil being the budget announcement, and without any remonstrance on the part of any deputy. This was precisely the situation which the appointment of the Wireless Committee had been intended to avoid. That the necessary expenditure and establishment arrangements had been approved and effected by default permits us to wonder at the lack of tenacity of those who believed that J.J. Walsh should be monitored in his procedure.

In introducing the Wireless Telegraphy Bill, Walsh (whose title, on foot of the Ministers and Secretaries Act, 1924, had now changed from Postmaster-General to Minister for Posts and Telegraphs) summarised the rapid development of wireless since the passing of the Wireless Telegraphy Act 1904. Due to 'the absence of legislation covering certain phases and also because of the uncertainty of existing legislation',[81] new legislation was necessary, partly to clarify existing ambiguities. It must have come as a major surprise to deputies when Walsh declared 'The Bill before the House to-day makes provision for the collection of licences. That is the main and outstanding provision'.[82] In other words, Walsh's preoccupation with the regularisation of an illegal situation had come to the fore in a Bill which was predominantly technical in its tenor.

The main provisions of the Bill, which re-affirmed the Minister's monopoly of every aspect of wireless telegraphy and telephony, were: control of wireless apparatus (section 3); control over signalling activity (S. 4); licensing of wireless for sale or ownership, and licensing of experimental broadcasting (SS. 5–6); control of wireless activity 'in times of emergency' (S. 10); prohibition of certain types of message of an indecent, obscene or offensive character (S. 11); regulations governing wireless activity which caused interference to other transmissions (S. 12); the establishment of broadcasting station(s) (S. 17); and the establishment of an advisory committee on broadcasting (S. 19).

In setting out the provisions of the Bill, Walsh went into careful detail on the niceties of the licensing system, so much so that he appears to have all the concerned pride of a parent displaying its baby, or of an inventor giving account of the intricacies of his new toy. In addition to the need to control distribution of receiving apparatus, was that of ensuring that broadcast matter was acceptable: in a neat reinstatement of the legal position which had been disrupted by the broadcast at Easter 1916, Section 11 of the Bill

---

81 DD 17, 30 November 1926, cols. 342-3.   82 Ibid. col. 343.

provided for the 'prohibition of certain classes of messages… subversive of public order'.

One must, however, credit Walsh with some prescience:

> I can conceive a situation in which the users of wireless will continue to defy the Postmaster-General's control in this matter, will not pay licence fees, will erect their miniature wireless stations as they please, and will bring the utmost chaos and confusion into the wireless world here.[83]

This was precisely the situation which arose in Dublin in the 1970s with the proliferation of unlicensed ('pirate') radio stations.

Only after describing sections 1–16 of the Bill did he reach Section 17 which 'provides for the establishment and maintenance of broadcasting stations'.[84] Here again, one might not have known that any debate had taken place, or that Walsh had intransigently promoted the opposite to what he now announced:

> Someone must have responsibility for what is proper in broadcast matter, and the Minister of the Department is obviously the person on whom that responsibility should fall.[85]

Introducing such legislation would, in Walsh's opinion, put the Department in 'a strong financial position'[86] – in marked contrast to his view two years previously. Since there were an estimated 40,000 sets in the country, and since only 4,000 people had voluntarily taken out the existing provisional licences, compulsory licensing, backed up by legal sanctions, would bring in up to £18,000 extra. As we can see from the figures given above, he was not entirely wrong in his estimates.

> I said … last year that, once this Bill was in operation and when we had the advantage of the import duties, broadcasting would pay its way. I am satisfied now that that statement was not wide of the mark, that broadcasting will, during the present year, and, as far as we can see, for the future, clear its own passage. Not only should it meet day to day outgoings but I venture to say we will be in a position to pay back to the State the capital advances which it has been, and will be, called upon to make in regard to the erection of the stations. In other words, broadcasting will stand on its own legs without any burden on the taxpayer.[87]

---

83 Ibid. col.1085. 84 Ibid. col. 349. 85 Ibid. 86 Ibid. col. 350. 87 Ibid. col. 351.

The first deputy to speak after Walsh, John Good (Dublin), moved straight to the unspoken part of the Bill:

> The Minister ... has not given us, so far, much indication of what the policy of the Department is in regard to broadcasting. In Clause 17 of this Bill very wide powers are conferred on the Ministry with regard to broadcasting. Before these powers are conferred one would like to know what exactly is the policy of his Department.[88]

In effect, Good was merely voicing concern at the Minister's previously announced intention of setting up four stations, whereas Good was of the opinion that 'in view of the rapid developments that are taking place, it would ... be better to concentrate on one station, to make the programmes in that particular station highly attractive, and then to relay from that central station to these other provincial stations'.[89] He was, in fact, advocating a financial policy rather than a concept of broadcasting, and Walsh was effective in arguing for the maintenance of the existing scheme which included a planned high-power transmitter in Athlone as well as the extant Dublin station and that under construction in Cork. Nevertheless, regardless of his reason for asking, it is astonishing to find Good asking 'what use is likely to be made of these Stations and what is to be the policy with regard to them?'[90] eleven months after 2RN had come on air.[91]

But it is a matter for the analyst of the political nous to establish how, in response, Walsh can have been so oblique on the question of the departmental mind: 'I do not know whether or not I would be justified in giving a very full explanation of the development of policy ... this Bill ... really has nothing to do with policy'.[92]

Nevertheless, the 1924 debate, and the direct experience of Irish radio since January, had clearly had an enlightening effect in some quarters, as George Wolfe (Kildare) indicated when he said:

> There is no discovery that has such possibilities before it as wireless for transmitting knowledge and of making the most wonderful difference to people who live in isolated places, and to young people especially living in districts where they have very little to do at night.[93]

As indicated in my Introduction, it was at this point that Walsh did enunciate a matter of policy which was otherwise to go unaddressed for the next fifty years:

---

88 Ibid. **89** Ibid. col. 352. **90** Ibid. col. 355. **91** Cf. A. Briggs, *The Birth of Broadcasting* pp. 110, 133ff., 150ff., indicating the difficulty in initiating a parliamentary debate in Britain on the formation of the BBC. **92** DD 17, col. 355. **93** Ibid.

The third station that we intend to provide is the one for the Gaeltacht. I believe it will be agreed that we cannot reconcile ourselves to a programme, largely in English, circulating in that district, seeing that we have set our minds to the maintenance of the Gaeltacht area ... The intention is that it should provide a programme in keeping with the language of the people.[94]

At the next stage of the Bill, on 7 December, Connor Hogan (Clare), expressing concern at the cost in general of setting up the stations, referred specifically to this plan: 'I confess that I have the feeling that if the Government could give bread to the people there it would be better than giving them a wireless station'.[95]

The Bill passed all stages on 15 December 1926, and on that day Walsh went to the Seanad to ask that the Bill be discussed as a matter of urgency, as otherwise the adjournment of the house until January would push back enactment until February. In his view it was still 'practically entirely concerned with the collection of licence fees'. That he should have told the Seanad that 'no single amendment was moved in the other House. As a matter of fact no one spoke on it' is a remarkable attempt to mislead it.[96]

It would be untrue to say that the Seanad debated the Bill the following day. Its proceedings began with objections by James Douglas and others that the status of the Seanad as a 'revising chamber'[97] was being undermined by precipitate introduction of Government bills as in the present case. This discussion took up half of the time allocated to the wireless matter. Much of the rest was devoted to Walsh telling the Seanad that it was urgently necessary to establish an income from licence fees to finance the new station: 'It is really a tough job, to say the least of it, to run broadcasting in this country, and to run it in competition with the free agents in every other country ... We are in the position of a man in a race with half a score of fetters around his legs, and if he does not keep up the pace he is blamed'.[98] The opinion of at least one senator – Sir Thomas Esmonde – was that he thought the Minister's speech 'a very pathetic one. He wants more money to amuse the people'.[99] The Bill was passed with almost no amendment, and proceeded into law without the Seanad having discussed in any way the matter of policy or of the direction of the State's broadcasting station.

---

94 Ibid. cols. 356–7. **95** Ibid. 7 December 1926, col. 485. **96** SD 8, 15 December 1926, cols. 1–2.
97 Ibid. 16 December 1926, col. 73. **98** Ibid. cols. 87–8. **99** Ibid. col. 90.

CHAPTER 5

2RN: the opening years

RECRUITMENT AND TEST BROADCASTS

In October 1925 the Post Office advertised for a Station Director and Musical Director of the emergent broadcasting station. The interview board (announced on 3 October 1925) consisted of P.S. O'Hegarty, T.J. Monaghan – (who had been seconded to the broadcasting station from the Post Office engineering branch to be Station Engineer), the managing director of the BBC, J.C.W. Reith and Sir Hamilton Harty, the Hillsborough-born composer, pianist and conductor of the Hallé Orchestra, plus three representatives of the Civil Service Commission.[1] The part-time post of Musical Director (with a salary of £400 per annum [£8,000 at 2000 values; €10k]) was given to Dr Vincent O'Brien (1870–1948), conductor since 1903 of the Palestrina Choir at the Dublin Pro-Cathedral and since 1906 of the Dublin Oratorio Society.[2]

Before his appointment (by Edward Martyn) at the Pro-Cathedral, O'Brien had been organist at the Catholic church in Rathmines (1885–8) and the Carmelite Church in Dublin's Whitefriar Street (1897–9). He had brought the Palestrina Choir (with John McCormack as a member) on a tour of the USA in 1904. As a singing teacher he had McCormack and Margaret Burke Sheridan (and very briefly James Joyce) among his students; his coaching was responsible for McCormack winning the gold medal at the 1902 Feis Ceoil, and he was McCormack's accompanist on his first world tour as a concert artist in 1913 as well as accompanying him in his 1914 gramophone recordings. One of McCormack's most popular items was a composition by O'Brien, 'The Fairy Tree'. O'Brien was to hold the post at 2RN-Radio Éireann until

1 On 6 October 1925 the *Irish Times* carried an announcement that the Board would report to the Minister, who would make the appointments. It also quoted a departmental statement that 'the Irish broadcasting undertaking will be administered wholly by the Minister for Posts and Telegraphs and the British Broadcasting Company will have nothing whatever to say to it'. It is probable that the presence of Reith on the panel had occasioned a suspicion that the BBC, or even the British Post Office, was to become involved in the operation of 2RN. 2 Together with Dr Annie Patterson, O'Brien had been the co-recipient of the inaugural organ scholarships at the Royal Irish Academy of Music in 1887. In 1899 he had, as conductor, won prizes with three different choirs at the annual Schools Choir Competition in Dublin (cf. R. Pine and C. Acton [eds.], *To Talent Alone: the Royal Irish Academy of Music 1848–1998* [Dublin: Gill and Macmillan, 1998] pp. 267–8).

1941 and was to exercise a significant influence on the development of the music content of the channel. Although the post was officially part-time, O'Brien in fact found himself working ten or more hours each day, which reflects both the onus and the importance of his input into the service.

The interview board which appointed O'Brien was unable to agree on a candidate for the post of Station Director. O'Hegarty's favoured candidate was W.G. (Willie) Fay, one of the founders and chief actors of the Abbey Theatre. After resigning from the Abbey in 1908 in disagreement with its artistic policy, Fay had lived in America before going to London in 1914, where he enjoyed a successful career as a stage and film actor. As Maurice Gorham observes, 'it is interesting to consider what the future of Irish broadcasting would have been if Fay had been its first director'[3] – a partnership between a musician of O'Brien's calibre and Fay's dramatic and media skills could have made 2RN much more creative and flexible than it actually became.

The post was re-advertised, stating that the Director would be 'a man [*sic*] of broad views and wide sympathies, interested in life and literature, and especially in Irish literature and culture'[4] with a salary of £750 per annum (£15,000 at 2000 values; €18,750). The interview board on this occasion included Roger Eckersley,[5] who had been appointed BBC Organiser of Programmes two months previously and Percy Pitt, BBC Music Director. On 25 November 1925 the Minister approved the appointment of Séamus Clandillon as Station Director.

Séamus Clandillon (1878–1944) was a native of Gort, Co. Galway.[6] He had attended St Flannan's College, Ennis, and in 1899 went to UCD, where he began to take an interest in Irish at the newly formed branch of the Gaelic League; by 1901 he had begun to teach Irish alongside Patrick Pearse. Simultaneously he started to collect Irish songs which he published with his wife, Maighréad Ní Annagáin, a singer and Irish speaker from Co. Waterford. Their first collection, *Londubh an Chairn*, was published in 1904; their second, *Songs of the Irish Gaels*, which was to be the subject of a notorious libel action, appeared in 1927. Clandillon won the gold medal for singing at the 1911 Oireachtas and went on to develop a career as a singer and recording artist[7] parallel to his employment as a civil servant – first in Clonmel and Clonakilty as a teacher under the Department of Agriculture and Technical Instruction (1903–12) and later as Senior Inspector of the National Health Insurance Commission in Derry and Limerick. Both husband and wife were to perform

---

3 M. Gorham, *Forty Years of Irish Broadcasting*, p. 20.   4 P. Clarke, *Dublin Calling*, p. 29.   5 Brother of P.P. Eckersley.   6 Information regarding Clandillon is derived from Fintan Vallely (ed.), *The Companion to Irish Traditional Music* (Cork: Cork University Press, 1999) pp. 72–3, and P. Clarke, *Dublin Calling*, p. 28.   7 F. Vallely op. cit. informs us that Clandillon made eleven 78rpm records for the Parlaphone and HMV labels.

on the opening night of 2RN and on many subsequent occasions. After his dismissal from the radio service in 1934 Clandillon was transferred back to the Department of Health.

Although he had no broadcasting experience, Clandillon clearly possessed two vital qualities – he had lived within the civil service environment and he was an acclaimed and accomplished devotee of Irish music. Even allowing for the fact that the initial appointment procedure had been fruitless, it is still surprising that the senior post was filled after those more junior: the Station Announcer and Assistant Engineer (W.A. Beatty)[8] had been appointed in October and work had been proceeding since September on installation of the transmitter. Not only did Clandillon have no voice in the location of the 2RN studio, but one of his staff, Monaghan, had sat in judgement on his, Clandillon's, candidacy. It suggests that the Post Office's determination to maintain control of the medium allowed it to see the engineering side as more important than the administrative or artistic.

Clandillon was to prove a popular Director; his staff recalled 'Clan' – as he was affectionately known[9] – as 'rather abrupt but very helpful' and extremely versatile: Nancy Bergin, a member of the clerical staff, observed him single-handedly undertaking an outside broadcast commentary in 1929 on the occasion of a parade to mark the centenary of Catholic Emancipation.[10]

The appointment of Séamus Hughes as announcer occasioned some comment, relating to anxieties such as we have examined in Chapter 2 in connection with 'propaganda' and the recent political situation. Hughes had first been a member of the Socialist Party of Ireland and active in the Volunteers 1913–16. He was imprisoned 1916–17 and on his release worked for the ITGWU, becoming its General Secretary in place of James Larkin in 1918; when he was deposed from this position he worked in the propaganda wing of the Free State government and became General Secretary of Cumann na nGaedheal.[11] An accomplished linguist and singer of Irish ballads, he had been defeated by Seán Lemass in a by-election for South Dublin in November 1924. León Ó Broin (whose wife had worked as Hughes' assistant in the Cumann na nGaedheal offices) called him 'an idealist, a 1916 man and Irish-Irelander'.[12] He wrote a weekly column (anonymously) for the *Irish Catholic Herald*.

Hughes had been in the thick of the ever-present threat of a split within Cumann na nGaedheal and, with his new political master, J.J. Walsh, had been

8 Cf. P. Clarke, *Dublin Calling* p. 10: 'William Arnold Beatty … who was then aged 28, had … worked in the Marconi Co. for six and a half years. He then returned to Ireland and served in the Irish Army Signals Corps. Immediately prior to his appointment to 2RN he had been in charge of the wireless department of the General Electric Co., Dublin. He was a member of the executive committee of the Wireless Society of Ireland … He resigned from 2RN in 1928.' 9 Recollection of Kitty O'Callaghan, RTÉ Sound Archives tapes B 92, 93 10 RTÉ Sound Archives tape B 76. 11 Cf. J.A. Gaughan, *Thomas Johnson* p. 160. 12 L. Ó Broin, op. cit. p. 58.

one of those most vocal in establishing a militia-style citizens' cadre to combat the possibility of further armed resistance on the part of anti-treaty factions.[13] As party secretary he was responsible for articulating and negotiating one side of the power-play which characterised the struggle for control of the government, and his eclipse (he was demoted in December 1924), along with that of Walsh, would have made him attractive to the latter in this new post.

On 26 November 1925 Bryan Cooper said in the Dáil that while he believed that Hughes 'was qualified for the post', and had 'satisfied a strong board that he was the best candidate', he felt that

> the Government are entirely ignoring public opinion if they make an appointment of that sort without giving a full and sufficient statement as to [his] qualifications ... I agree with the minister that the fact that a man has been a candidate for the Dáil, or was actively associated with any political party, should not debar him from taking up a position in the Civil Service. Having regard, however, to the immense possibilities of propaganda by means of wireless broadcasting, it would be better, I think, not to have persons associated with politics in connection with that work.[14]

He was, however, pleased to accept J.J. Walsh's assurance that the appointment had been quite regular. Nevertheless, the word 'propaganda' must have rung in Walsh's ears, not least because the appointment of such a person, with such obvious political affiliations, to a position of potential influence, would have repercussions in the form of a phantom announcement made on 2RN after the General Election of June 1927 (see pp. 170–1). Behind Cooper's seemingly searching comment on the appointment stands a column of unspoken suspicion of much more serious magnitude as to what a politically motivated and highly articulate person might attempt in a position of broadcasting power. Hughes was to become Assistant Station Director in 1929 (in succession to F.W. O'Connell who had been killed in a traffic accident) and in 1934, when Clandillon was in the process of being removed from his position, he was acting Director of Broadcasting (as the post had been redesignated) – a decision which we might not expect from a Fianna Fáil ministry at that time.

Appointed in March 1927, F.W. O'Connell was the son of the Church of Ireland Rector in Clifden, Co. Galway. A multiple prizewinner at TCD, he had embraced all things Irish, including converting to Catholicism, and changed his name to Conall Cearnach. Paddy Clarke records that 'in a European relay for the New Year 1929 he broadcast greetings in ten

---

13 Cf. J. Regan, op. cit. pp. 122–3, 168–9, 233. 14 DD 13, 26 November 1926, cols. 961, 966.

languages, Irish, English, French, Spanish, German, Italian, Russian, Greek, Turkish and Persian.'[15] Nancy Bergin described him as 'very simple in spite of all his learning'.[16]

Further appointments in 1927 included that of a Woman Organiser – Maighréad Ní Ghráda – to arrange women's and children's programming. She succeeded Séamus Hughes as announcer when he was promoted to Assistant Station Director and was in turn succeeded by Kathleen Roddy. Both these women were married, which had at first debarred their appointment, but under pressure from Bryan Cooper in the Dáil the regulation was suspended.

In the meantime Monaghan had been working on the establishment of the studio and the transmitter.[17] The transmitter – as envisaged, a Marconi 1½ kw 'Q' type, similar to that in most of the BBC stations – was located at McKee (formerly Marlborough) Barracks[18] on the northside of Dublin, and the studios and offices were in a Post Office premises at 36 Little Denmark Street, off Henry Street – the street was extinguished in the 1970s to allow the building of the Ilac Shopping Centre; the studio remained there until October 1928 when it moved into the main GPO which was to be the home of Irish radio until the purpose-built Radio Centre was opened in Donnybrook in 1973. The studio was equipped with two grand pianos and a 'Meat Safe' magnetophone microphone weighing over 30lbs, nicknamed after its perforated metal cover, which had been developed by one of Marconi's pioneers, Captain H.J. Round. A 'moving coil' instrument, its electro-magnet powered by four two-volt accumulators, it was cradled in a 'Sorbo' rubber sling suspended from a mahogany frame.[19] Dina Copeman remembered the studio as 'ramshackle, dark and dismal',[20] while Nancy Bergin described the approach staircase from the street entrance as 'winding ... like a crow's nest';[21] Joan Burke concurred: the stairs were 'rickety'.[22] The general impression was one of makeshift inadequacy, whereas the GPO facilities, in which studios were fitted out very successfully, were regarded by most as very convenient.

The first test transmission occurred during the Dublin Wireless Exhibition which took place at the Mansion House 11–14 November 1925. At 6.45p.m.

---

15 P. Clarke, *Dublin Calling* p. 54. O'Connell, who was allegedly drunk at the time of his death, was knocked down by a tram in Lansdowne Road. It is said that when his body was removed by train to Clifden station an unseemly tussle broke out between his father, the Rector-Archdeacon, and the Catholic parish priest Monsignor McAlpine, over who should take custody of the coffin. The Rector was victorious, but went off to the echo of McAlpine's cry 'You may have his body, but we have his soul!' **16** RTÉ Sound Archives tape B 76. **17** I am indebted to Paddy Clarke, *Dublin Calling*, for technical information regarding the 2RN transmitter and studios. **18** The hut in which the transmitter was located continued in use until October 1980. **19** The studio was also equipped with a Western Electric type 373 microphone which had been introduced in the BBC at Birmingham and Cardiff: P. Clarke, *Dublin Calling*, p. 38. **20** In a programme transmitted on 4 January 1976, RTÉ Sound Archives tape 1/76. **21** RTÉ Sound Archives tape B 76. **22** RTÉ Sound Archives tape B 96.

on the final evening 'listeners-in' could hear 'Sé seo stáisúin 2RN Baile Átha Cliath ag Triáil [This is 2RN the Dublin station testing]'. After modifications had been made to the modulations, tests continued with a variety of greetings up to 9.30p.m.

It immediately became apparent that existing listeners to overseas stations were apprehensive that the new service might block out foreign signals. Already one writer to the *Irish Times* had asserted over a year previously that

> the wave length has apparently been selected deliberately in order to cut off Manchester (375 wave length) and Bournemouth (385 wave length), the two stations best heard in Dublin. In fact, Manchester is the only station that can be readily picked up during the day-time with a one or two valve set. It is childish of Mr Walsh, or anyone else in office, to dictate to Irish people what they are, or rather what they are not, to listen to. King Canute tried to sweep back the sea waves, and Mr Walsh proposes to confuse the wireless waves. There is a wide range of selection – from Cardiff (353 wave length) and Aberdeen (495 wave length) – and I would suggest that a wave length of 410 would not interfere seriously with any broadcasting station.[23]

Now, a writer to the *Irish Independent* complained:

> Sir, I had the pleasure of hearing '2RN Calling' on Saturday night on a 4 valve set. The reception was exceptionally loud and clear. In fact it was so strong it completely drowned British and foreign stations of wavelengths of at least 50 metres above and below that of the Dublin station. This is to be deplored, for it means that when 2RN begins to function regularly, such stations as Manchester, Bournemouth, Breslau, and even London will be cut off from the Dublin 'listener-in', and he will be confined to the local station. One of the great advantages of broadcasting is that it takes us out of our parochialism and enlarges our international interest. One can switch on to British or Continental stations and suit one's taste, whether it be art, drama, music or languages. If the Dublin station retains its present wavelength the local 'listeners-in' will, accordingly, be deprived of the greatest benefit of broadcasting.[24]

2RN was transmitting on 390 metres, and thus its proximity to Bournemouth and Hamburg (395 metres) was particularly problematic.

23 *Irish Times* 2 April 1924. 24 *Irish Independent* 16 November 1925.

Although the *Irish Independent*'s wireless correspondent, 'Aether', thought that the advantages of having a local station outweighed the disadvantages of its interfering with such other stations, many Irish listeners who had developed a taste for a particular service were annoyed by the new development. Modifications were accordingly made to the wavelength: in March 1926 it moved to 397 metres, in November 1926 to 319m., in January 1929 to 411m. and in June 1929 to 413m., thus eventually vindicating the writer in the *Irish Times*.[25]

Listeners were highly critical of programme content, and they would continue to complain for years thereafter. A letter-writer to the *Evening Herald* said:

> On Saturday night ... the matter broadcasted was of the most trumpery description even for a test performance. Selections from *Maritana*, no matter by whom played, fill me with homicidal thoughts, and to hear an ultra-refined lady vocalist pronouncing the word 'vale' as if it meant the flesh of a calf made me weep aloud.[26]

On 21 November the PMG himself broadcast in Irish. On 13 December a one-hour programme was relayed from London 2LO, and on 15 and 16 December the first outside broadcasts (OBs) took place when concerts featuring 'The Irish Independent Male Voice Choir' and Renee Flynn were transmitted from the La Scala Theatre (also known as the Capitol Cinema, now demolished) and were received not only throughout much of Ireland but also in England, where listeners began to demand broadcasts of Irish folk music. The La Scala continued to be the source of further OBs which featured an orchestra and the Army No. 1 Band, while on 21 December Handel's *Messiah* was performed at the Centenary Methodist Church (now demolished) in St. Stephen's Green which included greetings from the first clergyman to broadcast on 2RN, Rev. W.J. Oliver. Some listeners noticed some humming during this transmission, which was attributed to the Inchicore tramline which ran close to the transmitter at McKee Barracks.[27] The final test was transmitted on 24 December with a performance of carols from St Mary's, Donnybrook under Vincent O'Brien.

Two days before 2RN officially came on air, the *Irish Independent* opined, in company with many Dáil deputies, that the innovation was 'especially welcome to those who dwell in rural parts, where dullness of life often makes for discontent, and sets youth along pleasure paths that lead to sin and crime ... Henceforth the possessor of a receiving set will have the pleasure of knowing

---

25 Information from P. Clarke, *Dublin Calling*, p. 34. **26** *Evening Herald* 17 December 1925. **27** P. Clarke, op. cit. p. 40.

that he can listen-in to a programme chosen to suit not the tastes and needs of neighbouring nations but to suit the Irish people'.[28] But what would suit the Irish people was far from clear to either Séamus Clandillon or 'the Irish people'.

INAUGURATION OF 2RN

'It is the earnest wish of the Minister for Posts and Telegraphs and of the Secretary, that you, above anyone else in Ireland, would do this for us, and, of course, it is my personal wish as well'.[29] Thus Clandillon wrote to Douglas Hyde, inviting him to inaugurate the new service, the Minister having decided that he would not do so himself.[30] When we note that Jeffrey Prager says 'an important prerequisite for political stability is the ability of political elites to organise popular sentiment and interests',[31] we can see in this invitation a form of cultural mobilisation, of which Douglas Hyde was regarded as the chief exponent, and which was concurrent with political mobilisation. With the phase described by Prager as the 'legitimation crisis' still evolving, it would not have been prudent or indeed possible for 2RN to have provided an explicit discussion of that crisis. The choice of Hyde, rather than, for example, Cosgrave, to inaugurate the service underlined both the cultural, rather than political, nature of the enterprise and the subliminal nature of what was being attempted.

Thus, in so far as the programming of 2RN in its first years demonstrates any attempt (whether tacit or overt) to signify a notion of identity, that signification was predominantly cultural and social, only marginally political, and determinedly non-ideological. In fact the *ex*plicit emphasis on culture can be interpreted as an *im*plicit suppression of ideology as a subject.

We can indeed confirm Prager's basic thesis that the accommodation strategy developed by Cumann na nGaedheal relied on the cultural admixture, rather than polarisation, of Irish-Enlightenment and Gaelic-Romantic values. Prager ignores Hyde's role in this, yet Hyde typifies the cultural integration necessary, in Durkheimian terms, to underpin the political order, and it was for this reason, we must assume, that he was invited to inaugurate the radio service.

---

28 *Irish Independent* 30 December 1925. **29** Translation of letter in Irish from Séamus Clandillon to Douglas Hyde, 22 December 1925, RTÉ Archives: I am indebted to my former colleague in the RTÉ Reference and Illustrations Library, Máire Ní Mhurchú, for this translation and of the letter of 23 December. In fact, it had been planned to open the station on New Year's Eve, as indicated in letters from Clandillon to the artists engaged to perform; there is no indication in the extant files of the reason for postponing the event. **30** Posts and Telegraphs file 711/53, now in RTÉ Archives. **31** J. Prager, op. cit. p. 25.

In 1925–6 Hyde was a university professor and a private citizen. A Protestant and a countryman by birth, he founded the Gaelic League, and became a folklorist and literary revivalist, helping to mobilise cultural nationalism through advocating 'the necessity for De-Anglicising the Irish People'.[32] He had had little exposure to politics (he had in fact been co-opted to the Seanad in February 1925 but, despite vigorous campaigning, he was defeated when he stood for election later that year)[33] and when he eventually became inaugural President of Ireland in 1938 it was with all-party agreement. His Seanad defeat was not his first taste of electoral failure: in 1919 he had been one of several prominent members of the NUI Senate who had been swept out by a raft of Sinn Féin candidates.[34] He was thus not a public figure, since he had also resigned as President of the Gaelic League in 1915 when, under Pearse and Eoin MacNeill, it had taken a decidedly militant turn. Not only was he a private figure, but he was also determinedly non-political, his militancy being purely in the cultural sphere. In Hyde's status at that time we can therefore detect the qualities which 2RN was to promulgate.

The correspondence from Clandillon to Hyde is quite explicit, and gives us an insight into the apparent lack of policy for the new medium.[35] Hyde's speech had been carefully commissioned by Clandillon. In two letters of succeeding days Clandillon, addressing Hyde in Irish as 'my old friend, a Craoibhin',[36] firstly expressed the need for 'telling the people of the world that we, the Irish, are again independent and showing that we stand among all nations'. Secondly, he emphasised that 'you ought to proclaim, to the Irish people and to the peoples of the world that we, the Irish nation, are on our own feet again although we have been long silent and that our language and our music will be heard all over the world from now on, in the midst of the languages and music of all other nations'. Hyde complied to the letter with this request.

Following the opening announcement by Séamus Hughes – 'Sé seo Radio Bhaile Átha Cliath ag Glaodhach; this is 2RN the Dublin Broadcasting Station calling' – Hyde spoke:[37]

> Our enterprise today marks the beginning not only of the New Year, but of a new era – an era in which our nation will take its place amongst the other nations of the world. A nation has never been made by Act of

---

32 Title of a lecture given by Hyde to the National Literary Society, 25 November 1892.   **33** Cf. J.E. Dunleavy and G.W. Dunleavy, *Douglas Hyde: a Maker of Modern Ireland* (Berkeley Ca.: University of California Press, 1991) pp. 354–6.   **34** Cf. A. Mitchell, op. cit. p. 121.   **35** Departmental minutes 17 December to 24 December 1925 on Posts and Telegraphs file no. 711/53, now in RTÉ Archives. **36** For the full text of the letters see Appendix 2. 'An Craobhin' ('the little branch') was a reference to Hyde's pseudonym, 'An Craoibhin Aoibhinn' ('the pleasant little branch') by which he was colloquially known.   **37** The full text is given in Appendix 2.

Parliament. A nation is made from the inside, itself, it is made, first of all, by its language, if it has one; by its music, songs, games and customs … The people of Ireland must understand that our nation is an exception, a nation that has its own rich language and will make its official business through Irish … It is a sign to the world that times have changed when we can take our own place amongst other nations, and use the wireless in our own language. Éire is not completely saved yet, and will not be until the foreign influence is wiped out.[38]

The sense of a cultural innovation (the broadcast was hailed by sections of the press as 'Beginning of a New Era')[39] had been anticipated in a fraternal message from the BBC, in which Reith (a Scot) had written:

We feel that the Irish Free State enters the ether at an opportune moment in the general development of broadcasting. We are now on the threshold of the international era, in the course of which the medium of wireless will permit a free exchange of thought and culture between all nations, continents and races. We are convinced that the Irish branch of the Celtic race has a definite contribution to offer in the full development of broadcasting for the benefit of humanity.[40]

The fact that 2RN could be successfully received in many parts of Britain gave confidence to the administration that an 'Irish voice' could send a cultural message to both Irish people abroad and to those who were as yet unaware of Irishness.

The commission from Clandillon to Hyde may in its turn have been coached by O'Hegarty. In *The Victory of Sinn Féin* O'Hegarty had written: 'Sinn Féin was founded on two things – on the Irish language and all the tradition and national individuality which that brings with it, and on the will to be free'.[41] The invitation to Hyde ('showing that we stand among all nations') carries a none too obscure reference to Robert Emmet's speech from the dock: 'When my country takes her place among the nations of the earth, then, and not till then, let my epitaph be written'. That aspiration, forwarded to Hyde a mere week after the Dáil, in the wake of the Boundary Commission crisis, had passed the Treaty Act which in Cosgrave's words was 'necessary for the immediate preservation of the public peace and safety',[42] was clearly one which the inauguration of 2RN could be employed to promulgate: to give voice to Irishness of a different order. Again, as O'Hegarty had said two years

38 *Irish Independent* 2 January 1926.　**39** Quoted in P. Clarke, *Dublin Calling* p. 46.　**40** *Irish Times* 11 November 1925.　**41** P.S. O'Hegarty op. cit. p. 119.　**42** DD 13, 15 December 1925, cols. 1957–8.

earlier: 'What has mattered in political freedom has been the power to develop our own resources, shape our own destinies, and preserve our own distinctive nationality ... There is no case known to history where a nation retained its individuality, its separateness, once its language had been lost'.[43] And even in Hyde's terminology we find an echo of O'Hegarty, who had said 'Jazz dancing, joy rides, fetes and bazaars have never built a civilisation, and never will build one'.[44]

In political and cultural terms, therefore, Hyde's speech represents a 'victory of Sinn Féin' in the sense of a reconstructive, accommodating integration of ideals and reality which echoes not only Emmet in spirit and O'Hegarty in the letter but also the Irish-language orientation of Walsh and the notion of Gaelic identity as expressed by George Russell and Darrell Figgis. It was a précis of the literature of independence, and as such it bore a distinct relationship to subsequent programming.

The performing artists for opening night had in fact been contacted before the invitation was extended to Hyde. Clandillon had written by 8 December to Dina Copeman, a young pianist who agreed to play two works for a fee of three guineas (£63 at 2000 values; €79).[45] He was not so fortunate in the case of Joseph O'Mara: 'my usual fee is twenty guineas, but I will accept fifteen guineas and perhaps might arrange a series of dates at a slightly reduced fee'.[46] Clandillon told Vincent O'Brien: 'I think his terms are very steep considering our wretched resources. What do you think? Is there any possibility that we could get him down to a five guineas fee?'[47] The departmental file does not record whether they were successful in this. One singer, J.C. Doyle, requested a rehearsal in the studio: 'I would like to get acclimatized to the "atmosphere" & make "Mick's" [the microphone] acquaintance – to see what he looks like. I understand from cross-Channel singers that, generally speaking, they consider it a gruesome experience'.[48] In only one respect was he unsuccessful: O'Hegarty had asked that Clandillon find 'a Gaelic League choir',[49] but none could be identified by Vincent O'Brien. The programme was sent to the Minister for approval. Walsh considered it 'excellent' and directed that it be sent to the newspapers for publication.[50]

The finalised programme which followed the official speech by Douglas Hyde was:

8 p.m.   Army no. 1 Band: Irish Fantasia by its conductor, Col. Fritz Brase (dedicated to John F. Larchet)[51]

---

43 P.S. O'Hegarty op. cit. pp. 126–7. **44** Ibid. p. 130. **45** D. Copeman to Clandillon, 21 December 1925, file 711/53 (RTÉ). **46** J. O'Mara to Clandillon, 14 December 1925, ibid. **47** Undated note Clandillon to O'Brien, ibid. **48** J.C. Doyle to Clandillon 14 December 1925, ibid. **49** O'Hegarty memorandum to Clandillon 21 December 1925, ibid. **50** Walsh memorandum to O'Hegarty 22 December 1925, ibid. **51** The Army No. 1 Band was relayed from Beggar's Bush Barracks.

8.15p.m.   Séamus Clandillon: three Gaelic songs

8.25p.m.   Arthur Darley: (violin solo), three Irish airs

8.35p.m.   Joan Burke (contralto): three Irish songs (accompanied by Arthur Duff)

8.45p.m.   Annie Fagan (harp): three Irish airs

8.55p.m.   Army no. 1 Band: Lament for Youth (by John F. Larchet) and Molly on the Shore (by Percy Grainger)

9.05p.m.   Joseph O'Mara (tenor): three Irish songs

9.15p.m.   James Ennis and Liam Andrews (uilleann pipes): selection of jigs and reels

9.25p.m.   Maighréad Ní Annagáin: three Gaelic songs

9.35p.m.   Dina Copeman (piano): Nocturne in G no.12 by John Field and Polonaise in E flat by Chopin

9.45p.m.   J.C. Doyle (baritone): three Irish songs

9.55p.m.   Arthur Darley (violin solo): Romance by Hugo Wolff and Boree [Bourree] by Alfred Moffat

10.05p.m. Palestrina Choir: Sanctus and Benedictus (Palestrina) and Regina Coeli (Aichinger)

10.20p.m. Army no. 1 Band: Prelude and Liebestod (Wagner, *Tristan und Isolde*) and The Soldier's Song.

The 'Fantasia', which was supposed to be of fifteen minutes' duration, actually lasted for considerably longer, thus extending the broadcast and throwing the schedule into disarray.

Superficially, it might appear that the programme was oriented heavily towards Irish traditional music, but there was much more subtlety to the selection than might appear, not least in the choice of artists, who were some of the most distinguished singers and instrumentalists available. Joseph O'Mara's claim to a twenty-guinea fee was not outrageous, given that he was, at the age of sixty, the leading Irish operatic tenor of his generation and the founder of a legendary touring opera company. Arthur Darley's career straddled both the 'classical' and the 'traditional' genres: a distinguished teacher at the RIAM, as a solo performer of Irish airs he had provided musical entertainment in the intervals at the Abbey Theatre before John F. Larchet established its house orchestra; his father played both the violin and the uilleann pipes, and the family was also connected to the nineteenth-century dramatist Dion Boucicault. On Darley's death in 1929 Annie Patterson recorded that 'he identified himself with the culling and preservation of what music the country still possessed in a somewhat fluctuating and unrecorded condition', while Katherine Tynan simply called him 'God's violinist for ever'.[52] James Ennis, an

---

52 Quoted in R. Pine and C. Acton, op. cit. p. 252. Darley's son, also Arthur, was a violinist and doctor and a friend of Samuel Beckett.

official of the Department of Agriculture, was a noted piper and a champion dancer, and was the father of the legendary piper Séamus Ennis (at that date only seven years of age). Joan Burke, who made a number of gramophone recordings and appeared frequently on 2RN in future years, was a half-sister of W.T. Cosgrave. Dina Copeman, the child of Jewish refugees from Lithuania and a protégée of Michele Esposito, was about to take up a teaching appointment at the Royal Irish Academy of Music, and to become one of the most influential teachers and pianists of her day, up to her death in 1982. J.C. Doyle was a prominent singing teacher in Dublin (and the uncle of Col. James Doyle who became the first Irish-born director of the Army School of Music and one of the earliest conductors of the Radio Éireann orchestra in the 1930s).

Colonel Fritz Brase, who had served as a conductor in the Imperial German Army up to 1919, was one of the founders of Irish musical life in the twentieth century, whose influence can still be observed in the Army School of Music and its four bands, which he established after accepting an invitation from General Richard Mulcahy (on the advice of Larchet and Denis McCullough) in 1923. The army wind and brass players would be an essential component of the fledgling orchestra which Vincent O'Brien would inaugurate in the 1930s for Radio Éireann's earliest concerts, as they also were of the amateur Dublin Philharmonic Society (incorporating an earlier Dublin Symphony Orchestra) which Brase set up in 1927. In the 1920s and 30s he gave considerable encouragement to conductors such as Arthur Duff and Michael Bowles who were the rising stars of the radio music department.

Exceptional in the range of performers, and of the music they chose to perform, is the quality and the diversity of interests which, without departing in any way from nationalist ideals, displayed a balance between traditional and classical, ancient and modern which would characterise the music output thereafter.

The following morning the *Irish Times* – still confining its terminology within inverted commas – commented:

> Last night the Dublin 'Broadcasting' Station began its regular service of 'wireless' programmes. During recent weeks aerials have been appearing on hundreds of house-tops, and the vendors of crystal sets have been doing a lively trade. The advent of a new station has aroused considerable interest even among 'wireless' enthusiasts across the Channel, and many thousands of 'listeners-in' assisted at last night's performance. The programme was very successful. Naturally enough, the Gaelic element predominated; but there was plenty of variety in the musical items, and, for a start, the entertainment was admirable. The

future of 'broadcasting' in the Free State lies in the hands of those who have been entrusted with the task of providing nightly programmes. 'Wireless' is a powerful instrument of culture, and we hope sincerely that it will be used to the very best advantage in the Free State. 2RN is not catering for the Free State alone. Probably, every item of last night's programme was heard by somebody in every country of Europe, and possibly by many in America. The object of the authorities, there-fore, ought to be not only to consider the immediate tastes of their Irish audience, but also to bear in mind that the country's musical and literary standards will be judged by critical audiences throughout the world. For that reason they ought to be satisfied with nothing less than the very best. There is no lack of talent in the Free State. We have a folk music second to none in the world, and Dublin boasts poets and men of letters whose names are famous in two hemispheres. The object of our 'wireless' directors should be to furnish programmes, which, while distinctively Irish, will escape the reproach of parochialism and to interpret the artistic genius of the nation not only to its own citizens, but to the whole of Europe.[53]

The critic of the *Irish Independent*, 'H.R.W.' (Harold White, the most influential critic of the time and a noted composer) considered that all the performances were satisfactory, with the exception of Maighréad Ní Annagáin, whose poor performance he attributed to nervousness.[54] The *Sunday Independent* published a 'Gallery of Broadcasting Artists' as a banner across its front page on 3 January and continued to do so almost continually for the next four months.[55]

During the meetings of the Wireless Committee in 1924, it had, surpris-ingly perhaps, been T.J. Monaghan, the engineer, who had had the most to say about scheduling:

> The beauty of broadcasting is that if you don't like the programme you can shut it off. You cannot guarantee if you broadcast any matter you will reach all. You must make your programme of such a holding char-acter that the man who is not particularly interested in it has his inter-est stimulated and he listens to the programme.[56]

To which, with some naïvety, Prof. Magennis responded

---

53 *Irish Times* 2 January 1926. 54 *Irish Independent* 2 January 1926; in a radio recollection of 1966 traditional fiddler Cormac McGinley, who broadcast during the first week of 2RN, said that her voice was troubled by a strained throat on opening night: RTÉ Sound Archives tape 32/68C. 55 P. Clarke, *Dublin Calling* p. 46. 56 *Report* para. 1875.

Therefore if it were known that at a certain hour each day this particular type of programme would be provided we should have a better
assurance that it would be listened to than if it were accidentally put in
or put in at random in the bigger programme. In that case it might
come as a hurtful shock to those who thought they were going to have
another jazz tune when they would get instead a lecture on Gaelic
literature.[57]

The concept of a schedule was of course new, as was the practice of arranging
for it to be published in the day's newspapers or, preferably, more in advance.
The idea of listener loyalty was born when that of dependability of service (in
both quality and quantity, technical and editorial) was conceived to stimulate
it.[58] Another point which was hardly articulated, but which was recognised
early on by Bryan Cooper, was that 'broadcasting is in a sense an art in itself',[59]
and to possess this art is more than half the business of creating the 'holding
character' which will attract and keep an audience. The attractiveness of some
of the voices of the presenters of sponsored programmes, such as Denis
Brennan and Leo Maguire, is ample evidence of that.

Perhaps the programme for the second evening is more indicative of the
general fare available on the average evening: popular musical selections
followed by 'Clery's Instrumental Trio', which was to form the nucleus of the
Station Orchestra; songs from Joseph O'Neill and Florrie Ackerman; a violin
solo by Rosalind Dowse; and the weather forecast. Among the other artists
who were to appear in the first few weeks and months were the distinguished
singers and teachers Jean Nolan and Turner Huggard, pianists Rhoda
Coghill,[60] Rhona Clarke and Dorothy Stokes (later to be influential teachers
at the RIAM), piper Leo Rowsome, comedians Jimmy O'Dea and Harry
O'Donovan and lecturer Walter Starkie, to whom the *Irish Independent* would
later refer as 'one of the finest of radio speakers'.[61]

---

57 Ibid. para. 1876. **58** Unlike the BBC (*Radio Times* and *Listener*) and the Finnish Broadcasting
Company, 2RN did not establish its own publicity organ early on. M. Gorham (*Forty Years of Irish
Broadcasting* p. 238) states that this development, recommended by the Advisory Committee and advocated by the Comhairle of Radio Éireann, had been blocked by the Department of Finance. The *RTV*
[later *RTÉ*] *Guide* was not published until 1961. Gorham also stated (in 1973) that in 1952–3, as Director
of Programmes, he had wanted to establish a radio journal or to purchase the *Irish Radio Review* but that
this had been vetoed by the Department of Finance: RTÉ Sound Archives tape 338/73. **59** DD 14,
28 January 1926, col. 281. **60** Rhoda Coghill was to become the official Station Accompanist, a position she would hold for forty years. **61** *Irish Independent* 15 August 1938. In the Dáil Bryan Cooper
had said in an oblique reference to Starkie: 'I know one friend of mine, a Fellow of Trinity College, one
of the greatest authorities in the British Islands on Spain, and an accomplished musician, told me he
would be glad to give a talk of a quarter of an hour on Spanish music, illustrating it on the violin' – DD
14, 28 January 1926, col. 283.

Philip Sayers had told the Dáil enquiry that 'we [the IBC] intend to have an independent concert party for broadcasting',[62] and this sole reference to the possibility of a 'station orchestra', as it came to be called, must be regarded as the kernel of the engagement with live and recorded serious music on the part of the future Radio Éireann.[63] Certainly, as in many other countries with similar schedules,[64] music in all its forms was to be the mainstay of the service. Another witness had even suggested that the station itself might be located in the 'prospective Concert Hall',[65] which had been a contentious issue for at least a quarter of a century,[66] and was to remain so until the opening of the National Concert Hall in the refurbished hall of the former Royal University in Earlsfort Terrace in 1980.

Again, we must not place too great a burden of expectation on the narrow shoulders of a fledgling radio channel. 2RN operated in a quite different cultural climate to the BBC, which at this time regarded itself as advancing 'the true democratization of Music',[67] nor could it hope – at that stage – to match the BBC's contribution to live music-making which the latter achieved by taking over the Promenade Concerts season in 1927. During the debate on the Wireless Report, Bryan Cooper raised the question of foreign relays of classical music:

> The Fifth Symphony [of Beethoven] was played in Dublin last year [1923], but I do not think that for ten years the other symphonies were played in Dublin for the reason that we have not an orchestra capable of the task. We have a first-class military band; we have the nucleus of a chamber orchestra ... but we have not any great orchestra, and if it is the intention of the Postmaster-General to deny us any opportunity of picking up these British and Continental concerts we will be at a great loss. I am sure the Postmaster-General, as a good patriot, would like to see some great musical genius arise in Ireland. But that genius is not likely to arise if we keep in a narrow circle and if the young composer never hears any of the first-class orchestras or any of the really great compositions of the masters, none of whom, with perhaps one exception, was English. By this extraordinary invention of wireless, you can

---

62 *Report* para. 838. **63** RTÉ's record of achievement in the creation of what became the National Symphony Orchestra (founded 1948) is described in Pat O'Kelly, *The National Symphony Orchestra of Ireland 1948–1998: a selected history* (Dublin: RTÉ 1998). A further monograph on RTÉ's role in music-making in Ireland will appear in the current series of 'Broadcasting and Irish Society'. **64** Cf. A. Briggs, op. cit. p. 251: 'Music accounted for by far the biggest single slice of broadcasting time. In November 1923, for example, London was broadcasting on an average each day 3 hours and 25 minutes of music to 2 hours and 5 minutes of everything else. In 1926 the figures were 4 hours and 40 minutes of music to 2 hours and 20 minutes of everything else'. **65** *Report* para. 2958. **66** Cf. R. Pine and C. Acton, op. cit. pp. 357–60. **67** Quoted in Scannell and Cardiff, op. cit. p. 195.

bring first-class music to the door of almost everybody ... An Irish station will never be able to provide this on a really satisfactory scale.[68]

Cooper could not have foreseen the separation of functions which saw the BBC, for example, establishing specialist channels such as the Third Programme (today BBC Radio 3) alongside the provision of orchestras, which has been recently undertaken by RTÉ with the repositioning of the National Symphony Orchestra and the creation of Lyric FM. In fact there were to be a significant number of relays from the BBC: over 35 hours in 1926, almost 14 in 1927, 23 in 1928, 5½ in 1929, 18½ in 1930, 7 in 1931 and 2 in 1932.[69]

As noted, the earliest schedules featured 'Clery's Instrumental Trio', a generic member of the 'Palm Court' type of afternoon entertainment in the restaurants of large department stores which continued to appear well into the second half of the twentieth century. This trio was replaced on an official basis at the end of the station's first month with the 'Station Trio', consisting of Rosalind Dowse[70] and Frederick Treacy, violins and Viola O'Connor, cello. A month later, re-titled grandiosely as the Station Orchestra, they were joined by Viola's sister, Terry O'Connor, and its exponential growth had begun. Four months later it numbered seven, with the addition of Maud Aiken (violin),[71] Moira Flusk (violin) and Zack Lee (double bass). Kitty O'Doherty was chosen as Station Pianist in preference to Dina Copeman, who had also applied for the job. She remained in her post until 1939 and, like Terry O'Connor (as formidable a person as she was musician), succeeded in avoiding the regulation which required retirement on marriage (she also rehearsed the station's 'opera chorus')[72]. Terry O'Connor went on to lead the Orchestra as it expanded, retiring in 1945 to be succeeded by Nancie Lord, a professor at the RIAM who had given the first performance of E.J. Moeran's violin concerto (1942).[73]

On 26 November 1927 Vincent O'Brien mounted his most ambitious venture, a symphony concert in Dublin's Metropolitan Hall, with the station orchestra hugely augmented for a performance of Weber's *Euryanthe* overture, Beethoven's first symphony, Saint-Saëns' *Danse macabre* and the Rossini/Respighi *La Boutique fantasque*. In keeping with the fashion of the day, this conventional symphonic fare was itself augmented with 'variety' items: bass Glyn Eastmann sang operatic numbers by Bellini and Mozart, Arthur Darley played Carolan's Concerto and a number of traditional Irish airs and Séamus

68 DD 6, 15 February 1924, col. 1119. **69** Rex Cathcart, 'Broadcasting – the Early Decades', in B. Farrell (ed.), *Communications and Community in Ireland* (Dublin: Mercier, 1984) p. 124. **70** Rosalind Dowse was a member of a numerous musical family: see R. Pine and C. Acton, op. cit. pp. 248–51, 322–26, 362, 395. **71** Née Davin; was Director of the Municipal School of Music 1931–4 when she married Frank Aiken (TD 1927–73, Minister for Defence 1932–45 and External Affairs 1951–4, 1957–69). **72** She describes this practice in detail in RTÉ Sound Archives tape B 96. **73** For details of the first student musical broadcasts, see Pine and Acton op. cit. p. 362.

Clandillon sang several songs in Irish. The Civil Service Choir assisted in audience participation in 'Adeste Fideles' and 'Let Erin Remember'.[74] Admission was one shilling (5p or £1 at 2000 values; €1.25) for 'working classes' and 2s. 6d. (12½ or £2.50 at 2000 values; €3.12) for 'upper classes' – a curiously discriminatory gesture.[75] The *Irish Times* critic commented 'the quality of playing in all departments was excellent and we have an orchestra that is worthy of high praise'. He continued 'Towards the end of the evening Mr Clandillon spoke as if further concerts of this kind are assured, and it may be hoped so. There is a place for such evenings, not only from the Free State Broadcasting programmes, but in the musical life of Dublin's fair city'.[76] Similar concerts were indeed given up to 1929, including a Homage to Schubert in 1928 to mark the centenary of the composer's death, but the series was then suspended for a number of years.

In the studio, however, O'Brien continued to grow his orchestra and to present a number of opera performances, including, in 1928, Donizetti's *The Daughter of the Regiment*, and in 1929 Offenbach's *The Tales of Hoffmann*, Balfe's *The Rose of Castile*, Mozart's *The Marriage of Figaro* and Verdi's *Il trovatore*, most of them featuring Joan Burke and William J. Lemass. The original trio had grown to 19 players by 1933; two years later, to 24; and by 1937 to 28.[77] Alice Brough, a student who went on to join the Radio Éireann orchestra, recalls that there were frequent calls at short notice from the GPO for augmentees whenever large works were being undertaken: 'you were always getting ready for something'.[78]

On St Patrick's Day 1926 the President of the Executive Council, W.T. Cosgrave, gave a formal speech which continued the tone set by Hyde, but also anticipated that to be adopted by Éamon de Valera in his own presidential broadcasts both as head of government and as head of state, in which the political dimension of culture was addressed.

> If we are to have a social order worthy of the teaching of St Patrick we must look upon all our citizens as Brother-Irishmen. If we are to conserve our traditions we must preserve our language, our games, our dances, our music in which our national culture is enshrined[79] ... In this little country we are inter-dependent; the employer and the employee, the producer and the distributer [*sic*]; the distributer and the consumer. The good of each is the good of all ... The building up of the State is a long task. It cannot be accomplished in a few years; it is the work of

74 Cf. Pat O'Kelly, op. cit. 75 P. Clarke, *Dublin Calling*, p. 56. 76 *Irish Times* 28 November 1927. 77 P. O'Kelly, op. cit. 78 Pine and Acton, op. cit. p. 249. 79 It is ironic that the Irish language section of Cosgrave's speech was written out phonetically, as he had little or no fluency in Irish.

many generations. It is but a little time since we undertook responsibility for our household – there have been many changes even in that short period. New institutions, consonant with our new responsibilities, have been set up; old institutions have been remodelled to bring them into harmony with our new conditions; big schemes of construction and development have been initiated ... The people are awakening to their responsibilities.[80]

In *The Victory of Sinn Féin* P.S. O'Hegarty had written: 'Whether Ireland will survive at all, will depend, not on further political changes, but on the character and the institutions which she produces. And that is the gravest problem which confronts her'.[81] There were, in fact, political changes (though not revolutionary ones) in the offing: in 1927 the assassination of Kevin O'Higgins led to a political watershed which saw Fianna Fáil taking its place in the Dáil and almost forming a coalition government; in 1932, indeed, de Valera took power and two years later deposed Clandillon as Director of the broadcasting service.

It was in this climate that the most significant cultural institution to be created by the new Ireland was to develop under the anxious eyes of its political masters.

2RN: 1926–32

'Whatever you do you will be subject to criticism', the Wireless Committee had been told,[82] and, as J.J. Walsh ruefully observed in his memoirs, 'as anticipated, our handling of this addition to public ownership was not a success'.[83] As expected, the spread of radio was rapid and thorough, and criticism was not slow to manifest itself. Walsh had not been persuasive in his attempt to preempt the begrudgery in the previous November (listeners 'ought not to embark at once in that destructive criticism which was more or less ready to the minds of most people, but should remember that the national prestige was at stake')[84]. Already by 6 January 1926 (five days after transmission had begun) letters of complaint were being published in the *Irish Times*. On 7 January a letter signed by 'Earth Wire' from Clontarf asserted that in return for the £1 licence fee, 'all we receive is a local programme of no variety';[85] a correspondent in Ballybunion, Co. Kerry, who clearly had extensive experience as a listener, observed that 2RN was being drowned out by the stations in Bournemouth and Hamburg, and that the establishment of a station in Cork

80 SPO S/5/111/1 (National Archives).   81 P.S. O'Hegarty op. cit. p. 127.   82 *Report* para. 2948.
83 J.J. Walsh, *Recollections* p. 67.   84 *Irish Times* 12 November 1925.   85 *Irish Times* 7 January 1926.

(eighty miles from Ballybunion) would not alleviate the situation;[86] and 'Willi', from Dublin, felt that for Hyde to have addressed foreigners in English and ' "my own countrymen" in Gaelic, which, of course was unintelligible to probably 95 per cent. of his Irish hearers' meant that presumably the broadcast was intended for non-Irish ears: 'the principal attraction of wireless is that by it we can get what would otherwise be unobtainable ... If Mr Walsh does not arrange to relay a reasonable proportion of "foreign" programmes, I am afraid there will be a slump in crystal sets'.[87]

On 8 January the *Evening Herald*, which had so enthusiastically supported the Wireless Exhibition and the advent of 2RN a couple of months previously, commented:

> Unless a more varied, interesting and educational quality is put into the programmes the public enthusiasm at present so obvious will flag and the benefits of broadcasting will be restricted. So far the fare has been poor. There has been more than enough instrumental and vocal items with never a humorous talk, a lecture, or an expert dissertation, or a business chat.[88]

The lack of resources seems to have been a greater impediment than any other factor to Clandillon's ability to enhance the schedules: he had only £3.3.0 (£3.15 or £63 at 2000 values; €79) to spend per artist or £20 (£400; €500) in total per evening, with a maximum of £120 per seven days. On occasions, he would take to the microphone himself, while the frequent appearances of his wife, Maighréad Ní Annagáin, led to her being dubbed 'Maighréad Ní On Again'. When Bryan Cooper said that 'the main criticism is that the type of entertainment every night is practically the same. It is what you might call the ballad concert'[89] he was not being unfair, and he was accurately describing what Clandillon was best at and most enjoyed.

The fact of his being a stressful job was certainly well established. It will be scarcely appreciated today that all programmes were transmitted 'live', since recording equipment as we know it did not exist, and, as with the BBC, there was considerable resistance to broadcasting gramophone records, which were employed during changeovers of speakers or performers in addition to the early evening programme in which they featured. (Sound recordings on tape were not generally available until 1934, and Radio Éireann did not acquire a machine until 1936.) There are apocryphal stories of Clandillon, in desperation, pulling in to the studio anyone passing in the corridor of the GPO who might adequately sing a song or relate an anecdote.[90]

---

86 Ibid. **87** Ibid. **88** *Evening Herald* 8 January 1926. **89** DD 14, 28 January 1926, col. 280.
90 M. Gorham, *Forty Years of Irish Broadcasting* p. 25.

The Department in its turn was controlled by Finance, which restricted Walsh's capacity for expenditure to £15 for the purchase of a musical instrument without prior sanction.[91] Towards the end of the first month of 2RN, Walsh told the Dáil:

> We try to run the station with skeleton material, and we cannot do it. We are merely working from day to day. To talk of great variety, to think out necessary schemes, to get the imagination in full play, is out of the question. Until such time as we have established a staff that will enable us to strike out in new directions, we will not be able to do anything.[92]

Walsh had clearly moved a considerable distance from the day when he had mocked the idea of 'a Director and an Announcer, and all their hangers-on'. He now envisaged an extension of broadcasting hours within three or four months from the present three hours per night to four-and-a-half hours, with a schools programme, children's programming and language classes, plus twice-weekly relays from the BBC at a cost of £14–15 per hour, and the introduction of Stock Exchange reports in the daytime.[93] 'We intend to extend slowly and to pick our steps carefully; in other words, we will not take on anything that we may have to recede from'.[94]

Ironically, he spoke on the day (28 January 1926) on which Ernest Blythe apologetically moved the retrospective approval of expenditure of £14,885 which had been incurred in the erection and installation of the broadcasting station.[95] The staffing level at that stage was already eighteen (of whom the Music Director and Announcer were part-time but were in fact working a twelve-hour day) and the additional appointment of an assistant Director and a 'Woman Organiser' was envisaged.[96] Once again, the inconsistencies on Walsh's part must be noted: 'the staff we have at present is not adequate for the purpose and must be increased, regardless of cost. I had no doubt about that fact myself for some time past, since I became acquainted with the conditions in other broadcasting stations'.[97] It is thus also obvious that at the time Walsh had proposed the IBC-led broadcasting station, he had *not* been 'acquainted' with such conditions.

The attitude of the administration itself remained an inhibiting factor in Clandillon's experience, however. During the heated exchanges between J.J.

---

91 Ibid. p. 27. **92** DD 14, 28 January 1926, col. 296. **93** Ibid. cols. 272–3. **94** Ibid. cols. 271–2. **95** Ibid. cols. 267–8. **96** Ibid. col. 268. In the event, a lengthy and acrimonious debate took place in the Dáil, largely sustained by Thomas Johnson and Bryan Cooper with Ernest Blythe as their adversary, when Blythe refused to appoint a married woman to the post in contravention of the Civil Service regulations (DD 15, 27 May 1926, cols. 2345–74). **97** Ibid. col. 270. Walsh mentioned (col. 271) that the staff at the Manchester station, with which 2RN was comparable, numbered 53.

Walsh and his critics in the debate on the Wireless Report, he had passed some scathing remarks on the proposed Advisory Board to assist the Director in preparing schedules, returning to his old argument about the popular desire for 'entertainment' or 'amusement' rather than 'improvement'.

> In England, when the Broadcasting Committees decided to get out on educational matters, they were overwhelmed with protests from the public ... They were told, for instance, that they did not need to be lectured on hygiene or the care of children or the care of fowl, or anything like that. They paid their money for concerts, and concerts only.[98]

In fact, Reith's book *Broadcast over Britain*, published later that year, showed that educational broadcasting was by no means an unreservedly popular choice although Reith does seem to suggest that he himself continued to see a justification for it:

> There has been a certain, but comparatively slight, amount of opposition to the Company's educational activities. We have been informed that people have no desire to be educated, and that in any case it is no function of ours to assume responsibilities of this order.[99]

Bryan Cooper was quick to point out that 'an Advisory Board is not a new thing in connection with Government'[100] – the Departments of Agriculture and Fisheries both consulted them. The concept was one of 'arm's length' and Cooper was a shrewd commentator on the possible fall-out of direct control:

> Another reason why I rather mistrust the Postmaster-General's censorship is because he declared before the Committee he would not allow any racing news and information. *Mr* J.J. Walsh has an absolute right to that attitude, but I am not quite sure that *Deputy* J.J. Walsh, who represents a large number of people in Cork who are interested in racing news, is entitled to take such a strong line ... The Postmaster-General on this matter has expressed what I know is a genuine desire to protect us from foreign propaganda. I am willing to go with him to a great extent; I would much sooner see genuine Irish propaganda, and see on the Advisory Board such people as the Minister for Education, Dr Larchét [*sic*], and Colonel Brasé [*sic*], the Director of the Army

98 DD 6, 3 April 1924, col. 2878; cf. Scannell and Cardiff, op. cit. chapter 8, 'Forms of Talk', for an account of the rise and fall in the fortunes of radio talks at the BBC. 99 J.C.W. Reith, *Broadcast over Britain* p. 148. 100 DD 6, 3 April 1924, col. 2885.

School of Music. They would give us the kind of entertainment that the Irish people would need.[101]

(Considering the political and cultural climate which favoured the indigenous Irish, it is amusing to see Cooper proposing the inclusion of a Huguenot descendant [Larchet] and a Prussian [Brase] on a Board intended to give the Irish people what they needed.) Another contributor to the Wireless Committee, Prof. F.E. Hackett, had given similar advice, advocating that experts such as the committee of the Feis Ceoil and the music committee of the RDS, 'with a fine ideal of public service',[102] should be included.

Paddy Clarke records that the Irish Agricultural Organisation Society asked 'that a broadcasting advisory committee be established, representative of the various interests in the country, including the agricultural and co-operative sectors', aiming for a twenty-minute programme on three evenings each week, and 'strongly support[ing] the suggestion that every village hall should have a ... valve receiver with loudspeaker'.[103]

All this was to rebound against the Minister since now, two years later, when 2RN was already on the air, Cooper raised the matter again, asking 'whether it was proposed to appoint an Advisory Committee to assist in framing the programmes of the Dublin Wireless Broadcasting Station, and, if so, whether [the Minister] is in a position to give the names of such Committee', to be told by Walsh that the upcoming Wireless Telegraphy Bill 'contains provision for the setting up of an Advisory Committee' which would include nominees of the Ministers for Education and Agriculture.[104]

In the interim, the departmental attitude to the question of an Advisory Committee, if not its mind, appears to have changed. A departmental note from P.S. O'Hegarty to Walsh commending the programme for the opening night of 2RN suggested that 'for later programmes an occasional talk or lecture will be advisable, but that aspect of the programmes will be more effectively tackled when the Advisory Cttee is established in the New Year'.[105] Walsh does not appear to have disagreed. On 28 January 1926 Bryan Cooper returned to the question of the Advisory Board, suggesting the inclusion of representatives of the universities, the Gaelic League and the RDS.[106] It would not require the anticipated legislation for the Minister to establish a consultative committee. Walsh could hardly disagree, but he made it clear that he did not want one, and was cruelly but appositely heckled:

---

101 Ibid. cols. 2885–6.   **102** *Report* para. 2968.   **103** P. Clarke, *Dublin Calling* p. 50.   **104** DD 14, 27 January 1926, col. 98.   **105** O'Hegarty to Walsh, 22 December 1925, departmental file 711/53 (RTÉ Archives).   **106** DD 14, 28 January 1926 col. 282.

— I see no objection to the early setting up of an advisory committee, none whatever, but I am not quite so enthusiastic about the idea as Deputy Cooper. It might happen that a committee of this kind would very seriously impede the work of the station. It might consist of a dozen, and the station may have to face a dozen extra obstacles every day. My experience in life is that the one-man show and the one-man direction usually beats the combination –

Deputy Magennis — Mussolini.

Deputy T. O'Connell [Galway] — Cumann na nGaedheal.

— If you want success you must have a central directing force without interference from a party of people who may choose to intrude their particular ideas. It may happen that in extending this experiment to our system here, we may be taking a step in the wrong direction, and one that may have to be discontinued. It has not been tried anywhere else so far as I am aware. I am, however, prepared to try it, because there are apparently so many well informed backers for the idea and I am not prepared to insist on my own ideas prevailing. But I do say again that I do not look upon it enthusiastically, nor do those in charge of the station; they fear the idea.[107]

Both the *Irish Radio Journal* and the *Irish Radio Review* strongly disagreed,[108] and on 8 March the *Evening Herald* said categorically that 'the establishment of an advisory committee ... seems to be the only remedy to bring about change for the better. This ... should be selected from the cultural and scientific classes'.[109] In September the *Irish Radio Journal* returned to the point, which clearly concerned Walsh's insistence on overall control: 'Unity of control need not be impaired by the presence of a knowledgeable representative body available in a consultative capacity'.[110]

Two months later, as the Dáil was debating the Wireless Telegraphy Bill (Section 19 of which related to the establishment of an Advisory Committee of five, two of whom were to represent the Departments of Agriculture and Education), Walsh was able to announce that a committee of eighteen was already in existence 'and it is a good committee ... likely to carry its weight and to be very helpful'.[111] Walsh was unwilling, however, to grant any membership of this committee to designated bodies: 'That would open up a great many difficulties ... We have no assurance that the rules and regulations governing particular societies are those with which we could find ourselves in full concurrence'.[112]

---

107 Ibid. cols. 296–7.   **108** *Irish Radio Journal* 13 February 1926; *Irish Radio Review* February 1926.
109 *Evening Herald* 8 March 1926.   **110** *Irish Radio Journal* 18 September 1926.   **111** DD 17, 30 November 1926, col. 350.   **112** Ibid.

In November 1929, after Ernest Blythe had taken over the additional port-folio of Posts and Telegraphs, his Parliamentary Secretary, Michael Heffernan,[113] was able to tell Cooper that the Committee had met eight times that year, and had made fifteen recommendations, almost all of which had been effected.[114]

However, the history of such committees was never as intended. As Maurice Gorham put it, the Committee 'had virtually ceased to exist in 1933' and thenceforth 'the Minister's statutory obligation to have such a committee … was formally fulfilled by appointing only the official members [of the relevant departments] with no outside members at all';[115] he has pointed further-more to the reluctance of Joseph Connolly (Minister in the incoming Fianna Fáil administration in 1932) and his successor Gerald Boland, to have anything to do with the Advisory Committee appointed to help in shaping the service.[116]

The debate on the establishment of 2RN at the end of 1926 brought out the nature of the difficulties faced by the administration. On one point during this debate Thomas Johnson took the Minister to task. 2RN (or rather the Post Office) had advertised the part-time position of news assistant, at a salary of £5–6 per week for a married man, £4–5 per week for an unmarried man or woman.[117] The job specification required the assistant to take notes of proceedings of the Dáil and Seanad and prepare summaries; to gather reports from the police and fire brigades; to obtain particulars of outstanding events from cultural and sporting organisations; and to edit these into a news bulletin, incorporating information (which would be supplied by the Department) on stock market and agricultural reports, and foreign and provincial news. Johnson made sarcastic use of these duties, suggesting that the assistant could hardly carry out all of them simultaneously:

> On the face of it, to any observer, however casual, it must be evident that it is not a part-time job. It is probably intended that it shall be a job for a man and his wife and his aunts and uncles, particularly the aunts who can ferret around for information … To judge by the tendency expressed in this advertisement, the object is to get the cheapest type, the poorest quality of State servant you can get … Nobody of quality or experience would pretend to do this work at the salary … These

113 Heffernan was now Chairman of the Farmers' Party.   114 DD 32, 6 November 1929, col. 706.
115 M. Gorham, op. cit. p. 140; A. Briggs *The Birth of Broadcasting* p. 225 indicates that the board envis-aged for the BBC suffered a similar fate, although (ibid. pp. 219ff.) programming committees did succeed in influencing policy.   116 M. Gorham, op. cit. pp. 82–3.   117 Women (with notable excep-tions – see above pp. 142, 154) were obliged to resign from the Civil Service upon marriage. The salary was thus equivalent to £260–312 per annum (married) or £208–260 (unmarried), or £5200–6240/£4160–5200 at 2000 values; €6500–7800/5200–6500.

things cannot be done by any individual person in this country ... The job is the job of an experienced newspaper-man who has knowledge of editing, a knowledge of the gathering of news, together with knowledge of precis writing and typewriting. Such a person in the employment of a newspaper would be paid probably double the salary, and the effect of this proposition is to do what has been done in other Departments of the public service, generally to depreciate the rates of pay ... This particular advertisement ... is entirely unworthy of any State service, and particularly one which is the subject of so much – I was going to say boastful – talk from the Minister this afternoon as to its quality, its value, and the kind of service it is rendering.[118]

In this he was supported by William Norton who was to succeed him as Labour leader in 1932: 'I think the House will unanimously come to one conclusion, and that is, that the Minister ... is at least a good judge of value'.[119] Walsh was able for once to see the irony of the situation and to respond in similar fashion:

One would imagine we had in mind the roping in of some defenceless citizen, some poor reporter out of work and hard hit, to drag the last ounce of life and energy out of him in the interest of the State and that we are, in fact, requiring him to do the job of a superman for a menial wage ... Before we can walk we have got to creep, and in employing a reporter on a part-time job we are embarking on the creeping stage ... We do not suggest for one moment that the reporter should cover that entire field. We say: 'There is the field that you may cover. You can cover one-tenth, or one-fifth, or one-third'.[120]

This was an example of experience getting the better of aspirations. Walsh had stated in December 1925 that 'the news service we propose to make second to none, and how much this will be appreciated by our country people will be understood when it is remembered that they are insatiable gluttons for news'.[121] Although there was a regular news service, staff shortages meant that much of it was poached from the BBC, ships in the area of Dublin Bay, and the Dublin newspapers (which printed the time of news transmissions only intermittently during 2RN's first year).[122]

Nevertheless, the prophetic words of Philip Sayers and others were being proved correct: during the debate on the Wireless Telegraphy Bill, deputy Wolfe could say 'all classes are now participating in wireless, and I am glad to see that it is going down to the very bottom',[123] and he was also able, in the

---

118 DD 17, 30 November 1926, cols. 360–5. **119** Ibid. col. 366. **120** Ibid. cols. 369–70. **121** Quoted in P. Clarke, *Dublin Calling* p. 50. **122** Cf. ibid. **123** DD 17, 30 November 1926, col. 353.

light of experience, to put practical, rather than the previously theoretical, points to the Minister:

> In my district a very considerable number of labourers have sets in their houses, and the amount of enjoyment and pleasure it gives to them, some of them tell me, is beyond description. But they all have their little grievances about it; a great many of them think that there is a little too much music that is above their comprehension in some cases, and that there might be lectures on subjects that would be useful to them, dealing with matters of agriculture, with which they are in daily contact … Another question which is very important to country people is this. At present the time signal and the weather forecast is given very late, at about 10.30. In the country districts it is the custom for the labouring classes to go to bed at about eight-thirty or nine, because they have to get up early. It would be a great advantage to them to have the weather forecast, the time signal, and all that kind of thing, given before the ordinary programme commences, instead of at 10.30 or later.[124]

And the Minister was able to state:

> Generally speaking, our programme is a good programme, and the proof of that is that we have received thousands of commendations in regard to it from people living in Great Britain. We have proof that a very considerable percentage of the listeners-in in Wales, Cumberland, Westmoreland, Lancashire, Yorkshire and the South of Scotland are regular listeners-in to the Dublin programme … We are very much inclined to depreciate the resources of our own land – very much inclined to see the long horns of the distant cow. If we had a little more respect for our own country and what it can produce, it would be all to the good. I think our programme is generally a good one and that, with the encouragement our artists are receiving, it will improve.[125]

Walsh revealed that he had invited the public to comment on the programme schedules and that 50% of responses had been favourable. Of the other half, 'some [were dissatisfied] because we had too much Irish, some because we had too little Irish and too much English; some because we taught German; some because we had not enough of jazz, and some because we had too much jazz'.[126] The reaction from the public was indeed mixed, but there was a notable series of complaints at the high level of Irish-language programming,

---

124 Ibid. col. 354.   **125** Ibid. cols. 358–9.   **126** Ibid.

which Walsh had arranged with the Gaelic League, and at the lack of variety and humour in the predominantly musical fare of 'violin solos, piano solos and traditional songs'.[127] Others, however, appreciated the 'unmistakable' Irish character of the schedule, which was 'like an oasis in a desert of tango and jazz from foreign stations'.[128]

Jazz was a subject which exercised the minds not only of music-lovers but also of many guardians of public morals in the 1920s and 30s, and was not merely a matter of listening but involved the issue of public association. Late-night dancing in foreign styles was seen as the chief danger to Irish society, with jazz as its main focus. Jazz – attributed to negroes and jews – was seen by the catholic church as a pagan danger to religion as well as to Irish indigenous traditions such as music and song. Irish music and jazz were polarised by the provincial press as symbolising on the one hand the character of Irish-Ireland and on the other the evils of cosmopolitan (and particularly English) culture.[129] Chief among the protagonists – who received messages of support from Douglas Hyde and Éamon de Valera – were the catholic clergy, the Gaelic League and some local authorities (seven county councils adopted the Gaelic League resolution urging the banning of jazz). Sligo Board of Health, for example, declared that jazz was contrary to the spirit of Christianity and Irish nationality.[130] Others questioned the right of the Gaelic League to make demands of the Minister for Posts and Telegraphs that he should ban jazz from 2RN. When the chief organiser of the campaign against jazz, Seán Óg Ó Ceallaigh, secretary of the Gaelic League, made an intemperate attack on the Minister for Finance, Seán MacEntee, Ó Ceallaigh's planned broadcast on 2RN, 'Irish Culture – its Decline' was dropped on the instructions of the broadcasting minister, Gerald Boland. The Gaelic League itself seems to have realised that the protection and promulgation of the Irish language was of more lasting concern than the issue of jazz (in 1931 it had called for equal airtime for Irish- and English-language programmes).[131] That there was a serious social problem, perceived in the phenomenon of the dance hall itself, was widely acknowledged, and led to the enactment of the Public Dance Halls Act 1935. As Michael Heffernan had pointed out at the beginning of 1926, 'one of the greatest problems that has to be faced in [country districts] is the provision of entertainment during the long winter nights. In recent years the people have broken out of bounds and insisted on getting entertainment. As a result, dancing goes on night after night'.[132] It was thus ironic that radio,

---

127 P. Clarke, *Dublin Calling* p. 48. 128 Ibid. 129 The subject is thoroughly addressed by Aidan M. Kennedy in an unpublished MA thesis (NUI/UCD) 1985, 'The dance hall and jazz music in Ireland 1925–1935' from which much of my information is derived. 130 *Irish Press* 26 January 1934, quoted in Kennedy, op. cit. p. 35. 131 *Irish Times* 8 April 1931, quoted in ibid. p. 45. 132 DD 14, 28 January 1926, cols. 289–90.

which might prove the means of bringing them in from the crossroads or the dance hall, should then be the medium by which their Irishness or their Christianity was subverted – not least because P.S. O'Hegarty had himself denounced jazz as leading to 'fatty degeneration of the morals, of the character, to inefficiency and extinction'.[133]

Members of the Dáil were not slow to make their opinions known to the Minister regarding relevant programming from a variety of viewpoints and interests. (We should recall that in 1924 Denis Gorey had warned of the need for vigilance: 'Recently we have had complaints about the harm the films have done. If we are not careful about broadcasting we will have the same complaints, and in addition to a film censor we will have to have a broadcasting censor ... The matter that will be transmitted should, in my opinion, be carefully revised from a moral and national standpoint. We do not want the minds of our youths contaminated with some of the stuff that the youths of other countries have been imbibing'.)[134] On 8 February 1927 Bryan Cooper sought assurances (which he received) that the rugby match between Ireland and England on the following Saturday would be broadcast.[135] Some deputies were concerned at the nature of advertising. On 14 November 1928 Barry Egan (Cork Borough)[136] complained about an advertisement for 'Royal Baking Powder' – had the Minister given permission to a foreign manufacturer to use an Irish State Service to advertise his wares, and what was the policy on advertising in general? Would he discontinue it in the case of foreign manufacturers competing with similar home-made articles? He was informed that 'the Department's policy is not to accept advertisements of foreign-made articles which are in competition with home-made articles. The Department was not aware that baking powder was manufactured in the Saorstát'.[137]

Advertisements were not in fact encouraged, although the kind of discrimination between indigenous and foreign goods and services in this case was reflected in the rates: £5 per five minutes for Irish companies, twice that amount for foreign companies.[138] Short advertisements as we know them today were not envisaged, although a one-guinea fee for short announcements of forthcoming functions was introduced: instead, the concept of a five-minute programme, which evolved into the 'sponsored programme', pioneered by the stations in Hilversum, Toulouse and Luxembourg, became a feature of radio in the 1940s, 50s and 60s. The Minister's announcement of such advertisements in fact described them as 'Lectures Advertising particular Irish Industries or

133 P.S. O'Hegarty op. cit. p.130.   **134** DD 6, 15 February 1924, cols. 1112–13.   **135** DD 18, 8 February 1927, col. 308.   **136** Barry Egan had been a member of the Cork Radio Company and a putative shareholder in Irish Developments Ltd.   **137** DD 27, 14 November 1928, col. 5. **138** Information on early advertising on 2RN is largely derived from Hugh Oram, *The Advertising Book: the History of Advertising in Ireland* (Dublin: MO Books, 1986) pp. 502–10. Additional information from Robert K. Savage, 'The Origins of Irish Radio', unpubl. MA thesis, UCD 1982.

National Concerns or Undertakings'.[139] In the first three months of 1927, advertising revenue amounted to a mere £200. In the whole of 1928 it attracted only £28 and in 1929 £50. It appears that P.S. O'Hegarty thought that advertisements should be allowed to die a natural death and Clandillon asserted that 'from a programme point of view they are a nuisance and are regarded by listeners as an impertinence'. The first sponsored programme, by Euthymol toothpaste, was transmitted on 31 December 1927. Thereafter, Independent Newspapers sponsored 'Slumber Hour', P.J. Carroll, makers of Sweet Afton cigarettes, sponsored 'Sweet Afton Varieties', 'The Savoy Minstrels' came from the Savoy Cocoa Company, and 'Rock Revellers' from the Blackrock Hosiery Company. Among the best-known and longest-running were the Irish Hospitals' Trust with its Sweepstake programme and 'The Walton's Programme' sponsored by the Dublin music shop of that name, which ran until 1981.

Comparisons between 2RN and the BBC were not necessarily appropriate, although their early experiences were similar: the BBC was a much larger organisation with access to much more extensive finance, but at its inception it was hardly more advanced than its Dublin counterpart. One tends to assume that, because it became the paragon of public service broadcasting, the BBC was born immutable and perfect. But, as Asa Briggs has documented it, its early history shows it to have encountered many questions similar to those of the fledgling 2RN. Even the question of *quality* was debatable: 'since "the policy of the Company was to bring the best of everything into the greatest number of homes", it followed naturally that genuine differences of opinion would be expressed about what constituted "the best" '.[140] In October 1924, two years after it started transmission, the BBC discovered that although radio talks had been generally favoured, with one quarter of programming consisting of speech, 'there are a few listeners who resent anything but Music Hall';[141] and 'political broadcasts and debates were always highly suspect'.[142] In April 1923 the British PMG had told Parliament that 'it is undesirable that the Broadcasting service should be used for the dissemination of speeches on controversial matters'.[143] Above all, it comes as a surprise to note, as Briggs informs us, that as late as the end of 1925 'the question of programme policy had never been considered by the Board'.[144]

With the opening up of a discussion of 2RN's programming we can also see the beginning of an articulation of what has come to be known as 'public service broadcasting'. In May 1928 Seán T. O'Kelly said during a Dáil debate:

---

139 15 April 1926, quoted in M. Gorham, *Forty Years*, p. 55.   **140** A. Briggs, *The Birth of Broadcasting*, p. 218.   **141** Ibid. p. 235.   **142** Ibid. p. 245.   **143** Ibid. pp. 154–5.   **144** Ibid. p. 352.

> Wireless is not a subject that interests me very specially, but, in
> common with everybody else, I have quite a number of friends who
> take a keen interest in it. Possibly because most of my friends are
> people with Irish-Ireland ideas, I hear a good deal of their criticism of
> the programmes broadcasted [*sic*] from the Dublin Station. I must say
> that generally they seem to be well pleased with the programme ... so
> far as it affects Irish-Ireland.[145]

In reply, Michael Heffernan (Parliamentary Secretary), while adopting the
same cautious approach to finance which had characterised the speeches of J.J.
Walsh, nevertheless pushed the concept of public service – and the consensus
on which it depended – into new territory:

> We are endeavouring, with very limited finances, with a comparatively
> small amount spent on programmes, to compete with other institu-
> tions, such as the British Broadcasting Corporation, which has an enor-
> mous fund at its disposal.[146]

Drawing attention to several operatic concerts, symphony concerts and a
performance of Haydn's *Creation*, and announcing the intention of using the
Army and Garda bands more often, he gave an example of the way in which
the Department might respond to public opinion:

> Our policy so far has been not to broadcast racing results.[147] It was
> considered undesirable to do so ... It is a matter which may have to be
> reconsidered ... We will have to get some idea of what public opinion
> generally is on the matter.[148]

Referring to the broadcasting of 'certain matters of general public interest'
Heffernan said:

> We have a policy in that regard. In that matter ... we gave the lead to
> the BBC by broadcasting matters which might be regarded as contro-
> versial to a certain extent. We broadcast a very interesting debate on
> 'Free Trade and Protection' some time ago from the Dublin Chamber
> of Commerce in which Deputy Lemass took part. If broadcasting is to
> be made interesting that is a policy we must continue and extend, but
> with considerable reservations and care. There are certain forms of

---

145 DD 23, 11 May 1928, col. 1300.   **146** Ibid. col. 1305.   **147** J.J. Walsh had spoken to the
Wireless Committee of his absolute refusal to allow this: *Report* para. 393–4: 'I consider racing to be the
deadliest element in the life of this country'.   **148** DD 23, 11 May 1928, col. 1306.

controversial matter which would probably be considered undesirable, but if we ever get hold of interesting controversies in which leading public men take part it is part of our future policy to see that such items are given to the public.[149]

In 1926 the Minister asked the Executive Council if the Budget debate could be broadcast 'on the grounds that it would greatly stimulate interest in the proceedings of the Oireachtas'.[150] The Executive Council in rejecting the application was 'of the opinion that such a course would not be desirable'. This, we can assume, was part of the impeding of democratic discourse, as Prager calls it,[151] and explains the almost total absence of current affairs broadcasting until the advent of television. It is also possible that this restriction contributed to, rather than prevented, the establishment of a stable democratic order. On one occasion Oliver St. John Gogarty delivered an impromptu talk which was considered improper: Nancy Bergin, who was secretary to seven successive Directors of Broadcasting, recalls that it was adjudged 'highly dangerous' for a broadcaster to speak without a written script[152] – a practice which was mandatory at the BBC. (The fact that broadcasting of Oireachtas proceedings did not materialise until 1986 indicates the measure of distrust which legislators had for the radio medium which they controlled, and the distance they wished to set between themselves and the public.)

It should not, however, be assumed that the Irish situation was unique. In Britain, too, as Asa Briggs puts it, 'political broadcasts and debates were always highly suspect'.[153] Britain, we should remind ourselves, was not itself a stable democracy during this period: the General Strike of 1926 had been a political crisis in which the BBC had had to establish a policy in regard to representation,[154] and the prevailing political and economic climate of the Depression, followed by the crisis caused by the abdication of Edward VIII, gave rise to civil unrest and social division which was immediately succeeded by wartime restrictions.[155] Reith had argued that broadcasting political speeches was 'in the national interest' and that by banning them 'the utility of broadcasting as a medium of enlightenment is prejudiced'.[156] In fact in the same month as Walsh's request to the Executive Council, Reith had asked the British PMG for permission to broadcast the Chancellor's budget arguments with a reply from the Opposition, but was refused without any reason being given. In the

---

149 Ibid. cols. 1306–7.   150 Letter of Clerk of the Dáil to Secretary of the Executive Council 23 March 1926, SPO S/7/321 (National Archives).   151 J. Prager op. cit. pp. 21–2.   152 RTÉ Sound Archives tape B 76.   153 A. Briggs, *The Birth of Broadcasting*, p. 245.   154 Cf. ibid. pp. 329–51.   155 Cf. Scannell and Cardiff op. cit. p. 32: '[The General Strike] focused the attention of everyone ... on the importance of radio. For the Government it showed the importance of radio as *the* means of controlling public opinion during a crisis. For Labour and the trade union movement it established a deep-seated suspicion of the bias of the BBC in favour of the powers that be'.   156 Ibid.

margin of the rejection letter Reith wrote: 'Isn't it absurd? What can we do by way of agitation?'[157]

One prominent broadcaster on 2RN was Sidney Czira, who wrote and broadcast under the pseudonym 'John Brennan'. Born Sidney Gifford, she was the sister of Grace Gifford who had married Joseph Mary Plunkett the night before his execution in 1916, and of Muriel Gifford who was the wife of the executed Thomas McDonagh.[158] She said of her family 'half became socialists … the other half went to Sinn Féin'.[159] In July 1927 she publicly impugned the government in a letter to the *Irish Times*. Her letter had referred to the fact that a Senate speech on the assassination of Kevin O'Higgins had mentioned the Irish Volunteers; some of the men awaiting trial for the murder were known to have been in the Volunteers, and thus the speech could be construed as prejudicing their trial. The matter might today be considered as a straight-forward one of civil liberty, but in the context of the time, and given Czira's own background, one can appreciate that any utterance on such a delicate matter would be regarded as controversial. The fact that her broadcasts had been concerned with traditional music might also be regarded today as innocuous; in 1927 it was an integral if subliminal part of national recon-struction. She was immediately removed from the airwaves by the Minister. Although (when the matter was raised in the Dáil the following May by Seán T. O'Kelly),[160] the Parliamentary Secretary, Michael Heffernan, undertook to consider her reinstatement,[161] it was not until 1932, following Fianna Fáil's electoral victory, that the ban was rescinded by Senator Joseph Connolly, who had been appointed Minister for Posts and Telegraphs.[162]

The most serious incident in early political broadcasting occurred in June 1927 when, after the General Election (in which Cumann na nGaedheal won 46 seats, with Fianna Fáil taking 44 and the balance held by Independents, Farmers and Labour), 2RN informed its listeners that Cumann na nGaedheal would not form a government either alone or in coalition:

> Information elicited from the Cumann na nGaedheal (Government
> Party) headquarters indicates strong opposition on the part of

157 Ibid. p. 244.   **158** Another sister, Mrs Gifford Wilson, was an unsuccessful applicant for the posi-tion of Woman Organiser at 2RN.   **159** Henry Boylan (ed.), *A Dictionary of Irish Biography* (Dublin: Gill and Macmillan, 1998 3rd edn.) p. 92.   **160** 'If people's political opinions are to be suppressed in this fashion, and their employment taken from them merely because they have the courage to express opinions not accepted by those in authority, and for no other reason, I think that is something one ought not to stand for. I do not know exactly what the political opinions of this lady are. I have an idea her opinions are not exactly the same as mine, but I know she has for a number of years given good service to the cause which eventuated to my regret in the setting up of this Free State. She gave good service in the early days of the movement'. DD 23, 11 May 1928, cols. 1301–2.   **161** Ibid. col. 1311.   **162** M. Gorham, *Forty Years.*, pp. 59–60. Gorham adds: 'the case forms an interesting anticipation of the Noel Hartnett case, which attracted much more attention when it occurred in 1946' – the case is outside the period with which this volume is concerned, but see Gorham pp. 154–6.

prominent members to any participation by Cumann na nGaedheal in a Government under existing circumstances. Under no conditions whatever will the idea of a coalition with any other element be considered ... The persistent demand for opposition to the late Government has now resulted in all opposition and no Government and Cumann na nGaedheal members see no reason why they should rescue the country from the position it has deliberately created.[163]

Neither Cosgrave nor Kevin O'Higgins would confirm or deny the authenticity of the statement, but the *Irish Times* – in an article headed 'Politics by Wireless' –understood that 'there was no authority for the announcement'.[164]

Two days later, the station announcer (Séamus Hughes) stated that the announcement had not been an official communique from Cumann na nGaedheal, 'but merely the result of investigations made in the ordinary way by the station's news correspondent on his own responsibility and without any intention that it was to be taken as an authorised expression of the Government's attitude'.[165] In order to cover up what the *Irish Times* called 'an indiscretion', 2RN then issued a statement by Éamon de Valera urging the removal of the oath so as to allow Fianna Fáil to enter the Dáil and thus, presumably, give effect to the electoral pact with Labour.

The *Irish Times* coverage continued:

> There may be some ground for the belief that opinion in the Cabinet is hardening against the idea of carrying on on 'terms' ... Cumann na nGaedheal probably now has less to gain from a second general election within a few months than any of the other political parties. Financially, it is in the poorest possible state to contest an immediate election, and even if its coffers were amply served, it could hardly be certain of better treatment from the second electorate.[166]

Maurice Gorham sustains the view that the announcement came from J.J. Walsh personally.[167] In this case, it is almost certain that Séamus Hughes was involved in it. The incident smacks of the kind of outburst of which Walsh was capable, and we are entitled to ask how a political crisis, with 2RN at its centre, was avoided. It is another episode in the history of the stabilisation of Irish politics which has yet to be explained.[168]

The end of the beginning of 2RN came two months later on the brink of the election predicted by the *Irish Times* when, on 29 August 1927, Walsh, with his family, without giving any notice, took the mailboat to France. His

---

163 *Irish Times* 21 June 1927.　**164** Ibid.　**165** Ibid.　**166** Ibid.　**167** M. Gorham, *Forty Years* p. 46.
168 Cf. J. Regan, op. cit. pp. 275, 308.

political career was over, and the man who had so strongly but strangely presided over the creation of this vehicle for 'propaganda' returned to private life, disillusioned and exhausted.

With the exception of folk music, in which it is generally agreed that the service has consistently excelled, the aspirations voiced in Darrell Figgis' essay on 'Irish Nationality' (above, p. 31) were seldom apparent in the 2RN schedules. Indeed, it can be argued that in some senses the radio programmes went counter to those aspirations, since there was little overt evidence of 'nation-building' by means of 'programme-building', and the heavy emphasis on traditional music tended to obscure developments in other areas. But conversely, there was tangible evidence of progress in the presentation of classical music, and in two areas, those of women's programmes (introduced in 1927) and of sports commentaries (which started in 1926)[169] the service was ahead of its time – as Michael Heffernan proudly stated in 1928, 'in that regard I believe we were ahead of the BBC. We gave the lead'.[170] No doubt Walsh was gratified that in 1928 2RN broadcast from the Tailteann Games, and that 1930 saw the first sports magazine pogramme.

It is likely that what began as being thought of as 'entertainment' came closer to embodying the Reithian concept of a cultural model. Having so great an experience of Irish traditional music in recent decades (and its permanent presence in our 'race-consciousness') and its huge international impact, we are apt to discount the significance of such music when it was heard, perhaps in the case of city dwellers, for the first time through the medium of radio. As Richard Hayward, an Ulsterman who had broadcast from BBC Belfast, wrote in the *Irish Radio Journal*, 'the regular transmission of a song or a play in the national language will be a powerful factor in the creation of a national being'.[171] One feature of broadcasting was that it introduced the variety of regional accents and of the variants in the Irish spoken in the different provinces. Songs – both accompanied and *sean nós* – and instrumental playing from different traditions and styles became widely known in many cases for the first time.

We have seen the Wireless Committee's reference to 'an Irish taste', and Hyde's insistence on the integrity of a nation inhering in its language, culture, music and sport. The early years of 2RN may well be regarded as bearing out

---

169 The first broadcast in Europe of a field game occurred on 29 August 1926, when P. D. Mehigan, who used the pseudonym 'Carbery', commentated the All-Ireland Hurling Semi-Final between Kilkenny and Galway at Croke Park (Kilkenny won by a margin of 6–2 to 5–1), P. Clarke, *Dublin Calling* p. 56. Mehigan had been in the Cork GAA organised by J. J. Walsh (Walsh, *Recollections* p. 19) and was succeeded in 1933 by another Corkonian who had been an anti-treatyite, Éamonn de Barra. The BBC broadcast its first field game (rugby) on 15 January 1927. **170** DD 23, 11 May 1928, col. 1306. **171** *Irish Radio Journal* vol. 2, no. 23, 16 November 1925.

the Committee's pursuit, as it was expressed by Pádraic Ó Máille, of 'national interests' *via* the medium of radio programming: bringing Irish music, sports and language to its audiences, yet also embracing other forms of music, other sports and languages.

Scannell and Cardiff discuss in their *Social History of British Broadcasting* the role of the incipient BBC in 'corporate national life' and in creating a sense of 'we-feeling' through portrayals of national events and, from 1932, Christmas Day speeches by the King.[172] In Ireland, approximately simultaneously, the radio service helped to bring together an 'Irish-Ireland' as a collective consciousness (and to stimulate a debate on that consciousness) without offending other cultures. Éamon de Valera's address on the occasion of the Eucharistic Congress may well have been Ireland's equivalent to the King's speech at the 1924 Empire Exhibition, and the presidential broadcasts on St Patrick's day were equivalent to the royal addresses at Christmas.

J.J. Walsh's retrospective consideration is instructive: even though he had witnessed the growth of Radio Éireann under the State control which he had so reluctantly put in place, he could say in 1944 'Even now, after a generation of experience, it is hard to say whether private or public control is the better way'.[173] Ironically, however, given that his strongly argued policy of providing separate facilities for Irish-language broadcasting had fallen on deaf ears, he also said:

> It must be conceded that, from the standpoint of national policy, such as the use of the Irish language and the introduction and maintenance of a strong Gaelic bias, it is better that the Station should be under public direction.[174]

Walsh had remained unrepentant on this issue, and saw his exclusionist policy as a success and a justification:

> Only in one respect did we succeed at least to the satisfaction of those who stood for Irish Culture in that we resolutely refused to admit the broadcasting of foreign games. Wherever and whenever Irish language, history, and general national characteristics have been featured, there was no hesitation in doing so.[175]

While the first year's transmissions may have been lacklustre, 1927 saw a major advance with the appointment of Maighréad Ní Ghráda – herself an

---

172 Cf. Scannell and Cardiff op. cit. pp. 277, 281, 288, 292.   173 J.J. Walsh, *Recollections*, p. 67.
174 Ibid.   175 Ibid. Walsh had obviously overlooked the issue of rugby matches.

Irish-language playwright and a former secretary to Ernest Blythe – whose remit included radio drama. She was responsible for producing an Irish-language version of Sophocles' *Antigone* on 3 April 1927 performed in an Outside Broadcast by students at St Patrick's College, Maynooth. Maighréad Ní Ghráda was able to attract actors of the calibre of F.J. McCormick and Sara Allgood to the fledgling service, thus bringing the resources of the Abbey (National) Theatre to the airwaves. 1927 also saw 2RN achieving a world-class 'scoop' (reminiscent of the Alcock and Brown landing in 1919) when it reported the sighting over Co. Kerry of Charles Lindbergh during the first solo transatlantic flight.

Parallel to the gradual increase in the size of the station orchestra was a somewhat controversial development in the encouragement of the céilí band – controversial because of the debated authenticity of the genre as a formal institution. Séamus Clandillon has been widely but erroneously credited with the 'invention' of the céilí band, which had in fact existed in one form or another since at least the late 1890s, and which can be documented defini-tively to 1918.[176] However, both Clandillon and (we may find it surprising)[177] Vincent O'Brien set themselves to stimulate the genre in order to have a vari-ety of traditional musical styles available to radio. The first to broadcast was the Dick Smyth Céilí Trio (Dick Smyth, fiddle; Tommy Breen, flute; Charlie Byrne, piano) who remained as a broadcasting group for five or six years. Clandillon also encouraged the Siamsa Gael Céilí Band (established by piper Leo Rowsome and pianist Leo Molloy under the auspices of the Garda Siochána)[178] by bringing them to London to make commercial recordings. In addition, a large number of solo performers of traditional music appeared from the start of 2RN, such as one of its first-night débutants, Liam Andrews; other pipers included Liam Breathnach and, slightly later, Seán Dempsey, who was to play at the World Folk Dance and Music Festival during the Berlin Olympics in 1936.

In stirring the Gaelic sentiment Walsh would have had the positive support of Clandillon, but there is, however, evidence that Clandillon's hands had been tied, mainly but not entirely, by the Department, where O'Hegarty, who had personal animosity towards Clandillon, reigned at least up to 1932. After only a few months, in September 1926, he asked to return to his old job as a health inspector, perhaps disillusioned not only by the meagre resources but by the hostile reaction to his brand of programming. In 1934, just before the Fianna Fáil government ousted Clandillon from the directorship, a BBC observer said:

---

176 Cf. F. Vallely, op. cit. pp. 60–4. **177** O'Brien's interest in céilí bands is discussed by Cormac McGinley in RTÉ Sound Archives tape 32/68C. **178** According to the recollection of Cormac McGinley (ibid.) who in 1966 mentioned Supt. Delaney of the Garda Band in this connection.

Clandillon seems to have attempted to keep broadcasting ... on the detached public service basis which we have adopted in this country but he has not had an easy time. As for the general position of broadcasting in the Free State, things seem to be pretty hopeless. They have got approximately 54,000 licensed listeners in a population of 3,000,000 ... Governmental control obviously makes for an unimaginative rigidity. For example, fees, of over three guineas have to be covered with the Secretary of the GPO and fees of over seven guineas with the Ministry of Finance ... Altogether the outlook is depressing. Clandillon has obviously for years chafed under an official clamp-down of initiative. There seems to be practically no desire to make broadcasting more popular or better equipped to take its rightful place as a public service.[179]

Clandillon's position, as León Ó Broin saw it, was hopeless: 'he struggled without successs to break away from the financial and staffing constraints ... and he found the continuous parliamentary criticism of the station's standards irksome'.[180] Clandillon's personal situation cannot have been helped by his failure to obtain a judgement in a libel action which he took against the *Irish Statesman* which had published a scathing review of his book *Songs of the Irish Gaels* by Donal O'Sullivan, then Clerk of the Seanad. The defendant's costs, amounting to £2,500, contributed to the closure of the *Irish Statesman*[181] and presumably Clandillon's own costs were comparable. Ó Broin recalls that 'when I last saw him, he was telling a porter at the Henry Street entrance to the GPO, in a voice loud enough to be overheard, how badly he had been treated'.[182]

Clandillon, under pressure, took sick leave and then received instructions to return to his former employment. The Government, after an interim which saw yet another interview board unable to agree on an appointment, transferred Dr T.J. Kiernan from the Department of External Affairs who was to hold the post for six years and to usher 2RN, under its new name, Radio Éireann, into a new era.

CONCLUSION

The period 1927–36 was one of both advance and retrenchment in Irish radio. The service expanded significantly in 1927 with the opening of a sister station

---

179 BBC Archives EI/947, quoted by Rex Cathcart in 'Broadcasting – the Early Decades' p. 44. **180** L. Ó Broin, op. cit. p. 168. **181** Although George O'Brien (J. Meehan, *George O'Brien* p. 110) points out that the financial support for the paper during the libel action contributed a surplus which actually prolonged rather than shortened its life. **182** L. Ó Broin, op. cit. p. 168.

in Cork (6CK) under the direction of Seán Neeson.[183] Cork had supplied some programmes to 2RN, including an entire evening relayed from the Cork School of Music (with which 6CK and its successors were to share premises for four decades from 1958). Initially 6CK was housed in the former Women's Gaol in Sunday's Well (today the home of the Irish Broadcasting Museum) and opened by J.J. Walsh on 26 April 1927. Cork provided up to one-sixth of 2RN's programmes until September 1930, when it became simply a relay station and remained so up to 1958.

León Ó Broin's view was that

> Irish broadcdasting ... spent its early years under the worst possible auspices – a department that didn't want the control of it, a Parliamentary Secretary, Heffernan, a Farmers' man, whose sole concern was to cut government demands on the farming community, and a Minister who happened also to be at the time Minister of the economy-conscious Department of Finance – Ernest Blythe.[184]

Later, as Roibeárd Ó Faracháin, who joined Radio Éireann in 1939 and became Controller of Radio Programmes in 1953, observed, Seán Lemass displayed open contempt for the radio service, saying to the then Minister, P.J. Little, 'How's the hurdy-gurdy?'[185]

From 1926, it had been the Minister's intention to set up a high-power station, similar to the BBC's major installation at Daventry, in the midlands near Athlone. Cost factors prevented this until 1932, when test broadcasts from 22 to 26 June were undertaken in order to carry the proceedings of the Eucharistic Congress in Dublin. This was one of the most important events in the consolidation of the democratic consensus under the newly elected Fianna Fáil government, and one of the first to demonstrate the power of radio to carry the papal messages, and their implications, into thousands of homes – by this stage over 30,000 licences had been issued.[186]

Joseph Lee has said that the Congress gave de Valera 'a timely opportunity to baptize his synthesis of republicanism and Catholicism'.[187] In 1921 de Valera had told the Dáil that he saw himself as 'a sort of connecting link' between the fundamentally opposed sides of Irish politics, and that he saw his role to be 'to try and harmonize these two voices as far as possible ... I felt that the unity of these forces was absolutely essential for national success'.[188] That

---

183 Like Clandillon, Neeson also sang Irish songs during broadcasts.   184 RTÉ Sound Archives tape 1/76.   185 Ibid. Ó Faracháin also said that under the extended secretaryship (1927–53) at the Dept. of Finance of J. J. McElligott, broadcasting was regarded as 'frivolous'.   186 The Athlone station had a Marconi 100kw transmitter which at that stage was operating on reduced power at 60kw.   187 J.J. Lee, op. cit. p. 177.   188 *Debate on the Treaty* p. 272.

the Civil War took place was confirmation that the entrenched problems of Irish history, on which Darrell Figgis had dwelt four years previously, would not be solved so easily. But that de Valera could speak so positively and optimistically on a document and on a political situation which would prove to be as divisive as his attempted constitution the following year, was an indication that, in the terms discussed by Jeffrey Prager, he himself could, and would, eventually embody the seeds of partial reconciliation, in which Cosgrave's capitulation in 1932 was a vital factor.[189]

The Athlone station was officially opened by de Valera himself on 6 February 1933, when the 2RN transmitter was closed down. So great was the response from the owners of crystal sets in the Dublin area who found the Athlone signal unsatisfactory that 2RN was reinstated.

The personality of de Valera needed no radio service to have already permeated the Irish mind. Yet radio was a powerful medium by which he arrived, in person and metaphorically, in many Irish homes. Already, the same broadcast on 20 June 1927 which had carried the phantom announcement purporting to come from Cumann na nGaedheal also carried a statement by de Valera: ' realising that unity is essential for national progress, the immediate aim of the Fianna Fáil organisation has been to re-unite the national forces. The first step is to get all the elected representatives of the people into the same assembly'.[190] One of his first actions, on forming the first Fianna Fáil adminstration, was to broadcast to the USA on 4 March 1932.[191] His next radio appearance was to supplant Cosgrave with a St Patrick's Day message on 17 March 1932 in which he capitalised on the circumstances of victory:

> The fifteenth centenary anniversary of the coming of St Patrick, the year of the Eucharistic Congress, the recent election by the people of this State of the first Fianna Fáil Government, all combine to make this year's celebration of the National Festival one of unique interest in our history… I most earnestly appeal to all Irishmen at home and abroad to close their ranks and to march forward with us. Let our desire to work for our country be our common bond, and let us be content to vie with each other for the honour of serving Ireland.[192]

---

189 J. Regan (op. cit. p. 256) suggests that this capitulation was consciously recognised within Cumann na nGaedheal as early as 1925.   **190** This was reported by *The Irish Times* in the article headed 'Politics by Wireless' referred to above, pp. 170–1. Muiris Mac Conghail has commented: 'it was an interesting and new role for broadcasting that a statement, by the leader of the second largest party in the State, should be afforded such a status in the State's broadcasting service and particularly so in the circumstances in which that party was not then seated in the Dáil' – 'Politics by Wireless – News and Current Affairs on Radio 1926–2001', Thomas Davis Lecture broadcast Monday 30 April 2001, RTÉ Radio 1. **191** M. Moynihan (ed.), *Speeches of Éamon de Valera* (Dublin: Gill and Macmillan, 1982) pp. 191–3.   **192** Ibid. p. 193.

When it came to the opening of the high-powered Athlone station on 6 February 1933, de Valera referred to the installation as 'Droichead nua Átha Luain is ea é, droichead idir na Gaeil in Éirinn agus Gaeil na himirce' – the new bridge of Athlone, a bridge between the Irish at home and those of the diaspora – and went on in English in the terms of Robert Emmet and Douglas Hyde:

> it will enable the world to hear the voice of one of the oldest and, in many respects, one of the greatest of the nations. Ireland has much to seek from the rest of the world and much to give back in return, much that she alone can give. Her gifts are the fruit of special qualities of mind and heart ... The Irish genius has always stressed spiritual and intellectual rather than material values. That is the characteristic that fits the Irish people in a special manner for the task, now a vital one, of helping to save western civilisation.[193]

Six days later, he was again broadcasting to the USA on the theme 'Ireland Free, Gaelic and United'.[194] Political mastery of the airwaves, and a personal 'holding character' of some style, had arrived.

So too had radio as a social partner. Terry de Valera remembers that in 1928, when he was six years old, his elder brother Ruairí called him into the family home in Dublin's Serpentine Avenue to share the headphones on the crystal set (made by their uncle-in-law, Richard Cotter) to hear the singing voice of John McCormack, telling him 'that's the greatest tenor in the world'.[195] Brian Friel, in his autobiographical play *Dancing at Lughnasa* (set in 1936), makes the radio apparatus, known simply as 'Marconi' – 'because that was the name emblazoned on the set'[196] – one of the central features of the play; its temperamental behaviour, its heavy use of batteries ('the man in the shop says we go through these things quicker than anyone in Ballybeg'),[197] and the stringing of the aerial from house to tree, are valuable illustrations of the practical side of radio reception. More so is the narrator's recollection of childhood: 'I remember my first delight, indeed my awe, at the sheer magic of that radio. And when I remember the kitchen throbbing with the beat of Irish dance music beamed to us all the way from Dublin'.[198]

And, as I mentioned in my Preface, Seamus Heaney's childhood was permeated by similar sensations:

---

193 Ibid. pp. 231–3. **194** Ibid. pp. 233–5. **195** Personal communication to the author from Terry de Valera. **196** B. Friel, *Dancing at Lughnasa* (London: Faber and Faber, 1990) p. 1. **197** Ibid. p. 16. **198** Ibid. p. 2.

When a wind stirred in the beeches, it also stirred an aerial wire attached to the topmost branch of the chestnut tree. Down it swept, in through a hole bored in a corner of the kitchen window, right on into the innards of our wireless set where a little pandemonium of burbles and squeaks would suddenly give way to the voice of a BBC newsreader speaking out of the unexpected like a *deus ex machina*.[199]

The 'Emergency', which Heaney mentions as a particularly vivid radio experience in Northern Ireland, also played a part in keeping discourse alive in the Free State (shortly to become the Republic), where, as Seán MacRéamoinn remarked, otherwise 'we would have lapsed into the worst kind of village idiocy'.[200] The war also brought a new political and financial crisis in Ireland's relations with the United Kingdom, Northern Ireland, Germany and the rest of the world, in which, eventually, radio was to play an historic part in carrying de Valera's reply in May 1945 to Churchill's attack on Irish neutrality. Thereafter, there was no further risk of radio being considered lightly.

Radio had achieved the distinction of becoming both a communal, gregarious activity *via* the valve set and the loudspeaker, and an intimate, individual pursuit *via* the crystal set. More than any agency responsible for deciding its direction, it had introduced itself into the Irish home.

---

199 S. Heaney, *Crediting Poetry: the Nobel lecture* (Loughcrew: Gallery Press, 1995) pp. 9–10. **200** RTÉ Sound Archives tape 1/76.

The text of the White Paper on Wireless Broadcasting, 1923

The first question which the Post Office had to consider in regard to wireless broadcasting was whether it should be worked as a Post Office monopoly, and after a careful consideration of the matter I came to the conclusion that the business of arranging concerts and general entertainment programmes was not one which a State Department ought to undertake.

In America and elsewhere, where broadcasting has been conducted as a private enterprise, a multiplicity of Companies has been found to lead to chaos and confusion and to an inefficient service. All experience has proved that there must be unified control in broadcasting if the public are to get an efficient service. The conclusion come to, therefore, was that an Irish Broadcasting Company should be established, the main capital of which should be provided by the chief firms interested in the industry, and with access to membership of the Company by the smaller manufacturers and traders on taking a share in the Company. This gives unified control, while at the same time ruling out no manufacturer or dealer who is interested in the industry.

The next problem was the problem of revenue. In Great Britain the Broadcasting Company gets its revenue from two sources: (a) it receives a proportion of its licence fees; (b) it receives a fee on each piece of apparatus sold. But in actual practice both (a) and (b) lent themselves to a good deal of evasion, and while 170,000 licences had been issued in Great Britain, more than 200,000 people had themselves put apparatus together and were receiving the benefit of the Broadcasting Company's outlay while making no contribution thereto, until the Private Contributor's licence was recently introduced there. On the other hand the trader, who is supposed to pay a contribution on each piece of apparatus sold, very often does not and the Company is thus defrauded of its legitimate revenue.

In order to meet this situation here, it was thought advisable in the first place to licence sets constructed by a private individual, which had not been done in Great Britain, and also to issue licences for other classes of user as hereinafter specified. And it was further deemed advisable that all apparatus should be imported through a Clearing House to be set up by the Irish Broadcasting Company, which should collect at the Clearing House the amount due to it on each apparatus as a contribution to broadcasting expenses.

On this basis negotiations were opened up with the various firms interested, and after many conferences the following constituent firms have agreed to join together in a scheme to work a system of broadcasting in the Irish Free State under licence from the Post Office:-

(1) The Cork Radio Company, 50 South Mall, Cork.
(2) The Irish International Trading Corporation, Ltd., 4 Lapp's Quay, Cork.
(3) Irish Developments, Ltd., 3 Molesworth Street, Dublin.
(4) Dixon and Hempenstall, Ltd., Suffolk Street, Dublin.
(5) Philip Sayers, Esq., 16 St Andrew Street, Dublin.

The main features of the proposed scheme are as follows:-

1. A Company called the Irish Broadcasting Company to be formed by the constituent Companies with a guaranteed capital of not less than £30,000, 25 per cent. of which is to be reserved for taking up by other manufacturers, traders and dealers, the maximum allotment to any such individual or firm not to exceed 20 shares. Membership of the Company to be open to any *bona fide* firm or person carrying on the business of manufacturing wireless apparatus, or trading or dealing in such apparatus, in the Free State on subscribing for one or more £5 shares in the Company and on paying a deposit of £50. This deposit to be invested in Free State Savings Certificates in the name of the Company. The Certificates, with interest, to be transferred to the depositor on his ceasing to be a shareholder in the Company.

2. The Board of Directors of the Company to consist of seven members nominated by the constituent firms.

3. The Company to undertake to erect and operate during the continuance of the licence a broadcasting station at Dublin, and other stations if found desirable. A suitable programme to be provided daily, except on Sundays, Good Friday and Christmas Day, to the reasonable satisfaction of the Postmaster-General.

4. A licence to be issued to the Company for five years and to be renewable thereafter at the pleasure of the Postmaster-General. Power to be reserved to terminate the licence at any time for failure to fulfil its conditions.

5. The importation of wireless sets or component parts of sets to be confined to the Company and its members. All wireless material, except Government material, to be consigned to the Clearing House of the Company at Dublin.

6. The Company to be at liberty to manufacture and sell wireless receiving apparatus.

7. The Postmaster-General to issue licences for wireless receiving sets to persons who comply with the conditions prescribed by him, and the Company to receive a share of the fees charged for licences in accordance with the following scale:-

Ordinary licence and Constructor's licence, fee, £1 a year; Company's share, 15s.

Schools and Institutions licence, fee, £1 a year, Company's share, 12s. 6d.

Hotels, Restaurants, Public Houses, &c., licence, fee, £5 a year; Company's share, £4.10s.

Occasional licences, fee, £1 each; Company's share, 12s. 6d. each.

Manufacturers', Traders', or Dealers' licence, fee £1 a year; Company's share, £1.

Amusement Purveyors' licence, fee, £1 a week; Company's share, 90 per cent.

8. The hours of broadcasting to be from 11.0 a.m. till 12 noon, and from 5.0 p.m. till 11.0 p.m. No news items save official news which the Government may desire, to be broadcasted before 7.0 p.m. The Company to obtain its supply of news from one of the recognised sources. The Company to be allowed to broadcast, for not more than 15 minutes daily, advertising matter relating to (a) products or topics concerning the Free State; (b) any foreign material to which the Postmaster-General has given his approval beforehand, and to pay to the Postmaster-General a royalty at the rate of 10 per cent. on any revenue derived from such advertising matter.

9. The Postmaster-General to have the right to send a representative to attend Directors' meetings or to inspect the processes of the Company when considered necessary.

10. The Company to pay a royalty of £50 a year in respect of each station operated by the Company.

It has been agreed by the promoters that the Memorandum of Association and the Articles of Association of the Irish Broadcasting Company shall be submitted for the approval of the Postmaster-General, and it will be provided in the licence issued to the Company that this

Memorandum and Articles cannot be altered without the consent in writing of the Postmaster-General.

The form of Agreement to be entered into between the Company and manufacturers, traders or dealers, who wish to become members, will also have to be approved by the Postmaster-General and will form a schedule to the licence. This Agreement will include a schedule showing the amounts payable on imported apparatus as a contribution to the expenses of the Broadcasting Company. Nothing will be payable on material imported by the Government, or on material imported by *bona fide* experimenters under licence from the Postmaster-General.

The licence will make provision for transmission by the Broadcasting Station on approved wave lengths designed to prevent interference with existing stations and to safeguard the telegraphic lines of the Post Office from damage or interference. The licence will also stipulate for the observance of the provisions of the Radio-telegraph Convention so far as they are applicable and of any regulations made by the Postmaster-General for the conduct of wireless telegraph business. The Company will be also required to transmit free from its station any communiqués, weather reports or notices issued by any Department of the Government, with the approval of the Postmaster-General.

Under this scheme there is prospect of the early establishment of a broadcasting service in the Free State for which a wide and growing demand is made. At the same time no monopoly will be created, as all manufacturers of wireless apparatus will be at liberty to share in the operations of the proposed Company.

It has been decided to erect the first and principal station at Dublin, as besides being central for a large part of the country, that city and surrounding districts have a much larger population than any other centre in the Free State. Cheap sets are adequate for reception within short range, so that with a station situation [*sic*] at Dublin broadcasting can be brought within the reach of the greatest possible number of people. Moreover, the success of the scheme will largely depend upon the character and diversity of the programmes provided, and Dublin undoubtedly offers greater facilities in this respect than any other town in the Free State.

The chief item of cost in the operating of a station is the provision of programmes of sufficiently high standard and variety as to attract and retain the interest of 'listeners'. This expense is felt by the Broadcasting Company in Great Britain, whose revenue from the large sale of apparatus and from licence fees is comparatively greater than an Irish Company can hope to gain. In this country at the best there will be a limited sale for receiving sets, especially expensive valve apparatus, and for this reason, in order that the proposed Irish

Company should earn sufficient revenue to afford to pay for good programmes it is considered necessary to charge a higher fee for licences for ordinary 'listeners' and for 'Constructors' than in Great Britain. The term 'Constructor' is applied to the person who either makes his own apparatus or assembles it from ready-made parts.

The other classes of licences mentioned in paragraph 7 of the scheme are not issued by the British Post Office and are intended to bring in new sources of revenue and to meet the special circumstances in this country.

The Post Office does not seek to make a profit out of the control of the service or the licensing of the receiving sets. The balance of the fees which it will retain after making the contribution to the Company will, it is estimated, only cover the cost of administration, accounting and inspection. The royalty to be paid by the Company is in recognition of the Postmaster-General's monopoly in respect of wireless communication and to meet the expense of administration and inspection. The Ministry of Finance and the Revenue Commissioners, who have been consulted, raise no objections to the proposals.

SEUMAS BREATHNACH Aire an Phuist, Samhain, 1923.

APPENDIX 2

(I) LETTERS FROM SÉAMUS CLANDILLON TO DOUGLAS HYDE

1. Invitation to open the broadcasting station. Letter dated 22 December 1925

STÁISIÚN CHRAOBHSCAOILEACHÁIN ÁTHA CLIATH 2RN
36-39 Sráid Denmarc
Baile Átha Cliath
Mí na Nollag
22ú lá, 1925

Don Chraobhin Aoibhinn,
An Doctúr Dúbhglas de hÍde,
Coláiste na hOllscoile,
Baile Átha Cliath

Dom' sheanchara, An Chraobhin, é seo,
 Seo achainí ort, a Chraoibhin, ón Aire Poist agus Telegrafa, a d'iarraidh ort a theacht anseo go dtí an Stiúideo chun an Stáisiún seo d'oscailt dúinn ar Lá Chinn Bhliana.
 Is é an rud a bheidh uainn ná óráid ghairid, bhríomhar, den saghas is eol duit féin, (óráid in nGaeilge, tá fhios agat), a sheasóidh ar feadh cúig nóiméad déag, nó deich nóiméad ar a laghad; a rá le muintir an Domhain mhóir go bhfuilimíd, na Gaeil, ag seasamh ar ár mboinn arís, agus chun a thaispéaint go bhfuilimíd i measc na Náisiún uile.
 Ceathrú chun a hocht sa tráthnóna caithfidh an chaint a thosú, agus má bhíonn tú sa Stiúideo roimh ré is amhlaidh is fearr é chun taithí a dhéanamh ar an nGléas.
 Is é mian Aire agus Rúnaí Poist agus Telegrafa, go mbeifeása againn thar aon fhear in Éirinn, agus, ar ndóigh, is é mo mhian fhéin é leis.

Mise, le hardmheas,

STIÚRTHÓIR

[To my old friend, An Craoibhin,

This is an appeal to you, a Chraoibhin, from the Minister for Posts and Telegraphs, asking you to come here to the Studio on New Year's Day to open the Station.

We would like you to deliver a brief lively speech, in Irish, lasting about 15 minutes or at least 10 minutes, telling the people of the world that we, the Irish, are again independent and showing that we stand among all nations.

The speech must begin at a quarter to eight o'clock in the evening and if you are in the Studio earlier you will be able to familiarise yourself with the equipment.

It is the earnest wish of the Minister for Posts and Telegraphs and of the Secretary, that you, above anyone else in Ireland, would do this for us, and, of course, it is my personal wish as well.]

2. Advice on the content of the inaugural speech. Letter dated 23 December 1925.

Don Chraoibhin Aoibhinn,
An Dochtúir Dúbhglas de hÍde,
1, Earlsfort Place,
Baile Átha Cliath.

A Chara,

Táimid go léir an-bhuíoch díot, A Chraoibhín, mar gheall ort a bheith ag teacht chugainn chun an Stáisiún nua d'oscailt. An chéad lá de Eanáir a bheidh an áit seo á fhoscailt againn, agus ceathrú chun a hocht an t-am, a bheidh tusa ag caint. Da bhféadfá óráid a dhéanamh a sheasódh ar feadh cúig nóiméad déag is é an rud atá uainn.

Bhuel, i dtaobh comhairle duitse, ní maith a thiocfadh comhairle ó mo leithéidse: ach deirim go mba cheart duit a rá ná gairm scoile a chur amach go dtí muintir na hÉireann agus muintir an domhain mhóir go bhfuilimidne, na sean-Ghaeil, ar ár mboinn arís, cé gurbh fhada dúinn in ár dtost, agus go gcloisfear ár gcaint agus ár gceol ar fud an domhain feasta, i measc caint agus ceol na Náisiún eile go léir. Is eol duit fhéin conas óráid bhríomhar a dhéanamh den scéal sin.

Beidh áthas ar Aire an Phoist a chloisteáil go mbeidh tú ag teacht chugainn.

Táimid go léir go maith sa mbaile, buíochas le Dia, agus guímid beannachtaí an Linbh ort fhéin agus ar do mhuintir.

We are most grateful to you, a Chraoibhin, for agreeing to open the new Station for us. The opening day is the 1st of January and your speech will be at a quarter to 8. We would like you to speak for 15 minutes.

Well, about advising you, I am not the best person to do so. However, I think that you ought to proclaim to the Irish and to the peoples of the world that we, the Irish nation, are on our feet again although we have been long silent and that our language and our music will be heard all over the world from now on, in the midst of the languages and music of all other nations. You will know how to deliver a lively speech on that topic.

The Minister will be delighted to know that you will come to us.

All are well here, thank God, and we wish you and your family all the blessings of the Christ Child.

(II) TEXT OF DOUGLAS HYDE'S INAUGURAL SPEECH, 1 JANUARY 1926

I have been asked to open this Broadcasting Station to-night in the national language of Ireland – Our enterprise to-day marks the beginning not only of the New Year, but of a new era – an era in which our nation will take its place amongst the other nations of the world. A nation has never been made by Act of Parliament. A nation is made from the inside itself, it is made, first of all, by its language, if it has one; by its music, songs, games and customs. So, while not forgetting what is best in what other countries have to offer us, we desire to especially emphasise what we have derived from our Gaelic ancestors – from one of the oldest civilisations in Europe, the heritage of the O's and Mac's who still make up the bulk of our country. This much I have said in English for any strangers who may be listening-in. Now I address my own country:

A mhná uaisle, a dhaoine uaisle, is ormsa a thit sé anocht an gléas nua seo, an craobhscaoileachán seo, d'oscailt. Is mór an onóir dom é sin. Dúradh liom é d'oscailt i nGaeilge, i sean teanga ár sinsear í. Caithfidh muintir na hÉirean go léir, agus lucht an domhain ar fad, a thuiscint anois gur náisiún a bhfuil a chaint bhréa bhríomhar mhilis féin aige, agus go mbainfidh sé obair as an gcaint agus go ndéanfaidh sé a chuid oibre oifigiúla inti. Tiocfaidh an lá le cúnamh Dé, agus b'fhéidir nach rófhada uainn é, nuair a fheicfimíd gach aon rud atá le déanamh ag an Rialtas á dhéanamh as Gaeilge.

Is mithid inniu fios a bheith ag sean agus óg, mór agus beag, go bhfuil Éire ag seasamh go láidir ar a cosa féin is í an Ghaeilge an leathchos eile a nósan-na, a ceol agus a cluichí féin.

Tá an t-am ag teacht go luath nach bhféadfaidh fear óg gan Ghaeilge a rá go bhfuil sé, ní hé amhain ina Ghael, ach ina Éireannach ann (ach an taobh thall den Teorainn mhí-ámharach, b'fhéidir) nach mbeidh teanga a shinsear aige – a bheag nó a mhór di – agus cibé áit san domhan mór a gcasfar Éireannaigh ar a chéile aithneoidh siad a chéile agus cabhróidh siad le chéile agus craithfidh siad lamh le chéile agus bgan I mbéal gach aon duine acu ach 'Go mbeannaí Dia duit', 'Go mbeannaí Dia agus Muire dhuit, a chara agus a chomh-Ghael as Éirinn'. Seo é an chéad lá den bhliain agus is comhartha don domhan mór é go bhfuil athrú mór ann nuair is féidir linne ár n-áit féin a ghlacadh i measc náisiún an domhain agus an gléas gan sreang seo a chur ag obair inár dteanga féin ar nós gach tíre eile.

Tá Éire ar bhóthar a sláinte ach níl sí slán fós. Is drochspota í gcorp na hÉireann an galldachas seo, agus ní bheidh Éire slán go ngearrfar amach aisti é. Tá súil agam go mbeidh an gléas-gan-sreang seo taitneamhach don chorp agus úsáideach don anam san am chéanna.

Tá dhá thaoide nó lán mara in Éirinn – ceann acu ag teacht isteach an taobh seo d'Éirinn agus ceann eile ag dul amach an taobh thiar di. Tá lán mara na Gaeilge ag dul amach ansin agus fágann sé trá lom fhuar fholamh.

[Ladies and Gentlemen, It is my pleasure to open this broadcasting station. I am doing so in our own national language. The people of Ireland must understand that our nation is an exception, a nation that has its own rich language and will make its official business through Irish.

The young and the old should know that Éire is standing on her own two feet – the Irish language being one and her culture, music and Irish sport being the other.

The time has arrived, almost, when no young man without Irish can call himself an Irishman – for there will be no Irishmen (the other side of the border being an exception) who will not have some knowledge of their own national language – and wherever in the world Irishmen meet one another, help one another and spend a lot of their time together.

It is a sign to the world that times have changed when we can take our own place amongst other nations and use the wireless in our own language.

Éire is not completely saved yet, and will not be until the foreign influence is wiped out. I hope this wireless will be an advantage both physically and mentally to the body.

There are two tides in Ireland – one is ebbing this side of the country and the other is flowing out in the west of Ireland, where the Irish language is ebbing, leaving an empty strand behind.]

Darrell Figgis: a profile[1]

Darrell Edmund Figgis was born in 1882 (the same year as Éamon de Valera and James Joyce) at 20, Grosvenor Road, in the Dublin suburb of Rathmines. He spent the first ten years of his life in India, and after he had been brought back to Europe he worked (1898-1910) for his uncle, a tea-broker in London. In 1905 he married an English nurse, Mildred, generally known as Millie. In London he started to develop a love of poetry and literature generally, and in 1909 his first volume of poems, *A Vision of Life*, was published, with a hyperbolic introduction by G.K. Chesterton, by the prestigious firm of John Lane.[2] This was the beginning of an extremely fertile writing career, which saw him publish two further collections of verse; five novels;[3] two verse plays; two collections of critical essays and the still worthwhile *Shakespeare: a study*;[4] three volumes of memoirs – two of them in the long-established tradition of 'jail journals' recounting his experiences in Stafford and Durham jails,[5] the third his posthumous *Recollections*; the study of George Russell (Æ) from which I have quoted; eight political pamphlets, several of them substantial, such as *The Gaelic State* and *The Irish Constitution Explained*, most of them published by Maunsel, and – again posthumously – his study of the paintings of William Blake.

Having given up his job in the tea trade in 1910, Figgis supplemented his income from writing by working as a literary adviser to the London publishing house of Dent (which published several of his books) and as a journalist

1 Information relating to Figgis' life and writings is derived from: Andrew E. Malone [Lawrence J. Byrne], 'Darrell Figgis', *Dublin Magazine* I, 1926; P.S. O'Hegarty, 'A Bibliography ... of Darrell Figgis' (privately printed, Dublin, 1937); Padraic Colum, 'Darrell Figgis: A Portrait', *Dublin Magazine* XIV, 1939; John J. Dunn, 'Darrell Figgis, A Man Nearly Anonymous', *Journal of Irish Literature* XV/1, 1986; Maryanne Wessel-Felter, 'Darrell Figgis: An Overview of his Work', *Journal of Irish Literature* XXII, 1993; Richard Burnham, entry on Darrell Figgis in R. Hogan (ed.), *Dictionary of Irish Literature* [2nd edn.] (Westport, Conn.: Greenwood Press, 1996) vol. 1, pp. 433–6. **2** *A Vision of Life* (London: John Lane) 1909. **3** *Broken Arcs* (London: Dent, 1911); *Jacob Elthorne* (London: Dent, 1914); *Children of Earth* (Dublin: Maunsel, 1918); *The House of Success* (Dublin: Gael Co-operative Publishing Society, 1921); *The Return of the Hero* [under the pseudonym 'Michael Ireland'] (London: Chapman and Dodd, 1923), published under his own name 1930 in New York by Boni. **4** *Shakespeare: a study* (London: Dent, 1911). **5** *A Chronicle of Jails* (Dublin: Talbot Press, 1917); *A Second Chronicle of Jails* (Dublin: Talbot Press, 1919).

and drama critic for *The Academy*, the *Fortnightly Review* and the *English Review*. As we have seen, his literary career was interrupted by his introduction to Irish history and politics and by his espousal of the Sinn Féin cause, which saw him return to Ireland and become involved in both the practical side of the independence struggle (such as buying arms in Hamburg for the Howth gunrunning in 1914) and the polemical side – his pamphlets occupying a considerable amount of his time and his jail journals recounting his experiences during his imprisonment 1916–17 (also addressed in his *Recollections*).

I have referred in my Introduction to the concatenation of fact and fiction in the proceedings of the Wireless Committee, which saw some of its members twigging Figgis in a none too friendly way about the possibilities of an imaginative writer bending the 'facts' or 'truth' into meanings which they ought not to bear. In his own life and words Figgis himself embodies this combination of substance and aura, of the concrete and the imaginative. This in turn is instructive for us as spectators of the entire process by which Irish radio came into existence, wherein the participants were at times so unsure of reality, so vulnerable to ideas and suggestions in the ether, that the uncertainty immanent in the concept and nature of radio (to which Reith had referred – above, pp. 12–13) became a characteristic of the process itself.

The misty sightings of Arthur Griffith which we gain from Figgis' evidence, the behind-the-scenes intrigues with the southern unionists, Beaverbrook and Churchill and the Independent Party, J.J. Walsh's alleged use of detective Moynihan, are all elements in a drama where the written word, the spoken word and the gesture shape and change the world in which they operate. Figgis was the author of many such ironies, not least when he wrote: 'What is that fabled dragon of a man's life, his worst enemy? The measure of his infamy, or the tribute of his quality?'[7] These ironies, depending as they do on a shared sense of context and experience, resonate throughout his work – both literary and political – and throughout his part in the Belton affair and the wireless inquiry. 'Andrew E. Malone' began his appreciation which appeared six months after Figgis' death with the observation: 'Some people are born fated to provide material for the scoffer and the maker of caricatures. Their every action, almost their every thought gives opportunity for malice; and all the time they seem to be quite unconscious of their fate'. We have seen Malone's commentary on Figgis' lack of political aura, and to this he added 'he had undoubtedly the gift, or the curse, of attracting attention to himself and an unusual facility for making enemies' – a judgement which was confirmed by both Robert Brennan and Ernie O'Malley. But

---

7 D. Figgis, *Recollections* p. 223.

what was Figgis' fate? Was it to go down in the history books as a mystery man, as a traitor, as a naïf, as a failed littérateur or as a failed politician? Was it his fate to kill himself after his life had become unsupportable with the suicide of his wife and the death of his mistress? Was it his fate to kill himself after the exposure of his misadventure with political reconstruction in general and with Belton in particular?

In his study of Æ he had written: 'The profoundest parts of a life are not its deeds but the long and slow preparations of personality necessary to those deeds; and these are untellable'.[8] Much of Figgis' life, although it was ostensibly lived in public, through his political career and his writings, seems now to be untellable. In one sense he never had the 'long and slow preparations' to fashion his personality, since he was only in his early thirties when politics took over the remainder of his life. In those years he had been predominantly a literary being, and when he met Sir Roger Casement in 1914 and was seduced into the cause of Irish freedom, he was more aware of the semantic consequences of his actions than the physical:

> As I spoke he left his place by the window and came forward towards me, his face alight with battle. 'That's talking', he said, throwing his hand on the table between us; and I remember the whimsical thought crossing my mind that language had wandered far from its meanings when one man could say to another that he was talking, when his appreciation and brevity betokened an end to talking.[9]

Beautifully expressed though such a sentiment may be, it also reveals a mind engaged with communication as its principal mode of action, with an intellectual, rather than a practical, grasp of – or grasping towards – the situation. Yet Figgis became a Sinn Féin activist, his name still echoing in the folk memory of Achill as the enemy of the landlord class, as recorded by John J. Dunn.

His concerns were primarily with what was communicated, and with how it was decoded, rather than with what was done. (In *The House of Success* he wrote with brilliant brevity: 'a man once saw something for himself, and he wrote a book about it'.)[10] Immediately after the passage which I have just quoted concerning Casement he made an observation which, given the context in which it appeared, seems to me to be a poignant, if not desperate, reflection of the artist, the maker and creature of the plastic, seeing himself caught up in a world which demanded definition but constantly escaped from it:

---

8 D. Figgis, *Æ* p. 13.   9 D. Figgis, *Recollections* p. 18.   10 D. Figgis, *The House of Success* p. 122.

> We may, and often do, use phrases identical with those used by other nations; but in many cases it will be found by the thoughtful student that what to them is often social theory, to us is a slumbering historic memory.

To Figgis, there was no such thing as a present or future, except it was an historical present or an historical future. Thus, what we say to others may be decoded into meanings other than that intended, depending on the individual's understanding of history, and therefore affecting how we interpret the future.

In the *Réamhrá* (Foreword) to *The House of Success*, Figgis wrote that he knew 'from experience the queer, permanent effect through life of isolated experiences in childhood'.[11] It is no wonder that Pádraic Colum considered that 'like many another man who has something in him that isolates him from his fellows, Darrell Figgis was moved by certain great abstractions'. In this, he shares something with J.M. Synge. In his novel *Children of Earth* he wrote (and the passage is possibly prompted by an experience in Achill) 'There was an infinity of music in the roaring that filled the night. The texture of sound was as complicated in its intimacies as it was terrifying in its vastness'. So too had Synge written of a musical conception during a night in Aran: 'The music increased continually, sounding like the strings of harps, tuned to a forgotten scale, and having a resonance as searching as the strings of a 'cello ... In a moment I was swept away in a whirlwind of notes'.[12] One of Figgis' difficulties as a writer was to translate these abstractions into text. His *The Return of the Hero*, although widely admired – and praised by James Stephens, to whom, when it was pseudonymously published, it had been attributed – was, in my opinion, flawed by the attempt to bring mythological characters into the present day, where, by contrast, Stephens himself had succeeded in *The Demi-Gods*. *Children of Earth*, a representation of the traditional Achill character, although generally considered to have been his finest work, and praised in this case by the hypercritical Daniel Corkery (no doubt for its exploration of what Corkery would call 'the hidden Ireland'), likewise commutes between the phenomena and the fauna in an ultimately unsatisfactory manner.

The *House of Success*, to which I adverted in my Introduction, is in my opinion Figgis' most successful novel, in the sense that it attunes closely with his understanding of where Ireland had come from and of where it was going; like Eimar O'Duffy's *The Wasted Island*, it belongs to a genre of the historico-present which takes a short historical perspective (in *The House of Success*, from

---

11 Ibid. p. 7.   12 J.M. Synge, *Collected Works* vol.II, *Prose* (Gerrards Cross: Colin Smythe, 1982) pp. 99–100.

the fall of Parnell) and brings the reader into a personal encounter with 'real' people in the immediate present. In the Irish circumstances it was a courageous undertaking. It was also profoundly autobiographical, not in the sense that it recounted the events of Figgis' own life, but in the uttering of the inner and outer thoughts of two Irelands, and in the desperately and typically characteristic way in which Figgis' own thoughts and emotions are expressed. He does so by surrendering to that most real and most compelling of abstractions, which he had mentioned in the *réambrá* – that of the 'other', imagined as self, which creates a symbiotic captivity between two attracted but mutually agonistic temperaments.

The House of Success is a haunted book. Figgis rightly saw Ireland as haunted by its past, and he portrays the character of Ireland itself in the divided personality of the narrator and his *Doppelgänger* as a bifurcated being, as a creature always looking over its shoulder at the conscience and failure which it carried within itself. This 'character' responds to voices within the book which are cruel but accurate portraits of the mixed emotions with which, at that historical point, the country was about to engage, in a bitterly destructive phase of attempted reconciliation.

Throughout the novel, Figgis moves between the physical and the metaphysical, addressing emotional problems with that abstraction which, we noted, he found in isolation:

> 'Those are just words'.
> 'Well, and didn't we begin with words?'
> 'You know very well what I mean. I mean that anyone can turn any subject into words'.
> 'No, that's just what you can never do. But you can give them different meanings with different words because there's never the same thing under each.'[13]

If he re-read *The House of Success* in the light of his evidence to the Wireless Committee, such notions must have struck him as being curiously personal. And yet, he knew that the real difficulty of life is something that cannot be communicated, that cannot be decoded from that Reithian ether:

> 'The things people talk about aren't of any consequence. That's the first thing your folk who write books never learned. They write books about what people say and discuss. But it's the things people don't say and won't discuss are the only things that matter. It's the old devil of fear

---

13 *The House of Success* p. 59.

again. If there's a whole roomful of folk all afraid of one thing, they'll surely all be talking eighteen to the dozen about every other thing but that one thing ... And that's the one thing that's so damnable hard to discover.[14]

In *Æ* Figgis had written: 'Men who are in debt are not only men in bondage but also men in fear; and men in fear are they who have lost the certitude or hope of success'.[15] In *The House of Success* he questions the concept of success, as indeed that of certitude and hope: already by 1921, it appears, Figgis was a profoundly disillusioned man whose isolation, in the sole company of Millie for most of the time, intensified his frustrations and his sense of failure. Meeting Andrew Belton, who seemed to truly represent the idea of 'success', the year following its publication, may have suggested to Figgis that political respectability, personal gain and a reconciliation between the two Irelands might be effected if he harnessed himself to this vehicle of reconstruction.

Two of the marks of a naïf, apart from his innocence, are his self-centredness and his capacity to dream, a point on which all observers of Figgis agreed. He was – and is – a perfect candidate for a critical biography, because, as Colum tells us, 'he was an unaccountable man ... Outwardly, he was candid, amiable, companionable; inwardly, he was self-centred to an astonishing degree'. Or, as Eimar O'Duffy painted him in the character of Cyril Umpleby in *The Wasted Island*: 'He's rather an ass ... He's not very discreet, he's a fair supply of brains, he's a sublime egoist and a snob of the first water'.[16]

When, as we saw, he asserted that he had been courted as a possible chairman for numerous committees but had declined, we can well imagine that he had dreamed of these possibilities because of his involvement with the Constitution Committee and the Resources Commission (where he was in fact the paid secretary – all others giving their services *gratis*). But Colum gives the lie to this and the notion of Figgis gaining political preferment:

> His self-centredness was such as to prevent his having any understanding of the public's estimate of him. After the death of Michael Collins, when the ministry of the Provisional Government was in disarray, I said to him 'They may make you Minister for External Affairs'. I should not have said it, for I knew perfectly well that Darrell Figgis was not the sort of man who is ever trusted by men who form ministries, and I knew that at that moment he was trusted less than ever.[17] With that assurance and deliberation with which he always spoke of political

---

14 *House of Success* p. 129.　**15** D. Figgis, *Æ* p. 68.　**16** E. O'Duffy, *The Wasted Island* (London: Macmillan, **2nd** edn. 1929) p. 305.　**17** This was in August 1922, when Figgis was severing, or about to sever, his connection with Belton.

affairs, he said: 'I should not take any ministry unless I were allowed to choose my colleagues'. That is, unless he was made president. When he said that I knew how isolated he was.

We are left with no doubt that Figgis could, a few months previously, have been perceived by at least some, as a potential candidate for a ministry, especially when Colum continues 'Arthur Griffith trusted him, and probably if Griffith had lived, Darrell Figgis would have been put in a position of responsibility'. One witness, however, questioned Griffith's regard for Figgis. Senator Joseph Connolly recorded:

> Darrell Figgis was to me something of an enigma in the movement ... He was clever as a writer and speaker and I had formed a high opinion of his administrative and executive competence ... [But] I could never get that sense of trust and comfort that I enjoyed with most of my other colleagues. I was not alone in that for, to be quite frank, Figgis was regarded generally by those who counted as something of an interloper, a careerist or an opportunist. There was one notable exception and that was Griffith ... I knew Griffith always appreciated men of keen intelligence and whose literary and journalistic contributions were of value to the national work, but Figgis had so many characteristics that were normally anathema to Griffith that I just wondered. Figgis had a double dose of vanity and egotism and seemed eager to dominate and hold the centre in whatever company he was. Most of us treated these characteristics with a good-natured tolerance and dismissed them as just the foibles of a clever but vain man. Normally I had always found that Griffith had little patience with anything that savoured of pretentiousness or vanity. Figgis was an intriguing study ... I cannot conceive that Figgis did what he did [in helping to break the Collins–de Valera pact] without the full consent and approval of Griffith.[18]

Figgis was quite able to see that there was some truth in the totalitarian view of Irish-Ireland – that 'the Gael is the element that absorbs': this, as Lennox Robinson had noted, was the way in which the non-Irish could be accommodated (but not assimilated) into the Irish future – Ireland would be 'racially more compact than any nation in Europe, with little of the colonial element remaining in it'.[19] And where Figgis the constitutionalist would be party to the examination of the charters of other countries which were assumed to be cognate within the British Empire, Figgis the nationalist, anticipating that

18 J.A. Gaughan (ed.), *Memoirs of Senator Joseph Connolly* pp. 227–8.   19 D. Figgis, *The Gaelic State* p. 5.

examination, could say 'The constitutions of English colonies such as Canada, Australia and South Africa may be good, bad or indiferent, wise or unwise, discreet or indiscreet; but they are as little applicable to the case of Ireland, and would eventually cause as much irritation, as Dublin Castle'.[20]

The idea of Figgis as a figure of caricature and the subject of malicious gossip is born out by a contemporary cartoon: when Pádraic Colum tells us 'he had a handsome beard and fine eyes and he dressed up to them; in a city where there is a good deal of carelessness in the matter of dress, Darrell Figgis was always fittingly and at the same time colourfully attired', we might consider him inoffensive. But when Colum continues 'I remember that when he came to Dublin first he donned saffron kilts, and he looked mighty well in them', we are entitled to question his intention in saying this, since we are immediately reminded of others, such as the second Lord Ashbourne, who 'went native' and provided the model for the dotty gael 'Monsewer' in Behan's *The Hostage*.

Unfortunately, the beard was to be a source of an event which precipitated Millie Figgis' suicide. Shortly before the General Election of June 1922, Figgis was accosted at his flat (at 17 Lower Fitzwilliam Street) by three anti-Treaty Republicans who had been instructed to intimidate him into standing-down, mutilating him by cutting off his beard.[21] When Collins related this to Kitty Kiernan, she replied that he was lucky it was only his beard. In the course of the attack, Millie Figgis was injured, apparently seriously, and this caused her suicide two-and-a-half years later. She had written to him:

> My Dearest Husband – I am heartfully sorry to cause you pain and sorrow, but the reaction to the events of the past ten years has at last broken down my barriers. I have not stressed the matter to you, but the injury to my neck when the men came to cut your beard has been a constant trouble to me, and sometimes my nerves have been unendurable. I would have ended long since but for the pain and suffering I should cause you ... I never felt more sane in my life. It is the only decision which an individual can ever make irrespective of his or her financial position.[22]

Having driven into the Wicklow mountains, she killed herself on 18 November with a revolver which had been given to them by Michael Collins 'as a protection against further raids'.

20 Ibid. p. 4.   **21** *Freeman's Journal* quoted by Michael Laffan, op. cit. pp. 391–2.   **22** Quoted in John J. Dunn, 'Darrell Figgis' – the letter was originally published by the *Irish Times* at the time of her death.

Almost the last line of *The House of Success* is: 'the meaning of life is the teaching of disillusionment'.[23] After her death, although apparently inconsolable, Figgis continued to work with the help of Millie's voice from beyond the grave. He wrote to Holbrook Jackson:

> She effaced herself, put herself out of the way, always, always, that I might be put forward; but I was only what she made me; and I knew it – and now I know it only too well ... Every pang and torture of her during the last night ... lives with, and in, me ceaselessly, for if things to do put them away, they only wait to return more terribly. Truly I am a fated man, whom folk should have little to do with. The very splendor of the things I have loved has undone me. It is better to be as the beasts, and not to create too great a love, and not to fail to satisfy the greatness of that which one has invoked. What hand shot her but mine, the hand that with a light caress on her brow might have saved all, and brought so simple a contentment with her pain?[24]

Figgis did recover, however, to the extent that he formed a relationship with Rita North, a dancer in her early twenties, and they went to London to attempt to remake his career as a writer – he was working on his study of Blake. But Rita died of septicaemia on 19 October 1925 as a result of an infection following an abortion, and eight days later, on 27 October, Figgis gassed himself in his rooms in Bloomsbury. Perhaps this was the final explanation of his cryptic remark to Andrew Belton: 'we are all snobs at heart'.[25]

23 *The House of Success* p. 318.   **24** J.J. Dunn, 'Darrell Figgis'.   **25** *Report* doc. 348.

Index

Abbey Theatre (Dublin) 44–5, 139, 149, 174
Aberdeen radio station xii, 143
Achill 191–2
Ackerman, Florrie 152
Aiken, Maud 154
Allgood, Sara 174
Alton, Ernest TD, 115
amateur radio activity 42
Andrews, Liam 149, 174
anti-Treaty parties 21, 28–9, 31, 32, 54, 62
'Apostles' *see* Twelve Apostles
Army crisis/inquiry 2, 29, 30, 62
Army No 1 Band 144, 148–9, 153
Army School of Music 150, 159–60, 168
Arnott, Edgar 45
Asgard (Howth gun-running) xv, 63
Athlone broadcasting station xii, xix, 105, 136, 176–8
Atlantic College (radio school) 43
Austria, broadcasting in, 40n., 49n.

Baird, John Logie xviii
Baldwin, Stanley 48
Ballycastle, Co Antrim 18
Baxter, Patrick TD, 115
BBC 5, 15, 32; reception in Ireland 37; relays from, 43–4, 130, 154, 158; as a model for Ireland 68, 70, 110, 112, 114; possibility of operating Dublin station 131, 138n.; message to 2RN 147; comparisons with 2RN 153, 167; source of news 163; and controversial items 169–70
BBC Belfast (2BE) xviii, 40, 43, 172
BBC Radio 3, 154
Beamish, Richard TD, 50; background 64; attendance at Wireless Committee 65, 102n.; as an Independent candidate 85n., 92, 107
Bean na hÉireann 64
Béaslaí, Piaras 32, 52
Beatty, W.A. 140
Beaverbrook, Lord 4, 45, 86, 98–9, 190
Beckett, Samuel 149n.
Behan, Brendan 198
Belgium, broadcasting in, 40n., 49n., 68
Bellingham, Sir Edward 85, 104

Belton, Andrew 4, 9, 34, 56–7, 64; relationship to Figgis, 66, 78–101; memorandum to J.J. Walsh 67, 103, 117, 124; plans for IBC 76; on 'influence' 89–93; plans for a casino 92–4; loan to Irish Free State 95–8; on Independent/Commercial Party 100–01; leaves Ireland 111; unsuitable character 89, 104, 110, 118
Bergin, Nancy 140, 142, 169
Berlusconi, Silvio 7
Blackrock Hosiery 167
Blythe, Ernest 52n., 103, 122–3, 126–7, 131, 174, 176; critical of broadcasting proposals 130–2; agrees to proposals 132; moves to approve capital expenditure 158; becomes Minister for Posts and Telegraphs 162
Boland, Gerard 55n., 162, 165
Boland, Harry 63
Bonar Law, Andrew 86
Boucicault, Dion 149
Boundary Commission 24, 29, 54, 63, 147
Bournemouth radio station 40, 143, 156
Bowles, Michael 150
Bracken, Brendan 37n.
Bradlaw, Isaac 56
Brase, Col. Fritz 148–50, 159–60
Breathnach, Liam 174
Breen, Tommy 174
Brennan, Denis 152
Brennan, Joseph 56n.
Brennan, Robert 190
Breslau radio station 143
Bridges, Robert 44
Briggs, Asa xii, 15, 44, 49–50, 75–6, 167, 169
Briscoe, Robert 78n.
British Broadcasting Company xvii, 6, 48, 61, 71, 76; *see also* British Broadcasting Corporation, BBC, BBC Belfast
British Broadcasting Corporation 6
'broadcast' as a verb 44–5 ; *see also* 'listening-in' broadcasting, characteristics of, xi, 5, 11–13; uses of 18, 50–1, 112–13, 119–20; on Sundays 76; *see also* public service broadcasting

199